Philosophy of Devotion

Philosophy of Devotion

The Longing for Invulnerable Ideals

PAUL KATSAFANAS

Great Clarendon Street, Oxford, OX2 6DP,
United Kingdom

Oxford University Press is a department of the University of Oxford.
It furthers the University's objective of excellence in research, scholarship,
and education by publishing worldwide. Oxford is a registered trade mark of
Oxford University Press in the UK and in certain other countries

© Paul Katsafanas 2022

The moral rights of the author have been asserted

First Edition published in 2022

Impression: 1

All rights reserved. No part of this publication may be reproduced, stored in
a retrieval system, or transmitted, in any form or by any means, without the
prior permission in writing of Oxford University Press, or as expressly permitted
by law, by licence or under terms agreed with the appropriate reprographics
rights organization. Enquiries concerning reproduction outside the scope of the
above should be sent to the Rights Department, Oxford University Press, at the
address above

You must not circulate this work in any other form
and you must impose this same condition on any acquirer

Published in the United States of America by Oxford University Press
198 Madison Avenue, New York, NY 10016, United States of America

British Library Cataloguing in Publication Data
Data available

Library of Congress Control Number: 2022942542

ISBN 978–0–19–286767–4

DOI: 10.1093/oso/9780192867674.001.0001

Printed and bound by
CPI Group (UK) Ltd, Croydon, CR0 4YY

Links to third party websites are provided by Oxford in good faith and
for information only. Oxford disclaims any responsibility for the materials
contained in any third party website referenced in this work.

Contents

Acknowledgments vii
1. The Longing for Devotion 1
2. The Nature of Sacred Values 23
3. Resisting Comparisons of Comparable Items 49
4. Devotion and Dialectical Invulnerability 64
5. Nihilism and the Abundance of Values 100
6. The Enlightenment Account of Fanaticism 127
7. Fanaticism as Individual Pathology 142
8. Group Fanaticism and Narratives of Ressentiment 163
9. Irony, Affirmation, and the Appeal of Inarticulacy 190
10. Conclusion 220

References 223
Index 235

Acknowledgments

I began thinking about the issues discussed in this book in 2015, when reading Nietzsche led me to have a vague suspicion that there might be some connection between nihilism, fanaticism, and the sacralization of values. Since then, my thoughts have been shaped by countless conversations with colleagues, students, and friends. I am sure I have forgotten many debts, but I want to thank Quassim Cassam, Berislav Marusic, Richard Moran, Matt Boyle, Béatrice Longuenesse, Francey Russell, Andreja Novakovic, Ben Roth, Patrick Murray, Ian Blaustein, Kathryn Tabb, Bernard Reginster, Lanier Anderson, Peter Poellner, Keith Ansell-Pearson, Kyla Ebels-Duggan, Keren Gorodeisky, Ken Gemes, Kaitlyn Creasy, Andrew Huddleston, Scott Jenkins, Maudemarie Clark, Ariel Zylberman, Colleen Cressman, Jacob Beck, Louis Philippe Hodgson, Kristin Gjesdal, Matt Meyer, Paul Loeb, Tom Bailey, Joel van Fossen, Ian Dunkle, Charles Griswold, Walter Hopp, David Eckel, Susanne Sreedhar, Michaela McSweeney, Daniel Star, Sally Sedgwick, Aaron Garrett, Marc Gasser-Wingate, Juliet Floyd, David Roochnik, David Lyons, Victor Kestenbaum, Ben Crowe, Victor Kumar, Rachell Powell, Allen Speight, Talbot Brewer, Olivia Bailey, Tamar Schapiro, Ruth Rebecca Tietjen, Hans Bernhard Schmid, Thomas Szanto, Leo Townsend, Anne Reichold, Pol Pardini Gispert, Casey Grippo, Amber Sheldon, Jaleel Fotovat-Ahmadi, Alexa Li, Nick Buscemi, Erin Seeba, Danielle Slevens, participants in the Boston University Center for the Humanities Faculty Fellows Workshop, and students in various graduate seminars at Boston University. Anonymous reviewers for Oxford University Press provided exceptionally comprehensive and insightful comments on the manuscript. I had the pleasure of presenting material from this book at the following venues: Princeton University, The University of Wisconsin Milwaukee, The University of Vienna, George Washington University, Northwestern University, Roma Tre University, University of Rome Tor Vegata, John Cabot University, The University of Southampton, Georgia State University, York University, Bard College, SUNY Binghamton, Temple University, The College of the Holy Cross, Warwick University, UMass Boston, Milton Academy, Tufts University, and Columbia University. I thank the audiences for their many helpful comments.

An earlier version of some of the material in Chapters 6 and 7 was published as "Fanaticism and Sacred Values," *Philosophers' Imprint* 19:17 (May 2019), pp. 1–20. An earlier version of Chapter 8 was published as "Group Fanaticism and Narratives of Ressentiment," in *The Philosophy of Fanaticism: Epistemic, Affective, and Political Dimensions,* ed. Leo Townsend, Ruth Rebecca Tietjen, Hans Bernhard Schmid, and Michael Staudigl, Routledge Press (2022). I gratefully acknowledge the publishers' permission to reuse this material.

1
The Longing for Devotion

1.1 Devoted Agents

Reading philosophical and psychological literature on human motivation, we are confronted with long lists of things that people want. We want happiness and freedom from pain; acceptance by groups; a sense of achievement; perhaps self-determination or self-actualization; perhaps a sense of power.[1] But there is something that often goes unmentioned in these lists: we seek a form of *devotion*.

Consider a famous excerpt from George Orwell's 1940 review of *Mein Kampf*. Orwell warns that Hitler

> has grasped the falsity of the hedonistic attitude toward life. Nearly all western thought since the last war...has assumed tacitly that human beings desire nothing beyond ease, security, and avoidance of pain.... [but] human beings *don't* only want comfort, safety, short working-hours, hygiene, birth-control and, in general, common sense; they also, at least intermittently, want struggle and self-sacrifice... Whereas Socialism, and even capitalism in a more grudging way, have said to people 'I offer you a good time,' Hitler has said to them 'I offer you struggle, danger and death,' and as a result a whole nation flings itself at his feet.
>
> (Orwell 1968: 14)

Anyone who considers the rise of nationalist politics, extremism, and jihadist movements in our time can see that these tendencies are not mere historical curiosities. It's certainly true that human beings are moved by considerations of happiness, comfort, and so forth. But we also seek something else, something for which we are at times willing to set aside these other ends, something for which we will undertake toil, struggle, violence, opposition, and self-sacrifice. We seek something to which we can *devote* ourselves.[2]

Consider three examples.

---

[1] Representative works from empirical psychology include Maslow 1962, Deci and Ryan 1985, Baumeister and Vohs 2007, Snyder and Lopez 2011, and McClleland et al. 1989.

[2] We might wonder which factor comes first in the order of explanation. I will suggest that we seek a form of devotion and that our craving for devotion explains some cases in which we are attracted to toil, struggle, violence, and so on. But an alternative explanation would be that we seek (for example) violence for its own sake, and are attracted to devotion insofar as devotion enables or justifies this violence. The examples I give below won't decide this issue; they are merely suggestive.

* * *

In the summer of 2016, protesters began gathering at Standing Rock, North Dakota. They objected to the federal government's plan to construct a large oil pipeline underneath a section of the Missouri River that lies only a half-mile from the border of the Standing Rock Indian Reservation. The protesters feared contamination of the Reservation's water supply as well as destruction of areas of cultural and religious import. As Standing Rock's Historic Preservation Officer Ladonna Brave Bull Allard put it, "if we allow an oil company to dig through and destroy our histories, our ancestors, our hearts and souls as a people, is that not genocide?" (Allard 2016).

In October, the protestors found themselves confronted by hundreds of police officers and National Guardsmen. Marching in columns behind five armored military vehicles, brandishing clubs and shields, firing rubber bullets and tear gas, armed with concussion grenades and tasers, the officers advanced on the protestors. One hundred and forty-two protestors were arrested; many more were injured. A month later, the process was repeated: columns of officials once again marched toward the protesters, this time spraying them with water cannons in subzero temperatures, firing rubber bullets, and allegedly using concussion grenades.

As images of peaceful protesters confronted by militarized police forces circulated through the media, many viewers were shocked and appalled. Some of them organized: Michael A. Wood, Jr. and Wes Clark, Jr. formed a group called Veterans for Standing Rock. Their goal was to join the protestors and provide some measure of protection by using themselves as human shields. Initially expecting a small turnout, Wood and Clark were surprised to find that over 2000 US military veterans turned up at Standing Rock.

What attracted these veterans? "You might as well die for something that means something," said Vincent Emanuele, a thirty-two-year-old former Marine (Healy 2016). Emanuele had served in Iraq and had come to regard that war as futile. He sought something more, something that would give his life significance and direction, some weighty cause to which he could sacrifice himself: "A lot of people here are willing to sacrifice their body, willing to give their life," he noted. And his potential sacrifice didn't go unnoticed: the tribal chairman, Dave Archambault II, said "You guys are very symbolic…What you're doing is sacred" (Healy 2016).

Most of the veterans had no direct connection to the area. They were drawn by something else. "You might as well die for something that means something" (Healy 2016).

* * *

Until early 2015, Kadiza Sultana, Amira Abase, and Shamima Begum had been living ordinary, comfortable lives in London. These fifteen- and sixteen-year-old girls had been doing well in school, earning praise from their teachers, and enjoying their popularity: "they were the girls you wanted to be like," said a student from the grade below theirs (Bennhold 2015). By conventional standards they were flourishing. Yet in February 2015, the three students left their homes, flew to Turkey, and made their way across the border into Syria. There, they joined ISIS. They were quickly married off to ISIS fighters and began having children. They were also confronted with all the horrors of life under ISIS. In a 2019 interview with *The Times* of London, Shamima Begum said, "When I saw my first severed head in a bin it didn't faze me at all... It was from a captured fighter seized on the battlefield, an enemy of Islam. I thought only of what he would have done to a Muslim woman if he had the chance" (Mueller 2019). Begum reportedly joined al-Hisba, ISIS' female morality police, which was known for inflicting brutal punishments: violations such as using makeup, traveling without a male companion, or wearing the wrong clothing were punished with forty to sixty lashes.

What led these teenagers to ISIS? An earlier article offered this account:

> Asked by their families during sporadic phone calls and exchanges on social media platforms why they had run away, the girls spoke of leaving behind an immoral society to search for religious virtue and meaning. In one Twitter message, nine days before they left Britain, Amira wrote, "I feel like I don't belong in this era." (Bennhold 2015)

They sought something more, something that would give them purpose and direction, something that the tedium of their ordinary lives in London did not provide. And ISIS appeared to offer just that. A few months before they left, ISIS' online magazine *Dabiq* published this call:

> The time has come for those generations that were drowning in oceans of disgrace, being nursed on the milk of humiliation, and being ruled by the vilest of all people, after their long slumber in the darkness of neglect—the time has come for them to rise. The time has come for the ummah of Muhammad (peace be upon him) to wake up from its sleep, remove the garments of dishonor, and shake off the dust of humiliation and disgrace, for the era of lamenting and moaning has gone, and the dawn of honor has emerged anew. The sun of jihad has risen. The glad tidings of good are shining. Triumph looms on the horizon. The signs of victory have appeared.[3]

And the calls continued: the twelfth issue of *Dabiq* refers to its followers as "the brothers who have refused to live a life of humiliation" (Al-Ushan 2015). The ninth issue claims that ISIS has established a true Caliphate, with "honor and

---

[3] "The Return of Khilafah." *Dabiq*, July 5, 2014, 3.

pride for the Muslim and humiliation and degradation for the kaffir [apostates]" (Al-Muhajirah 2015; cf. Stern 2016).

The conditions that these teenagers encountered were perhaps not what they expected: confronted with the collapse of the Islamic State and the deaths of all three of her children, Shamima Begum spent several years trying to return to London. And yet something of that longing for purpose remains in her: "I don't regret coming here," she says (Loyd 2019).

Kadiza Sultana, Amira Abase, and Shamima Begum weren't alone. A July 2018 study counted over 41,000 foreigners who traveled to Syria or Iraq to join ISIS. Around 19,000 were from the Middle East, 13,000 were from Europe, and 300 were from the United States.[4] The attraction was perhaps obvious: the "revival of the Caliphate gave each individual Muslim a concrete and tangible entity to satisfy his natural desire for belonging to something greater."[5] The goals may be abhorrent, the conditions horrific; but the "natural desire" for subordinating oneself to a greater purpose was satisfied.

* * *

In August 1996, twenty-two-year-old Julia "Butterfly" Hill was struck by a drunk driver. She was severely injured, with the steering wheel of her car penetrating her skull; she spent nearly a year in recovery. And this gave her plenty of time to dwell on the life she had led:

> As I recovered, I realized that my whole life had been out of balance...I had graduated high school at 16, and had been working nonstop since then, first as a waitress, then as a restaurant manager. I had been obsessed by my career, success, and material things. The crash woke me up to the importance of the moment, and doing whatever I could to make a positive impact on the future. The steering wheel in my head, both figuratively and literally, steered me in a new direction in my life. (Martin 1998)

And she found that new direction. A few months after her recovery, in December 1997, she joined protests against the Pacific Lumber Company's plan to clear-cut 60,000 acres of ancient redwoods in Humboldt County, California. To prevent logging, she climbed nearly to the top of a 200-foot-tall, 1000-year-old redwood tree; there, she constructed two rudimentary six foot by six foot platforms out of scrap wood. She spent the next 738 days living on those platforms, 180 feet above the ground, enduring freezing temperatures, harassment by logging company workers (sometimes via helicopter), and other difficulties.

---

[4] https://www.bbc.com/news/world-middle-east-47286935.
[5] "The Extinction of the Grayzone," *Dabiq*, February 12, 2015, 57.

What motivated her? In December 1999, after two years in the tree, Hill spoke to reporters: "There's no way to be in the presence of these ancient beings and not be affected... There's something more than profit, and that's life" (Dundon 2017).

Hill descended only when the logging company finally agreed to spare her redwood as well as any trees within 200 feet of it. But Hill didn't end there: in the years that followed, she devoted her life to conservation efforts throughout the world.

Reflecting on her time in the tree many years later, she said:

> I really do see so much in people. The desire to have something worthy of giving our lives to; because we give our lives to so much that really is not worthy of it. And I think even if people are not completely conscious of that, their spirits, their hearts, their souls feel it. And that is why we turn to self-medicating and numbing ourselves with shopping, over-consumption, movies, television, drugs, alcohol, and all these things we do. Because there is something deep within us, even if we do not recognize it and cannot name it, that wants to have something worth giving our lives to. So something powerful about that arc of what takes the ordinary and makes it become extraordinary.   (Taggart 2014)

Hill focuses on the need to find something worthy of sacrifice and struggle. She claims that the yearning for this is widespread, even when it is not consciously experienced as such; and we see this in the joy that comes from finding a goal worthy of devotion.

* * *

Putting oneself in danger and subjecting oneself to extreme conditions in order to protect people one does not know; fleeing the safety and security of a London suburb to join a violent war in Syria; living in a tree for two years in order to prevent logging. What's remarkable about these events is just how *unsurprising* they are. It's rare, of course, for people to go to such extremes. But it is not incomprehensible, not shocking. We are not stunned by the fact that these people are putting aside conventional values in favor of something that strikes them as more important. We have some sense of what the people are after; we have some sense of what they are seeking. They want something to which they can devote themselves, subordinating their comforts, their happiness, their pleasures. They find different outlets: protecting the territory of a nation to which they do not belong; enforcing barbaric laws; saving trees. The content is various but the form is the same: they crave something to which they can subordinate their mundane desires and pursuits.

From one perspective, these actions look manifestly irrational: why put yourself at risk of abuse and imprisonment to protect a bit of land from development? Why join a violent and oppressive regime, suffering from abuse and deprivation, instead of pursuing a comfortable life in London? Why give up two years of your life to save one acre of trees, while the world experiences 70,000 acres of deforestation *per day*?[6] Why commit to these courses of action when the costs are so grave? And why *stay committed*? Why not give up the commitment when the costs begin to mount?

Those are just three examples, of course. Like any examples, they can be resisted, redescribed, or viewed as mere idiosyncrasies with no larger import. But they are suggestive: they give some support to the idea that human beings—at least in some cases and in some circumstances—crave a form of devotion. My hope is that the remainder of this book will convince the reader that these kinds of cases are ubiquitous.

* * *

But how should we describe this form of devotion? Here is the most obvious possibility: we try to identify the *contents* of the individuals' pursuits. We try to pick out the persons, properties, or states of affairs that the devoted individuals value. And we say that the individuals value these persons, properties, or states of affairs so highly that they are willing to sacrifice lesser goods in order to achieve or preserve them. So, the Standing Rock veterans value a form of freedom or the defiance of oppressive government agents, and are willing to risk their own lives to achieve this; the British teenagers value the sense of purpose or meaning that ISIS provides, and will endorse violence and risk extreme dangers in order to secure it; Hill values the preservation of certain elements of the natural world, and will forgo conventional comforts in order to promote this goal.

If we can explain the devoted actions in this way, then they would raise no special problems. There's nothing especially mysterious about the fact that people weigh costs and benefits, forgoing some conventional pleasures or comforts in order to achieve things they regard as having greater value. That's routine.

Yet I think this explanation is too easy. It fails to explain a striking feature of the above cases. Notice that the individuals I've mentioned above are to some extent inarticulate about the contents of their goals. It's not obvious that they *first* identify something immensely valuable and *then* decide to undertake sacrifices in order to attain it. It looks like things go the other way around: they first seek something to which they can devote themselves, and then happen upon opportunities to express this devotion. In other words, *they choose particular ends for the sake of expressing devotion, rather than expressing devotion for the sake of attaining particular ends.* This is completely explicit in Hill and Emanuele and is strongly suggested in Begum's self-descriptions. But again the particular examples don't matter. What matters is this: I will argue that people often adopt ends for the sake of expressing the devotion that these ends require, rather than first

---

[6] The UN estimates that between 2015 and 2020, the worldwide deforestation rate was approximately 25 million acres per year. See http://www.fao.org/documents/card/en/c/ca8642en.

identifying valuable ends and then deciding to devote themselves to these ends. Put differently: many people are more interested in finding an opportunity to express devotion than in identifying things of great value.

That's my first claim. It can be understood simply as a claim about the psychological priority of two goals: does the person seek to express devotion, and then go about looking for a way to do so? Or, conversely, does the person identify highly valuable things and then decide to devote herself to them? If we understand the question that way, it will look like we have two psychological items—devotion and value—and are merely asking which typically comes first. But I want to suggest that things are more complex: when devotion comes first, we tend to be dealing with a distinctive *type* of value. Let me explain.

1.2 A Distinction among Normative Commitments

It is a striking fact that our normative commitments divide into the trivial and the profound. Compare the normative significance that you place upon enjoying your morning coffee with the normative significance that a violent white nationalist places upon establishing a racially "pure" society, or that a committed jihadist places upon establishing a conservative Islamic state, or that a social activist places upon protection of the oppressed, or that a devoted environmentalist places upon preservation of the biome. We use the same term to describe all of these individuals, saying that they value certain ends or take there to be reasons to do certain things. And yet it's obvious that the normative significance that you place upon your morning latte pales in comparison to that which the jihadist or the nationalist sees in his action. This is a perfectly familiar point: the actions that we label valuable or reason-supported vary in their perceived significance.

Philosophers have offered ways of marking this distinction. We can speak of the *weight* or *strength* of our commitments. We can speak of their *import*. We can order them lexically, saying that some always override others. We recognize, then, that some commitments seem to be imbued with a special force. They tend to override competing concerns; they tend to be fixed points in deliberation, which we refuse to compromise; in some cases, they are objects of passionate attachment.

So we all recognize distinctions among our normative commitments. It's not news that some normative commitments are profound and others trivial. But I want to ask a question about this distinction. Does accounting for this distinction require anything more than the familiar philosophical machinery? Does it require anything more than speaking in terms of the weight, intensity, or strength of the commitments? I will argue that it does. Our commitments do not sort exhaustively into the *weighty* and the *unweighty*. There is another dimension: there is an important distinction between ordinary values and what are sometimes called *sacred* values.

In moral philosophy, it is commonly assumed that all normative phenomena are roughly on par. They are all weighable, perhaps with a few complications. There may be some incommensurables or incomparables: perhaps we can't compare the value of a Picasso with the value of the Grand Canyon. There may be some normative commitments that are overriding: perhaps there's an absolute prohibition on murdering innocent people. But all of our normative commitments can enter into deliberation as potentially weighable items, can be deployed as premises in reasoning, can be defended. Insofar as they can't be, they are problematic. So, considerations that are exempted from deliberation, or that aren't weighed against competing concerns, or that aren't deployed as premises in reasoning, or that aren't critiqued and defended in the usual ways—all of these will be problems.

But there is a striking mismatch between these theoretical claims and the way in which our evaluative lives actually proceed. Let's illustrate this with a valuation that's central to us: the valuation of human life itself. Most of us agree that human life has great value. But there are different ways of understanding this value. The Catholic Church holds that "human life is sacred and inviolable at every moment of existence" (John Paul II 1995: 61). "The absolute inviolability of innocent human life is a moral truth" (John Paul II 1995: 57), so that "the direct and voluntary killing of an innocent human being is always gravely immoral" (John Paul II 1995: 57). Peter Singer, by contrast, writes that "during the next 35 years, the traditional view of the sanctity of human life will collapse under pressure from scientific, technological, and demographic developments. By 2040, it may be that only a rump of hard-core, know-nothing religious fundamentalists will defend the view that every human life, from conception to death, is sacrosanct" (Singer 2009). Singer is not denying that human life is valuable; on the contrary, he thinks it has great value (Singer 1972). But for Singer, tradeoffs, weighings, and balancings are perfectly fine: to use one of his examples, "We may not want a child to start on life's uncertain voyage if the prospects are clouded" (Singer 2009). For example, Singer thinks it can make sense to decline to preserve the life of a severely disabled child. According to the Catholic doctrine, which treats human life as having an inviolable value, this is perverse.

There is a clear difference between the way in which the Catholic doctrine and Singer's theory treat the value of human life. Can we draw this distinction merely in terms of the weight of the value? Not obviously. Singer and the Catholic Church *agree* that human life is immensely valuable. Singer thinks that human life outweighs many competing concerns, and indeed that great sacrifices are often required so as to ensure its preservation: in a famous article, he argues that we are morally obligated to sacrifice much of consumer society—nice clothes, comfortable homes, restaurants, vacations—in order preserve human life by alleviating dire poverty (Singer 1972). He believes that almost no sacrifice is too great for this: we ought to give up our disposable incomes and severely curtail our non-essential expenditures in order to preserve human life. So there are limits, but Singer does accord human life immense weight. The Catholic doctrine is, in that respect, analogous. While professing belief in the inviolability of human life, the Catholic Church does not treat it as infinitely valuable: it does, in fact, accept limitations on the quantities of other goods that must be traded to preserve or protect human life.[7]

Nonetheless, there's a difference between the way that Singer and orthodox Catholics are envisioning the value of human life. How should we capture this difference?

We could say that whereas Singer assigns human life a value of weight W1, the Catholic Church assigns it a value of weight W2, where W2 is somewhat greater than W1. This is true, but it misses the point. There is a disagreement between Singer and the Catholic Church, but it's not well captured by speaking of variances in weight. That would obscure the distinction. Human lives are valuable and apples are valuable. If Singer's weighting of a human life is just somewhat lower than the Catholic doctrine's, then Singer's valuation of a human life *plus* a number of apples should, for some quantity of apples, equal the Catholic Church's valuation of human life. But this is absurd. Even if we could, in fact, find some point at which these purported weights would be equal, we wouldn't have revealed anything interesting about the disagreement between Singer and the Catholic Church. (I am not denying that it's *possible* to draw this distinction in terms of weights. I am claiming that it's *inadvisable* to do so; it doesn't illuminate anything. While there is a difference in weights, that difference is explained by something more fundamental.)

So there's not a good way of drawing the distinction between Singer and the Catholic Church merely in terms of the weights of the relevant values or reasons. We might try to account for the distinction in other ways. For example, the Catholic position involves deontological norms, whereas Singer is a consequentialist. So we might speak of absolute prohibitions on using human lives in certain ways, where these prohibitions would be accepted by Catholics but denied by Singer. And we will find some differences here. But again, this won't illuminate the difference. After all, there are deontological views that allow human lives to be traded against competing goods. To mention one notorious example, Kant, the paradigmatic deontologist, recognizes certain cases in which considerations of honor seem to outweigh the value of human lives: he claims that if a military

---

[7] For example, consider these rules, taken from the 2009 edition of *Ethical and Religious Directives for Catholic Health Care Services* (a guidebook published by the United States Conference of Catholic Bishops): "56. A person has a moral obligation to use ordinary or proportionate means of preserving his or her life. Proportionate means are those that in the judgment of the patient offer a reasonable hope of benefit and do not entail an excessive burden or impose excessive expense on the family or the community. 57. A person may forgo extraordinary or disproportionate means of preserving life. Disproportionate means are those that in the patient's judgment do not offer a reasonable hope of benefit or entail an excessive burden, or impose excessive expense on the family or the community." Notice that "extraordinary" and "disproportionate" means of preserving life are not required.

officer kills someone in a duel in order to preserve "military honor," or if an unwed mother kills her newborn infant in order to avoid "the disgrace of an illegitimate birth," then they should be exempted from the usual punishments for murder (*Metaphysics of Morals*, 336–7).[8] So the mere fact that the Catholic position involves deontological claims doesn't explain the phenomenon in which we're interested. The status that the Catholic doctrine is bestowing upon human life, while it does involve a deontological claim, also involves something more.

We might describe this by saying that the Catholic doctrine treats human life as absolutely inviolable. Or we might focus on the way in which human life has a kind of sanctity, dignity, or meaning for Catholics that it lacks for Singer. This, I think, is getting closer to the real difference, but these phrases are obscure; we need an explanation of what they mean.

So there's something here, some kind of difference between the way that Singer values human life and the way that the Catholic Church does. The Catholic Church treats human life as absolutely inviolable, and accords it a form of dignity. It is exempted from material exchanges; it is not a fit object for tradeoffs; it is not to be bartered or weighed. Moreover—and this is a point to which I will return in later chapters—human life is described in a way that is at least somewhat obscure: for what does it mean for something to be sacred, to have dignity, and so forth? It's not obvious. Singer's position, by contrast, has the appearance of clear-headed rigor (though I will later argue that this appearance is deceptive).

If this disagreement about the value of human life were a local curiosity, it would be of limited import. But in fact these kinds of commitments are pervasive. Empirical psychology has studied them under the headings of "sacred values" or "protected values." There are a number of cases in which people seem to bestow this special status on particular objects of value.

Psychologists typically elicit these judgments by asking people to consider tradeoffs. Ordinarily, for any two valued goods, we can find circumstances in which we would trade one for the other. I value happiness and I value money; but there's some point at which I would trade an uncompensated night of happiness for a tedious evening accompanied by a quantity of money. Most values operate in this way. But there are exceptions. Some individuals are unwilling to trade certain goods at any cost. Consider cases such as these: buying and selling human body parts for medical transplants; buying votes for political office; prostitution; lowering your own insurance rates by declining to offer insurance policies to members of certain races; auctioning babies for adoption; giving up part of a nation's territory in exchange for peace; giving up an object of religious significance in

---

[8] The illegitimate child "has, as it were, stolen into the commonwealth (like contraband merchandise), so that the commonwealth can ignore its existence…and can therefore also ignore its annihilation" (Kant, *Metaphysics of Morals* 6: 336).

order to end violence.[9] In studies, a significant percentage of subjects refuse to engage in these tradeoffs regardless of the circumstances.

Whereas most values are fungible, these values aren't. People won't trade them for other values, regardless of the quantities involved. Psychologists call them *sacred values*.[10] We will examine the features of these values in more depth in the following chapters, but for now let me give a typical example of the way in which they are defined: a sacred value is "any value that a moral community explicitly or implicitly treats as possessing infinite or transcendental significance that precludes comparisons, tradeoffs, or indeed any other mingling with bounded or secular values" (Tetlock et al. 2000: 853).

I am not entirely happy with the label "sacred": it obviously has religious connotations, and many of the things that qualify as sacred values have nothing to do with religion. So the label is potentially misleading. Unfortunately, the term "sacred value" is firmly entrenched in empirical psychology. Although I think alternative labels such as "protected value" and "higher value" are better, it's too late to resist the standard label. So I will use "sacred value," hoping that the reader bears in mind that sacredness shouldn't be taken to have religious implications.

Some of the empirical studies of sacred values have the traditional flaws of social psychology: the studies are run on undergraduates, who are disproportionately drawn from predominately white, educated, industrialized, rich, democratic societies.[11] Moreover, these studies often ask students to give quick judgments about cases which may be of little import to them (does an undergraduate in an introductory psychology class really have any stake in whether adoption of children is run by auction? How seriously are they taking these questions?). So we might be skeptical that real attitudes are being uncovered here.[12]

In an effort to counteract these problems, Jeremy Ginges and Scott Atran conducted "experiments using realistic hypothetical scenarios involving values that were central to the lives of our participants and their communities who were sampled from key populations involved in political disputes" (Ginges and Atran 2012: 278). Consider a few results. Jewish Israeli settlers (defined as people who choose to live in territories that Israel occupied after the 1967 war) were asked whether they would exchange land for peace. Specifically, they were asked: "Do you agree that there are some extreme circumstances where it would be permissible for the Jewish people to give away part of the Land of Israel?" In their sample of 601 settlers, roughly half (46%) said no. Ginges and Atran took this as indicative

---

[9] These are just a few of the cases studied by Tetlock et al. 2000 and Tetlock 2003.
[10] In addition to being nonfungible, psychologists often claim that sacred values have several other features. I will discuss these below.
[11] See Henrich, Heine, and Norenzayan 2010.
[12] Some of the researchers actually share this conviction: Tetlock (2003) suggests that sacred values may be merely avowed, rather than actual. People are generally sincere when they claim that a value is sacred; but, when forced to choose, there are always circumstances in which people will compromise the value.

of a sacred value: after all, these individuals claim that there are absolutely no circumstances—in particular, no tally of human lives saved by an end to hostilities—that would motivate them to give away land. And that's not all: trying to sweeten the deal by offering additional material incentives (e.g., an end to conflict *plus* a donation of 100 billion dollars from the US to Israel) increases hostility and *decreases* the willingness to compromise (Ginges and Atran 2012: 279).

In another experiment, Palestinians were asked whether they would give up the right of return[13] in exchange for a Palestinian state in the West Bank and Gaza. Eighty percent said no, which Ginges and Atran interpret as indicating that "the right of return [is] a sacred value" (Ginges and Atran 2012: 283). As Atran puts it in a related article:

> Rational cost-benefit analysis says the Palestinians ought to agree to forgo sovereignty over Jerusalem or the claim of refugees to return to homes in Israel in exchange for an autonomous state encompassing their other pre-1967 lands because they would gain more sovereignty and more land than they would renounce. They should support such an agreement even more if the United States and Europe sweetened the deal by giving every Palestinian family substantial, long-term economic assistance. (Atran 2017: 73)

But again, that isn't the case: "the financial sweetener makes Palestinians more opposed to the deal and more likely to support violence to oppose it, including suicide bombings" (Atran 2017: 73).

The values implicated in these cases are exceptional: they are uncompromisable and are held despite immense costs. Of course, that alone doesn't demonstrate that these values are distinctive: it may just be that one thing (such as sovereignty) is valued so highly that the costs of giving it up massively outweigh the gains. But that alone doesn't explain the second feature: tradeoffs and attempts at mitigation make things worse, rather than better. That's peculiar.

We could try to explain away these cases by focusing on the particulars. Maybe the "financial sweetener" makes the deal seem like a trick (the opposite side must really be desperate for this!); or maybe there are fears about the stability of the deal (they're trying to make us more vulnerable!). While we might question any particular case in these ways, the body of research is by now so large that it seems foolish to deny that this is a real phenomenon. To give a sense of just how extensive sacred values are, I will mention a few disparate cases.

---

[13] The right of return is typically defined as the idea that both Palestinian refugees—defined as those whose place of residence had been British Palestine, but who were displaced in 1948—and their descendants have a right to return to what is now Israel. Sometimes, the right of return is interpreted as including a right to the property that was abandoned in 1948.

In the United States, a prime candidate is gun rights. Most Americans are happy to accept significant restrictions on freedoms in exchange for safety. Few object to laws requiring us to fasten seatbelts and drive at posted speed limits. Few object to prohibitions on purchasing explosives, toxins, and so forth. In these cases, the reasoning appears to be a simple cost/benefit analysis: the dangers are so great that prohibitions are acceptable. However, in large segments of the American population, gun rights are not given an analogous status.[14] Suppose it could be conclusively established that prohibitions on gun ownership would save a significant number of lives. Australia is often used as an example to support this claim. After a mass shooting in 1996, Australia introduced certain restrictions on gun ownership. Between 1995 and 2006, gun-related homicides dropped 59%. Given that there are somewhere around 34,000 gun homicides per year in the US, we could easily imagine restrictions on gun ownership saving thousands of lives. Nonetheless, some gun rights proponents object that this would not be justified. After a 2008 Supreme Court ruling that the Second Amendment protects an individual's right to gun ownership, Senator John McCain claimed that "Unlike the elitist view that believes Americans cling to guns out of bitterness, today's ruling recognizes that gun ownership is a fundamental right—sacred, just as the right to free speech and assembly." The National Rifle Association routinely promotes the idea that gun ownership is a sacred right; its bylaws state that it will defend the "inalienable right of the individual American citizen guaranteed by such Constitution to acquire, possess, collect, exhibit, transport, carry, transfer ownership of, and enjoy the right to use arms." These rights are treated as unrestricted and independent of the consequences: no costs are too great. Even minor restrictions on these rights are treated as monstrous, as threats to the rights themselves.

Another domain in which sacred values arise is in certain environmental movements which oppose not just some, but *all* impacts on the environment. *Earth First!* is often interpreted as committed to this position. Distinctive here is *Earth Firsts!*'s absolute refusal to compromise the environmental values for other values. Their slogan is "no compromise in the defense of mother earth!", and they endorse acts of sabotage and violence.

But I don't want these examples to give the impression that sacred values are isolated. There are even more mainstream examples. Human rights are candidates: "We hold these truths to be self-evident, that all men are created equal, that they are endowed by their Creator with certain unalienable Rights, that among these are Life, Liberty, and the pursuit of Happiness" (US Declaration of Independence, 1776). Or consider the First Article of the German constitution, which begins as follows:

---

[14] For statistical data, see https://www.pewresearch.org/social-trends/2017/06/22/americas-complex-relationship-with-guns/.

(1) Human dignity is inviolable. To respect it and protect it is the duty of all state power.

(2) The German people therefore acknowledge inviolable and inalienable human rights as the basis of every community, of peace and of justice in the world.

Or take the United Nation's 1948 Universal Declaration of Human Rights, which claims that "recognition of the inherent dignity and of the equal and inalienable rights of all members of the human family is the foundation of freedom, justice and peace in the world." It continues: "All human beings are born free and equal in dignity and rights." Or consider John Rawls' widely quoted claim that "each person possesses an inviolability founded on justice that even the welfare of society as a whole cannot override... the loss of freedom for some is not made right by a greater welfare enjoyed by others" (Rawls 1971: 87). Dignity, rights, and justice are taken to have lexical priority over other considerations. Regardless of how great a gain in welfare would be produced by acting unjustly or by violating rights, this is prohibited. Tradeoffs are not to be entertained. And the language of sanctity, dignity, and inviolability routinely arises in these contexts. These look like candidates for sacred values.

So I am suggesting that when we examine social and ethical life, we find widespread commitment to a distinctive sort of value. In the following chapters, I will analyze the structure of this type of value more precisely. But for now, we can say that there seems to be a domain of sacred values. We can initially distinguish these values by focusing on the way in which they are exempted from tradeoffs and held independently of costs. Prospects of massive casualties, staggering environmental destruction, and crippling economic burdens do not sway people from maintaining commitment to their sacred values. In being immune to tradeoffs, sacred values differ from ordinary values. But not just in terms of this immunization; there's also the fact that an aura of mystery surrounds many of these values. There is an ethos surrounding gun ownership. It is connected, sometimes in inarticulate ways, to a sense of identity. And words such as "dignity" have a whiff of the portentous and ineffable; they are redolent and it's not obvious what they mean.

I want to investigate these phenomena. What are these things that psychologists call sacred values? How should they be understood?

Sacred values aren't just things that are taken to be extremely valuable, for things can be extremely valuable without being sacred. Sacred values aren't identical to moral values, for the same reason: many of our moral values are not treated as sacred (though some are). Nor are sacred values identical to commitments that are perceived as meaningful: things that are very meaningful, that are taken to imbue one's life with significance, can nonetheless be non-sacred. (I can view athletic achievement or literary skill as imbuing a person's life with significance, without thinking that sports or books are sacred.) Sacred values needn't be associated with religions, though they often are; environmentalist movements, the Second Amendment, and political stances can involve sacred values.

The presence of sacred values is most obvious when people maintain them at great cost, as in the Palestinian/Israeli and gun-rights cases discussed above. But actual costs needn't arise; if we're lucky, they will only arise in counterfactual circumstances. Thus, we sometimes need to consider counterfactual scenarios in order to determine whether a given value is sacralized. And once we do this, many more sacred values appear. I will return to this point in Chapter 3.

For now, though, let's just note that sacred values present a puzzle. It's not clear what, exactly, they are. One possibility is that they're nothing, or, more precisely, no *one* thing. Perhaps the things that get labeled "sacred" are just a motley assortment of things that are objects of passionate attachment for some, considered meaningful for others, taken to warrant sacrifice by others, and bound up with a sense of identity for some. Perhaps there's no unified class here.

But I think there is. I think we can single out something essential about sacred values and use that feature to uncover some important features of our thinking about value and the craving for devotion. In the following chapters, I argue that we can distinguish sacred values by their formal features: they prohibit certain kinds of tradeoffs, including merely contemplated tradeoffs; and they are invulnerable to the effects of certain forms of rational argumentation. I will explain these points in the next chapter, but for now we can think of sacred values as inviolable, incontestable, and resistant to ordinary modes of rational critique.

1.3 Sacred Values and Devoted Agents

But why bother? Why should we analyze sacred values? People engage in all sorts of strange, foolish, and irrational behavior. They display quirks and peculiarities. Shouldn't we class sacred values with these phenomena? And if so, aren't they a better topic for empirical psychological investigation than for philosophical study?

I argue that this would be a mistake. In ignoring sacred values, moral philosophy operates with a distorted picture of ethical life.

Although there are exceptions, a great deal of moral philosophy over the past century is concerned with the trivia of everyday life: should I keep my promise? Should I tell a lie? Or it is concerned with artificial dilemmas: suppose there's an avalanche and my child and I are trapped in wreckage. Can I use a stranger's body as a shield to save my child's life, without that person's consent, if doing so would crush one of his little toes? How about if crushing two toes would save two lives? (This is an actual discussion; Parfit 2011, Volume I, pp. 222–31.) Left untheorized are the questions that drive many of us to moral philosophy in the first place:

questions about significance, meaning, commitment; questions about the objects of passionate commitment; questions about what drives the jihadi, the nationalist, the committed proponent of human rights, the devoted environmentalist.

And I think there's a reason for this. Philosophers assume that these are just more extreme or more complicated instances of the trivial phenomena. If we can figure out whether we can compel toe-sacrifices to save children, then we can figure out what's going on with the commitments involved in nationalism, authoritarianism, terrorism, and so forth. We just have to start small, teasing out the differentiating factors. We don't start with the big questions; we build up to them.

But perhaps not. Perhaps these aren't just more complex, more extreme versions of the same problems. Perhaps the focus on trivial and imaginary cases distorts ethical theorizing. We start formulating our ethical theories and distinctions by considering these trivial cases. We assume that the grave questions that animate our actual ethical lives will be answered in analogous ways: they will have more variables, they will involve additional factors, but at root they will be the same. And I think this makes us incapable of seeing how deliberation and reasoning actually proceed in these cases. It blinds us to the way in which our deepest normative convictions actually function. We assume that these convictions can enter deliberation as rationally assessable, weighable points; that they can be defended in ways that are analogous to the way that the trivial concerns are defended; that they stand in need of the same kind of justification as these trivial concerns do; and that we can typically articulate them with at least some degree of clarity and precision. And all of that, I will argue, is mistaken.

But my conclusions won't just be descriptive. I won't just be arguing that people *do in fact* operate with sacred values. I will argue that there are ways in which they *should*. After all, many philosophers will be tempted to think that while people do display the behaviors I've described above, these are pathologies, rational failures, things to be overcome. Not so, I will argue. It's not just that philosophers have failed to notice sacred values and have thus given inaccurate descriptions of ethical life; it's also that, in virtue of the distorted picture of ethical life, their normative claims have gone astray.

So, in part this book will be about philosophers' difficulties in acknowledging the existence of sacred values. When I say that philosophers fail to acknowledge sacred values, I don't mean that philosophers have explicitly denied that there can be any such thing. Rather, I mean that philosophers have operated with assumptions that constrain the deliberative space. As we go on, we'll see that a group of apparently heterogenous phenomena—incommensurable values, lexical priority rankings, moral remainders, tragic choices, questions about importance and meaning in life—all of these, which seem to be at the edge of ethical theorizing, turn out to be related, to be manifestations of the phenomenon that I am investigating. Moreover, central features of ethical theories—the way in which arguments for the core assumptions proceed, the aspects of the theory that philosophers focus upon—are puzzling until we recognize the role of sacred values in theories that fail to acknowledge them.[15]

In short: I think sacred values play a crucial role in ethical life and that our failure to recognize this distorts ethical theorizing. While the real argument for this point is not shorter than the entire book, let me try to give some indication of how this is so.

A central idea in many religions is that a satisfying human life requires wholehearted commitment to values or ideals that cannot be justified in the ordinary ways, that perhaps cannot even be fully understood. These values cannot be justified by reason alone; nor can they be established by empirical inquiry; instead, they require revelation, or divine insight, or the acceptance of dogmas, or some sort of ability to limn the structure of reality. So we need not just reason, but faith. This is an exceedingly common way of understanding the difference between religious and non-religious approaches to life.

Against this, many philosophers argue—again at a very high level of generality—that we can do without faith. The most optimistic of philosophers believe that we can (or eventually will be able to) justify wholehearted commitment to certain values by reason alone.[16] Others back off just a small step, claiming that although of course there will be controversies about particular goods, we can get overlapping consensus on a number of shared goods.[17] Others tell us that we can detach our desire for rational justification from our wholeheartedness: we can live as "ironists," or "free spirits," or existentialists, who remain wholeheartedly committed to values that we freely admit are not rationally justifiable.[18] And others think we are doomed to vacillation or fragmentation or anomie: we have to choose between wholeheartedness and clear-headed rationality; we can't have both.[19]

---

[15] A good example of this is *All Things Shining* (Kelly and Dreyfus 2011). This extremely popular book opens with a promise to cure us of nihilism and despair: "Anyone who is done with indecision and waiting, with expressionlessness and lostness and sadness and angst...anyone with despair that they would like to leave behind, can find something worthwhile in the pages ahead" (xi). Kelly and Dreyfus deny the possibility of objective sources of meaning and propose that we instead content ourselves with the ordinary: the experience of communal cheering at a baseball game; the taste of coffee; the grain of a nice piece of wood. While there's much to be commended in this book, it arguably fails to appreciate the distinction between sacralized commitments and trivial commitments. For reasons that will become clear as we proceed, there is all the difference in the world between being *devoted* to coffee connoisseurship, baseball, etc., and merely treating these things as valued yet fungible goods. See Ebels-Duggan 2011 for an argument that, while phrased differently, effectively makes this point.

[16] Parfit 2011 is a good example. But the aspiration is also present in many others: see, for example, Korsgaard 1996, Smith 1994, and Scanlon 1998.

[17] See, for example, Rawls 1993 and Berlin 1990.

[18] Rorty 1989, Kierkegaard 1841/1989, Camus 1955, Sartre 1948, de Beauvoir 1976, perhaps Nietzsche 1974.

[19] Schopenhauer 1844 and 1891, perhaps Nietzsche 2003, Benatar 2017.

Depending on which philosophical position seems tempting, sacred values will look different. Sacred values do involve a particular form of wholehearted commitment: we are completely committed to them in the sense that they are treated as uncompromisable. Moreover, they involve a particular form of dogmatism: I will argue that we treat them as incomparable and as invulnerable to ordinary rational argumentation. Finally, they often imbue our lives with a sense of purpose or direction, and thereby give us a way of attaining a form of contentment with life. So they have the features that many of us associate with traditional religious values. But sacred values needn't be religious; they are far more pervasive.

In virtue of these features, I will suggest that sacred values enable us to stave off the forms of nihilism, anomie, and vacillation that I've mentioned above. This is why they play a crucial role in ethical life. But the sacralization of a value is typically premised upon the idea that commitment to the value *cannot* be fully justified by ordinary modes of rational thought. I think this is true and important. More precisely: I will argue that although we have reason to embrace *some* sacred values, we don't have a good justification for picking any *particular* sacred values. And there is where the need for insulation from questioning and critique arises: in order to fulfill their psychological function, sacred values have to be shielded from the effects of certain kinds of inquiry. But this doesn't mean that we need to seek some religious or metaphysical foundation for them. Instead, it can just mean that we delimit the quest for foundations. Nietzsche famously wrote that the ancient "Greeks were superficial—*out of profundity!*" (*The Gay Science,* Preface, 4). I will develop a version of that thought. To lay my cards on the table: as you might expect from someone who has spent much of his career writing on Nietzsche, I am an atheist devoid of religious sentiments. So the solution I propose at the end will attempt to preserve a version of the religious form without the religious content.

In particular: I will argue that there is an intimate connection between sacred values and devotion. Although you can be devoted without having sacred values, if you do have sacred values you will experience devotion as required in certain circumstances. Sacred values make devotion non-optional. There are other ways of manifesting devotion—in Chapter 9 I will explore a way of manifesting devotion without holding sacred values, and aside from that it is possible to devote yourself to something that you regard as entirely valueless—but they are more complex and potentially more tenuous.

Of course, we might respond to this conclusion in different ways. Some will view it as a reason to abandon the quest for the forms of devotion that are based upon sacred values: if those forms of devotion require sacred values, we had better learn to live without them! Others will view it as a reason to preserve certain forms of devotion. And others, still, might seek some kind of compromise or balancing of these desires. I will explore these possibilities in the final chapters.

1.4 Plan of the Book

I pointed out that some of our commitments involve sacred values. To understand this point, we need to clarify the notion of sacred values. **Chapter 2** reviews the psychological and philosophical work on sacred values and related phenomena. I argue that sacred values are commitments with three distinguishing features: they are overriding, incontestable, and invulnerable to certain forms of critique. In particular, we can analyze sacred values as follows.

(**Sacred value**) Let V1 be a value. Then V1 counts as sacred iff it meets the following conditions:

1. <u>Inviolable</u>: If V2 is an ordinary value, then it is prohibited to sacrifice V1 for V2, regardless of the quantities of V1 and V2.

2. <u>Incontestable</u>: It is prohibited to *contemplate* trading or sacrificing V1 for most or all other values.

3. <u>Dialectically Invulnerable</u>: The agent insulates her commitment to V1 from the effects of justificatory reasoning. That is, while the agent may think about V1's justification, consider objections to V1, consider alternatives to V1, engage in thought experiments with respect to V1, and so on, the agent does not stake her commitment to V1 on the outcome of this justificatory reasoning. There is no dialectical move that would disrupt the agent's commitment to V1.

Chapter 2 explains these features. In addition, I review several other factors that are characteristically but not inevitably associated with sacred values. These include certain types of emotions (such as reverence and awe); a sense of subjective import or meaning; and inarticulacy about the contents of or justification for one's sacred values.

With that, we will have an account of a distinctive type of normative commitment, the *sacred value*. But sacred values might seem paradigmatically irrational: isn't it problematic to treat values as inviolable, incontestable, and dialectically invulnerable? **Chapter 3** argues that it can be rational to hold sacred values. I start with features (1) and (2), the prohibition of exchanges and comparisons. The commitment to sacred values conflicts with views according to which every normative consideration can be assigned a weight (you are forbidden to weigh or even entertain the idea of weighing sacred values). Moreover, the commitment to sacred values conflicts with views according to which it is always problematic to refuse to compare things which are in fact comparable. I explore how it can be rational to have commitments that exhibit these features.

This still leaves feature (3), dialectical invulnerability. **Chapter 4** examines the peculiar way in which sacred values are insulated from the effects of justificatory reflection. I begin by analyzing the concept of *devotion*. I argue that being devoted requires treating one's commitment to the object of devotion as dialectically invulnerable. I further argue that it can be rational to manifest devotion, for devotion is a precondition for the preservation of central features of ethical life. If it can be rational to devote oneself to things, and if doing so requires treating one's commitment to these things as dialectically invulnerable, then it can be rational to render certain commitments dialectically invulnerable.

The arguments in Chapter 4 turn on the idea that we need to treat certain commitments as fixed and immutable. One way of treating commitments as fixed is by immunizing them from critique, in the ways that Chapter 4 examines. But another way would be by decisively establishing these commitments through rational argumentation. Suppose, for example, that Kant's ethical theory were successful: we begin with some undeniable facts about agency and then show that some analogue of enlightenment values follow from them. If this worked, then we could do away with the dialectical invulnerability component of sacred values: we wouldn't *need* to treat the values as dialectically invulnerable, because dialectic would decisively establish them.

I think this strategy has no hope of success. In **Chapter 5**, I explain why. In essence, I argue that reasonable people can always find good grounds for questioning their basic normative commitments. In particular, I argue that there is a sense in which we are unable to justify weightings or lexical orderings of competing basic normative claims. Reaching an all-things-considered judgment about what ought to be done in a particular case typically requires assigning relative weights to competing normative claims; and yet, according to a view that I call *Normative Weighting Skepticism*, we lack sufficient justification for assigning these relative weights and thus are unable to reach all-things-considered ought judgments. Although Normative Weighting Skepticism rests on certain assumptions about moral uncertainty, I argue that it is a reasonable philosophical position. I further argue that people who accept Normative Weighting Skepticism will experience a motivational problem that I label Normative Dissipation: roughly, they will find that normative entities (reasons, values, or principles) formerly treated as overriding cease to function as overriding. Having sacred values is one way of insulating one's values from these effects and thereby preventing the relevant form of dissipation.

Chapters 2 through 5 thus jointly show that it can be rational to have sacred values. But sacred values are not wholly positive; they have their costs. In Chapters 6 through 8, I examine pathologies that can arise from defective relations to sacred values. In being immune to rational critique, sacred values can foster and promote oppositional tendencies in individuals and groups. In particular, sacred values can easily give rise to a form of fanaticism.

Chapter 6 examines individual fanaticism. Several philosophers in the early modern period, including Shaftesbury, Locke, and Kant, argue that fanaticism consists in a certain type of dogmatism: one takes oneself to have an incontrovertible justification for some ideal but simultaneously insists that this justification outstrips ordinary rational standards, being based instead on personal experiences of divine communication, insight into the nature of reality, or some such. I call this the *Enlightenment account of fanaticism*. I argue that it is inadequate: while the Enlightenment account does identify one type of epistemic failing, this failing is not correlated with fanaticism. So we need a new account.

Chapter 7 offers that new account. I argue that fanaticism is based upon a constellation of psychological traits including a form of personal fragility, group orientation, and a view about the status of values. I argue that the fanatic is distinguished by four features: the adoption of one or more sacred values; the need to treat these values as unconditional in order to preserve one's identity; the sense that the status of these values is threatened by lack of widespread acceptance; and the identification with a group, where the group is defined by shared commitment to the sacred value. I explain how these features are mutually reinforcing and tend to promote the types of violent intolerance that we typically associate with fanaticism.

In **Chapter 8**, I ask how individual fanaticism relates to group fanaticism. The simplest view would be that fanatical groups are groups all or most of whose members are fanatics. But I argue that there is a more promising view. According to my *generative* view of group fanaticism, a group qualifies as fanatical iff it promotes individual fanaticism. But how, exactly, might a group promote individual fanaticism? I explore the way in which certain kinds of group narratives can promote ressentiment. Analyzing this notion of ressentiment, I explain how the production of ressentiment encourages individual fanaticism. Thus, my account runs as follows: a group counts as fanatical iff it promotes individual fanaticism; a common (though not necessary) way of promoting individual fanaticism is by promoting ressentiment; thus, a common characteristic of fanatical groups is their tendency to promote ressentiment. I argue that this account helps us to identify a disturbing feature of certain contemporary groups, movements, and political ideologies.

Chapter 9 draws these points together. We have seen that devotion plays an important role in ethical life; that devotion is fostered by sacred values, which are inviolable, incontestable, and dialectically invulnerable; that close examination reveals that sacred values pervade ethical and social life; and that sacred values stave off normative dissipation. More worryingly, we have seen that the person who holds sacred values risks meeting the Enlightenment conditions for fanaticism; that, when the person with sacred values displays certain additional features, he does indeed become fanatical; and that fanatical groups encourage individuals to display these additional features and thereby lapse into fanaticism. So we now need to ask: are there ways of holding sacred values without risking fanaticism? I suggest that there are. There are ways of rendering values dialectically invulnerable, and thereby enabling devotion, without generating the most problematic forms of life that can be associated with sacred values. For I suggest that there are non-fanatical ways of expressing devotion, ways that differ from fanaticism in that they enable the agent to recognize a form of contingency, optionality, or revisability in her basic commitments. I investigate whether you can be devoted through irony; through affirmation; and through what I call the deepening move. Each of these stances preserves a degree of flexibility and openness in the objects of devotion; each one tries to preserve a wholehearted form of devotion despite this openness.

Finally, the **Conclusion** considers what lesson we should draw from these reflections. I began by arguing that we yearn for devotion. My ultimate recommendation is to achieve devotion in non-pathological forms, via affirmation and the deepening move. By doing so, we would avoid the dangers of fanaticism on the one hand and normative dissipation on the other. But this is always a fragile and precarious state: affirmation can slide into a focus on rejecting that which isn't affirmed, and the deepening move can deform into rigidity. Only the perpetual quest to maintain a form of existential flexibility, in which we may need to oscillate between affirmation and deepening, can stave off these dangers.

2
The Nature of Sacred Values

"No one dies for mere values" (Heidegger 2002: 77). Heidegger's words are extremely ominous when we consider that they were delivered in a June 1938 lecture, a few months after Nazi Germany annexed Austria. People were dying, by the thousands and later by the millions, for the sake of some kind of commitment—but, Heidegger suggests, not for the sake of ordinary values. Ordinary values are "powerless and threadbare," seen by their adherents as the mere "objectification" of individual or cultural goals, so that what is labeled valuable is merely what we take ourselves to desire (Heidegger 2002: 77). Heidegger suggests that devoted actors, those willing to endure suffering and hardship and even death for the sake of their ends, are moved not by mere values but by a different form of normative commitment.

There's something right about this; there's something right about the idea that our normative commitments don't all take the same form. As I pointed out in Chapter 1, we value coffee, naps, sunsets; but these values are trivial, exchangeable, fungible. When we compare these values to the ideals of the devoted nationalist, the committed jihadist, the ardent environmentalist, the advocate of social justice, it looks like significant differences arise. These latter ideals don't look trivial, don't look exchangeable, don't look fungible. But how should they be understood? What features do they possess?

In the last chapter, I suggested that we could make progress on these questions by drawing on a research program in empirical psychology. Over the past three decades, psychologists have been developing a concept of "sacred values." In a classic paper, Philip Tetlock tells us that a sacred value is

> any value that a moral community implicitly or explicitly treats as possessing infinite or transcendental significance that precludes comparisons, trade-offs, or indeed any other mingling with bounded or secular values.
>
> (Tetlock et al. 2000: 853)

The evangelical Christian who treats human life as sacred; the German constitution's opening lines, which state that human dignity is inviolable; the Universal Declaration of Human Rights, which treats human rights as inalienable and inviolable; the Aryan nationalist, who treats racial purity as an unquestionable ideal; all of these are prime candidates for sacred values. For the values implicated in these stances are not treated as fungible, compromisable, or tradeable; they are, instead, treated as exempt from comparisons, and as having a special status.

But what *exactly* is involved in treating a value as sacred? Answering this question is not as easy as it might seem, for the psychological and philosophical literature on sacred values is rather imprecise. Psychologists mainly focus on the way in which sacred values resist being traded against competing values. Sometimes, psychologists link sacred values to a certain set of emotional responses, including disgust, horror, and repugnance.[1] In the philosophical literature, the few authors who discuss sacred values typically associate them with a form of inviolability.[2] Philosophers sometimes link sacred values to a set of emotions, but the list is rather different than that drawn up by the psychologists: reverence, honor, and awe figure prominently. And there are other features as well: sacred values are sometimes understood as requiring particular metaphysical views, divine sanction, links to religion, and so on. Finally, sacred values tend to be exempted from certain kinds of rational critique: their proponents are sometimes held to be dogmatic or resistant to engaging in critical reflection.[3]

In short: sacred values are associated with a cluster of claims about tradeoffs, the emotional concomitants of valuing, metaphysical or religious views, and dogmatism. To achieve a better understanding of sacred values, we need to figure out which of these features are essential and which are inessential; and we also need to state each feature more carefully. That will be the task of this chapter.

That task can be carried out in two ways. First, we can locate and make more precise the concept of sacred values as it figures in psychological and philosophical work, trying to tease out the essential features. Second, working from a different direction, we can locate features that show up in certain evaluative experiences and show that, when jointly present, these features constitute a type of normative commitment that deserves philosophical attention. Working from that direction, we can use the term "sacred value" to mark out things with those features. I will begin by working in the first direction and then move on to the second.

The structure of the chapter is as follows. Section 2.1 investigates the sense in which sacred values are inviolable: unlike ordinary values, there are no circumstances in which it is permissible to act against a sacred value. Section 2.2 examines the way in which sacred values prohibit certain kinds of comparisons and thereby issue restrictions on permissible types of reflection. Section 2.3 analyzes the dogmatism that often seems to be associated with sacred values, discussing the ways in which sacred values are immunized from the effects of justificatory reflection. With that, we arrive at the three core features of sacred values: they are inviolable, incontestable, and invulnerable to justificatory critique. Section 2.4 argues that recent philosophical and psychological discussions have erred in arguing for necessary connections between sacred values and purity-related emotions. Section 2.5 examines the connection between sacred values and

---

[1] Haidt 2012, Graham and Haidt 2012.   [2] Tessman 2014, Dworkin 1995, Uniake 2004.
[3] Skikta 2010, Tetlock et al. 2000, Baron and Spranca 1997.

a sense of meaning; Section 2.6 asks why sacred values often seem inarticulate or inchoate. Finally, Section 2.7 offers the full account of sacred values.

2.1 The Inviolability of Sacred Values

Let's begin with the idea that sacred values are immunized from tradeoffs. Those who profess belief in sacred values often explicitly state that these values are inviolable, as in the Catholic claim that "human life is sacred and inviolable at every moment of existence" or the German constitution's claim that "human dignity is inviolable." A number of philosophers agree. Hume repeatedly claims that certain rules pertaining to property are "sacred and inviolable" (Hume 1739/2000: Book 3, Part II, Section VI; and Book 3, Part II, Section X). Just so, Adam Smith calls the rules of justice sacred and inviolable (Smith 1759/1976: 161). Kant tells us that "the moral law is holy (*inviolable*)...In the whole of creation everything one wants and everything over which one has power can also be used *merely as a means;* a human being alone, and with him every rational creature, is *an end in itself*" (1788/1996: 5:87).[4]

And these associations continue in more recent philosophical work. Ronald Dworkin claims that the central feature of the sacred is that it is inviolable (1995: 24). Richard Norman writes that "it is this idea of 'inviolability' that seems to me to be the key. What is distinctive about the 'sacred' is that it sets up boundaries or barriers which must not be crossed" (2017: 10). Suzanne Uniacke agrees: "'Inviolability' refers to the way in which a sacred thing ought to be treated: it ought not to be violated or attacked" (2004: 75).

Many psychologists and philosophers thus agree that the sacred bears some connection to the inviolable. But there are different notions of inviolability at play in the above quotations. Let me try to tease out some features.

First, inviolability should be understood in a normative sense: it's not that sacred commitments cannot be violated; it's that they *shouldn't* be. So we can put the inviolability point as follows: if V is a sacred value, then violations of V are always prohibited.

But there's some unclarity here. What counts as a *violation*? We often see commitments or demands as excused by competing concerns. Consider cases like this: I shouldn't break my promises, but I also shouldn't put someone's life at risk; if the only way I can avoid breaking my promise is by putting someone's life at risk, I am no longer obligated to keep the promise. The soldier should follow orders, but he also shouldn't murder innocents; if the only way he can follow

---

[4] Kant associates the sacred with that which cannot be fulfilled once and for all: "for, a moral object is sacred if the obligation with regard to it cannot be discharged completely by any act of keeping with it (so that one who is under it always remains under obligation)" (Kant 1797/2017: 6:455).

orders is by murdering innocents, he is no longer obligated to follow orders. The company should maximize profits, but it also should avoid poisoning the water supply; if the only way it can maximize profits is by poisoning the water supply, it should refrain from doing so. In conflicts between competing duties, we typically don't see the agent as *violating* a duty; we see one duty as overridden or cancelled by a more important concern.

One thing that's notable about sacred values is that they aren't cancelled or overridden by competing concerns. We might put the point as follows: if V1 is a sacred value, then in any case where V1 conflicts with some other value V2, sacrificing V1 for the sake of V2 is wrong.[5]

So understood, sacred values would be absolute requirements or absolute prohibitions. This would explain why we're tempted to describe cases of trading a sacred value for some other good as a "violation": the obligation to act as the sacred value dictates is not cancellable. It has priority over other obligations.

And this priority would obtain independently of the quantities of the goods involved. Psychologists often emphasize this feature of sacred values. In a representative paper, Baron and Spranca claim that sacred values are distinguished by their "resistance to trade-offs" (Baron and Spranca 1997: 4). They are resistant to tradeoffs in the sense that the "quantity" of consequences is irrelevant for sacred values.[6] That is, suppose we can preserve commitment to value V1 only by abandoning value V2. Most normative commitments are quantity-sensitive: whether you ought to trade V1 for V2 depends on the quantities of these values. I've promised to help my friend move to a new apartment, but I wake up with a very mild headache. Presumably my desire to stay home doesn't override or cancel the promise. But now suppose the pain is severe and incapacitating. It seems fine to cancel the promise. Or, another example: perhaps a government shouldn't seize a person's home in order to prevent extremely minor environmental damage; but it should do so in order to prevent major environmental damage. Quantities typically matter. But with some values, quantities don't matter.[7]

Psychologists often express this point by claiming that individuals holding sacred values ignore the consequences or "utility" of compromising these values;

---

[5] Values can conflict in different ways and accordingly what counts as sacrificing one value for the sake of another can vary. The most straightforward cases occur when we consider temporary, contingent clashes that arise from our circumstances and abilities. For example, suppose I value the saving of this child's life and also value being on time for my meeting; I cannot do both; so I must choose. More complex cases arise when the conflicts reside in the nature of the values themselves, so that the conflicts aren't localized to particular circumstances. To give some standard examples: perhaps there's a conflict between the requirements of justice and those of mercy, or between liberty and equality, or between self-interest and duty. The above remarks on inviolability should be understood as pertaining to both kinds of cases.

[6] Baron and Spranca actually list five features; this is just the first of them. I will return to the others later in this chapter.

[7] For discussions of purportedly absolute requirements and how they might be cancelled once certain "thresholds" are reached, see for example Alexander 2000, Moore 1997, and Sen 1982.

no matter how high the utility of compromising the sacred value is, they will see this as prohibited. For example, Graham and Haidt claim that "sacredness refers to the human tendency to invest people, places, times, and ideas with importance far beyond the utility they possess. Tradeoffs or compromises involving what is sacralized are resisted or refused" (2012: 14). Atran and Axelrod write that "sacred values are moral imperatives that seem to drive behavior independently of any concrete material goal" (2008: 226).

So we can make our definition a bit more precise: if V1 is a sacred value, then in any case where V1 conflicts with some other value V2, acting against V1 so as to achieve V2 is wrong regardless of the quantity of V2.

Is this sufficient? Not quite: there's another complication.

Despite philosophers' frequent emphasis on inviolability and absolute prohibitions, the language of absoluteness is rather overblown. Most psychologists working on this topic think that tradeoffs involving sacred values are *restricted*, rather than absolutely prohibited. For example, Ginges and Atran write that the

> defining characteristic [of sacred values] is a taboo against considering sacred values as *fungible with economic things or valuing sacred values along a material or monetary scale.* (Ginges and Atran 2014: 274, emphasis added)

And Sheikh writes:

> The term "sacred value" denotes a way of thinking about a preference. Specifically, the application of a decision-making rule that treats as prohibited any attempt to value that preference *along a material scale*.
> (Sheikh et al. 2012: 110, emphasis added)

Here, it is not *all* tradeoffs that are prohibited, but just tradeoffs of sacred values for material or economic values. Analogously, Tetlock writes that

> sacred values as those values that a moral community treats as possessing transcendental significance that precludes comparisons, trade-offs, or indeed any mingling *with secular values.* (Tetlock 2003: 320, emphasis added)

Again, it's not that all tradeoffs are prohibited, but that trading a value from one class (the sacred) against a value from another class (the non-sacred) is prohibited. So, while I can't trade a sacred value for money or material comfort, I can trade one sacred value so as to realize another.

With that in mind, we can formulate the inviolability claim as follows:

<u>Inviolable</u>: if V1 is a sacred value and V2 is an ordinary value, then it is prohibited to sacrifice V1 for V2, regardless of the quantities of V1 and V2.

This is what's sometimes referred to as a lexical preference ordering: V1 is lexically preferred to V2 if a person is unwilling to give up any amount of V1 for any amount of V2. As Elizabeth Anderson puts it, "lexical preferences prohibit trade-offs of one good against another" (Anderson 1995: 67). Quantities don't matter.

Of course, this immediately raises a question: we have been discussing cases in which a sacred value conflicts with an ordinary value, but what about cases in which two sacred values come into conflict?

These conflicts between sacred values operate in an importantly different way. In order to mark the difference, psychologists distinguish between "taboo tradeoffs" and "tragic tradeoffs." A *taboo tradeoff* occurs when an individual trades (or considers trading) a sacred value against a non-sacred value. A *tragic tradeoff* occurs when an individual trades (or considers trading) one sacred value against another sacred value. We can generate an example by returning to the Palestinian and Israeli case mentioned in the last chapter. Recall that the study (Atran 2017) found that many Israelis treat territorial integrity as a sacred value. Accordingly, if a government official considered trading territory for a monetary payment, this would constitute a taboo tradeoff. By contrast, if we assume that human life is also considered to be a sacred value, then a government official who considering trading territory for human lives would be entertaining a tragic tradeoff.

There is empirical evidence that individuals exhibit moral outrage, disgust, anger, willingness to punish those who make these tradeoffs, and so forth when asked to consider taboo tradeoffs. Crucially, individuals perceive these as *easy* choices: they take it as obvious that the sacred value should not be sacrificed for the non-sacred value. In part for that reason, they tend to judge people more harshly when they spend more time contemplating particular taboo tradeoffs. I will say more on this below.

Tragic tradeoffs are different, though: in these cases, individuals respond more positively to those who dwell on the tragic tradeoff at length, who feel guilty or conflicted about the tradeoff, and who make attempts to atone for their failure to respect whichever value they choose to violate. So: if the government official quickly decides that he will sacrifice lives for territory and is happy and confident with his choice, this is perceived as objectionable. If, on the other hand, he dwells on the choice, lingers over it, feels torn, but ultimately makes the same choice, this is likely to be perceived as better; and the more so, to the extent that afterwards he experiences guilt and regret.[8]

I mention this phenomenon because it marks a crucial difference between sacred values and standard lexical orderings of values. Tradeoffs between two

---

[8] For discussions of this phenomenon, see for example Tetlock 2003, Tetlock et al. 2000, Hanselmann and Tanner 2008, and Haidt 2012. There is a related literature on "moral residue": for classic discussions, see Williams 1965 and Marcus 1980. More recent discussions include Greenspan 1983, Hill 1996, Sinnott-Armstrong 1988, and Tessman 2014.

sacred values involve "moral residues": regardless of which choice is made, remorse and guilt seem appropriate. This is *not* a typical feature of lexical preferences. Consider, for example, John Stuart Mill's distinction between higher and lower pleasures (Mill 1861/1998: 2): roughly, pleasure A counts as higher than pleasure B if an experienced judge would be unwilling to trade A for any quantity of B. For example, Mill thinks that experienced judges would be unwilling to trade the pleasures of intellectual discovery for the pleasures of eating, regardless of how great the quantities are on either side. This is often interpreted as a lexical preference ordering.[9] So the higher pleasures form a set that is lexically preferred to other pleasures. However, exchanges within the set of higher pleasures seem perfectly fine. If Mill trades a night of reading for a night at the opera, he wouldn't see this as a tragedy; it's a simple exchange of one higher pleasure for another. So, whereas tradeoffs between sacred values result in moral residues, tradeoffs between other lexically ordered values needn't.

In light of this, we can see the sacralization of values as partitioning the agent's values into two sets: the sacred and the non-sacred, where the sacred enjoy lexical priority over the non-sacred but do not enter into further lexical orderings with one another. In other words: on one side of the lexical ordering, we have all of the person's sacred values; on the other, we have all of the person's non-sacred values. The set of non-sacred values may itself contain various lexical orderings (the person may lexically prioritize the obligations of her job over the requirements of her hobbies), but not so with the set of sacred values. Another way of expressing this point would be as follows: if we find that a person's values exhibit multiple lexical orders, the candidates for sacred values will be only those values at the top of the lexical ordering.

2.2 Sacred Values as Involving Prohibitions on Particular Forms of Deliberation

The first feature of sacred values, then, is that they are lexically prioritized over all non-sacred values but do not enjoy any lexical prioritizations over one another. But this lexical ordering has a distinctive structure, which we can bring out by considering what happens when the agent deliberates about his values.

As the remarks on taboo and tragic tradeoffs suggest, sacred values involve specific kinds of prohibitions not just on action, but also on *thought*. So far, we've focused on prohibitions on tradeoffs. This refers to behavior: I shouldn't act so as to compromise sacred values in exchange for ordinary values. Doing so would be wrong. But consider a further feature, which some psychologists emphasize:

---

[9] Though see Anderson 1991 for a good argument against interpreting it in that way.

prohibitions on *comparisons*. There is a range of research indicating that merely *thinking about, deliberating about,* or *comparing* sacred values with ordinary values is viewed as prohibited.

While empirical studies of this phenomenon are relatively new, the phenomenon has been recognized since antiquity. Consider a passage from Epictetus:

> When Florus was deliberating whether he should go down to Nero's spectacles, and also perform in them himself, Agrippinus said to him, "Go down": and when Florus asked Agrippinus, "Why do you not go down?" Agrippinus replied, "Because I do not even deliberate about the matter." For he who has once brought himself to deliberate about such matters, and to calculate the value of external things, comes very near to those who have forgotten their own character.
>
> (Epictetus 2008: Chapter II)

What is Agrippinus saying? Florus is deliberating about whether he should participate in Nero's gladiatorial spectacles, which involve the thrills of violence, pageantry, and ritual. Agrippinus himself won't go, won't even consider going. But what's his advice to Florus? Why not simply tell Florus not to go? Agrippinus' point is that insofar as Florus has seriously entertained the possibility of going, the important questions have already been settled. Once he's opened deliberation on this topic, it doesn't matter how the deliberation is resolved; merely deliberating about the matter shows him to have a deficient character.

Consider an example with more contemporary relevance. Suppose I deliberate about whether I should murder my rich uncle in order to collect an inheritance. I ultimately conclude that I shouldn't. Still, something has gone wrong. I shouldn't have entertained murder as a serious possibility; having done so already shows that my character is problematic. Or suppose Bill considers whether he should cheat on his wife, drawing up a list, weighing the pros and cons. Again, something has gone wrong. His relationship is defective if he takes the possibility seriously.

Focusing on these sorts of considerations, Steven Lukes writes,

> to treat something as sacred is not simply to accord it unconditional or absolute value relative to other values or lexical priority relative to other goods; it is, rather, to view it as incommensurable in a specific way: that is, *as set apart from comparison with other items*. It is to have a specific attitude to such comparisons, namely, to denounce, even anathematize them.
>
> (Lukes 2017: 110, emphasis added)

For Lukes, treating something as sacred involves viewing its value as *not to be compared* to other values. If I seriously deliberate about violating a sacred value so as to secure some other good, this alone constitutes a moral deficiency.

There's a large psychological literature on this point. Psychologists have found that for a certain class of values, merely contemplating tradeoffs generates feelings of contamination. In a classic paper, Tetlock et al. showed that when observers believe that decision makers have entertained the possibility of trading sacred values against mundane ones, "they respond with moral outrage, which has cognitive, affective, and behavioral components: lower thresholds for making harsh dispositional attributions to norm violators; anger, contempt, and even disgust toward violators; and enthusiastic support for both norm enforcement (punishing violators) and metanorm enforcement (punishing those who shirk the burdensome chore of punishing deviants)" (Tetlock et al. 2000: 855). For example, in one experiment, participants were asked to consider a medical administrator in a cash-strapped hospital who had two options: he can spend $1,000,000 to save a single five-year-old child; or he can spend the money to purchase better medical equipment and enhance salaries in order to recruit talented doctors to the hospital. In one iteration of the experiment, the participants were told that the administrator decided to save the child; in another, that he chose the salaries and equipment. Participants were asked to rank their agreement with certain questions, such as "the administrator should be removed from his job," "the administrator should be punished," "if the administrator was a friend of mine, I would end my friendship over this issue." In addition, they were asked to rank whether the decision was fair or unfair, whether they were disgusted or not disgusted, whether they were sad or happy, and so on.

As one might expect, the study revealed that participants were most outraged when the child was not saved. But, for our purposes, the interesting point is that the studies found that individuals felt that decision makers were "tainted by merely contemplating" these tradeoffs and needed to "engage in symbolic acts of moral cleansing designed to reaffirm their solidarity with the moral community" (Tetlock et. al. 2000: 855).[10] In this particular experiment, there was "a surge in moral cleansing in the two conditions in which decision makers thought long and hard about a taboo trade-off and either affirmed the sacred value or allowed the secular value to trump the sacred value" (2000: 859). That is, the outcome of the decision (whether the money is spent to save the child or to buy equipment and boost salaries) didn't have a significant effect on the desire for moral

---

[10] Psychologists use the term "moral cleansing" to refer to behaviors that are aimed at restoring a positive sense of self-worth in response to past moral transgressions. The basic idea is simple: if I have a negative sense of myself as a result of some past misdeed, I may try to restore a positive sense of myself by performing various compensatory actions. These actions can take many forms and in some cases are only very loosely related to the original misdeed. For example, suppose my sense of self-worth has been damaged because I take myself to have mistreated a friend. I might engage in moral cleansing in any number of ways: I might apologize to her; I might buy her a gift; I might try to be especially kind to her in the future; I might perform supererogatory acts in order to compensate for the past misdeed; I might even do things entirely unrelated to the friend I've wronged, such as donating to various charities without ever telling her.

cleansing; rather, the length of time spent contemplating the choice did. Thus, even when people who hold sacred values do contemplate tradeoffs, they "are not happy with themselves for doing so" (Baron and Spranca 1997: 1).

We can see this in my hypothetical examples as well. If the thought of murdering my uncle passes through my mind, that's bad; if I dwell on the possibility for days, weighing the pros and cons, that's much worse. If I cheat on my spouse in a moment of passion, that's bad; if I draw up detailed plans to do so and carry them out, that's worse.

I will treat this as an essential feature of sacred values. If we let V be a value, then:

Incontestable: It is prohibited to *contemplate* trading or sacrificing V for most or all other values.

I say "most or all other values" in order to account for cases in which the agent is forced to consider trading one sacred value for another sacred value. As I pointed out in the last section, things are different in these cases. In tragic tradeoffs, contemplation is still found objectionable: best of all would be to find some way of avoiding the need to contemplate these tradeoffs. But, if forced by circumstance to contemplate tradeoffs of two sacred values, agents are judged more positively when the contemplation is long-lasting, laborious, conflicted, reluctant, and agonized. Presumably this is a mark of the prohibited nature of the contemplation: if the world forces you to do something wrong, it's better to do it reluctantly and begrudgingly than eagerly and gladly.

One final clarification: we should distinguish Incontestability from cases in which an agent refuses to make certain comparisons but views this merely as a matter of personal preference. For example, suppose I enjoy yoga and refuse to contemplate trading or sacrificing my yoga classes for anything else that I value. Suppose I view this merely as a personal preference, rather than as a requirement. I don't see others as making a mistake when they engage in comparisons of yoga and running or yoga and going to the gym. This is *not* a case of Incontestability, for I don't see the comparisons as *prohibited*; I merely see the refusal to entertain comparisons as grounded in my personal preferences.

2.3 Justificatory Reasoning

This refusal to contemplate tradeoffs of sacred values can be seen as a restriction on the types of thoughts that we're permitted to have. And there is another such restriction. As I mentioned in the introduction, people who embrace sacred values often seem in some sense dogmatic about their values. While we expect most values to be adjusted in light of thoughts about their justificatory standing, sacred values seem to resist this. Let's explore this feature.

At first glance, it might seem that sacred values prohibit justificatory reasoning. After all, we've just seen that sacred values prohibit the contemplation of tradeoffs and exchanges with non-sacred values. Just so, we might think, sacred values will prohibit their adherents from contemplating the justification of these sacred values. Some have endorsed this view. For example, in her fascinating book about moral dilemmas, Lisa Tessman considers sacred values at length. She writes that sacred values

> must be shielded from the inappropriate thought that they are commensurable with non-sacred values. Thus, *values that have been sacralized can be betrayed through engaging in justificatory reasoning about them*, with further insult when this reasoning takes the form of weighing costs and benefits.
>
> (Tessman 2014: 5, emphasis added)

The first line of this quotation points out that sacred values are Incontestable: they prohibit contemplated tradeoffs. But notice that in the italicized portion of the quotation, Tessman additionally claims that agents with sacred values will object to engaging in justificatory reasoning about them.

While this view might seem tempting, I think it is incorrect. Many of the paradigm cases of sacred values involve a great deal of justificatory reasoning. In the last chapter, I cited certain Christian values that seem to be sacralized (such as the valuation of human life). Yet these Christian values have long been subjected to detailed, scrupulous justificatory reasoning: there are two millennia of theological and philosophical commentary on these values, much of which takes the form of inquiring into the justificatory standing of particular values.[11] Or, if we step outside the religious context, consider the way in which *human dignity* arguably functions as a sacred value. There is no shortage of defenses and critiques of this notion. So, too, with the political examples we've been considering: it would be absurd to suggest that Palestinians who treat the right of return as a sacred value are thereby barred from engaging in justificatory reasoning about this claim. And we all know that extremists with sacred values often produce staggeringly long justifications of those values: Anders Behring Breivik completed his 1518-page manifesto (*2083: A European Declaration of Independence*) shortly before beginning his terrorist attacks in Oslo and Utøya;[12] and Ted Kaczynski (the Unabomber) wrote a 35,000-word essay "Industrial Society and its Future" defending his values.

---

[11] Not all of this reflection is overtly justificatory. Much of it consists in an attempt to achieve a deeper understanding of the relevant values. Consider the difference between *trying to justify some value that you take yourself to understand* and *trying to come to a fuller understanding of some value that you take to be justified*. Those are different stances, though they are often blended together and can easily transition into one another. I will explore this in more detail in Chapter 9.

[12] These attacks took place on July 22, 2011. Breivik killed 77 people and injured over 300.

As these examples illustrate, sacred and non-sacred values may enjoy comparable amounts of justificatory reasoning. Indeed, the fact that a value is sacred might prompt one to reflect on its justificatory standing all the more.

I will suggest that what distinguishes sacred values is not the *quantity* of justificatory reflection but the *effect* of justificatory reflection. The agent with a sacred value can engage in arbitrarily large quantities of justificatory reflection; indeed, in an extreme case the justificatory reflection can be the central occupation of his life. What matters is not how much justificatory reflection occurs but whether the agent genuinely stakes his degree of commitment to the value on the outcome of this justificatory reflection. Let me explain.

To start, let's introduce some terminology: an attitude is *dialectically invulnerable* when there is no dialectical move that would alter the agent's degree of commitment to the attitude. That is, while the agent may think about the attitude, engage in thought experiments with respect to it, consider its justificatory standing, and so forth, the agent does not stake his commitment to the attitude on the outcome of these thoughts.

In some cases, attitudes appear to be dialectically invulnerable simply because the agent cannot find any good grounds for doubting them. Consider straightforward factual beliefs. I can't seriously question whether 1+1=2 or whether triangles have three sides. I don't have any real grasp on what it would be to doubt these propositions. And this needn't be restricted to apriori matters. For example, I can't seriously doubt that the earth is round or that emeralds are green. I can, of course imagine scenarios in which these beliefs are false: I might engage in the standard thought experiments from introductory philosophy classes, imagining massive conspiracy or inverted spectra. But none of these seem to me live doubts. The evidence for the contrary position is just too overwhelming. So considering these skeptical scenarios has no effect on my beliefs.

Some people have similar attitudes toward their evaluative beliefs. For a person who thinks that a certain ethical view is definitively correct, something similar could follow for propositions directly entailed by the theory. For example, if you accept a divine command theory and think you have incontrovertible proof that God commands that you refrain from murder, then there would be no way of seriously doubting whether murder is wrong. Or, if you're a committed utilitarian, perhaps you think there's no way of seriously doubting whether happiness is good.[13]

---

[13] Bentham seems to endorse this view. Consider his remarks on the principle of utility: "Not that there is or ever has been that human creature at breathing, however stupid or perverse, who has not on many, perhaps on most occasions of his life, deferred to it [the principle of utility]" (Bentham 2007: 4). Or take Sidgwick: "the propositions, 'I ought not to prefer a present lesser good to a future greater good,' and 'I ought not to prefer my own lesser good to a future greater good of another,' do present themselves as self-evident; as much (e.g.) as the mathematical axiom that 'if equals be added to equals the wholes are equal'" (Sidgwick 1981: 383).

These are cases in which the inability to entertain genuine skeptical doubts about a proposition arises either because you believe that you have decisive justification for it, because you cannot find any good arguments against it, or both. In these cases, you are willing to critique the proposition in abstract, detached contexts. You are willing to go into the philosophy classroom and entertain skeptical scenarios concerning the proposition. But you don't take these skeptical scenarios to have any real implications. They don't affect your degree of commitment to the proposition.

But we can distinguish two possibilities. Perhaps if you *were* convinced by one of these skeptical scenarios, you would modify your beliefs. In that case, you are genuinely willing to modify your beliefs in light of justificatory considerations; it's just that you haven't yet encountered any convincing arguments for revising them. Your attitudes are *not* dialectically invulnerable, for certain dialectical moves (which you haven't yet encountered and might never encounter) would disrupt the beliefs.

On the other hand, you might not do this. You might go through the motions of critiquing your belief, but not allow the skeptical scenarios, arguments, and so forth to dislodge the belief regardless of how persuasive you judge them to be. You might think the evidence or arguments for a claim are very weak, that good arguments against the claim exist; but you might retain your belief in that claim nonetheless. In the extreme version of this stance—when there is *no* dialectical move that would disrupt the belief in the claim—the belief is dialectically invulnerable.

In general, there is a presumption that a person's credence in p should track p's perceived justification. That is, if I think I have only very weak justification for p, I ought to decrease my credence in p; if I think I have very strong justification for p, I ought to increase my credence in p. When an agent treats her belief that p as dialectically invulnerable, this connection is severed: degree of credence in p is dissociated entirely from p's perceived justification.

With this notion of dialectical invulnerability at hand, we can see why it is a mistake to think that justificatory reasoning about one's sacred values is prohibited. There are many individuals who are happy to engage in justificatory reasoning about—let's say—the dignity of human life, who are willing to admit that they don't have decisive justifications for this value, who even acknowledge grounds for doubting the value, but who nonetheless treat it as a sacred value. Their degree of credence in the proposition "human life has dignity" is dissociated entirely from the perceived justification of this claim.

If we like, we could make this point by distinguishing *genuine critique* from *inauthentic critique*. We could say that *genuine critique* of p involves staking one's acceptance of p on the outcome of justificatory reflection. If I find good reasons for p, I preserve my belief that p. If I find considerations against it, my credence in p is reduced. Then we could say that an agent with sacred values may go through the motions of critically assessing the justificatory standing of his values, but, crucially, doesn't stake the acceptance of the value on the outcome of the deliberation. So he doesn't engage in genuine critique of the value.

Of course, it will be difficult to identify these cases in practice. The distinctions won't be sharp and there will be borderline cases. Moreover, it is often difficult to distinguish genuine critique from mere pantomime. Consider new parents having an exceptionally difficult night: they've managed to snatch only a few moments of sleep amidst the bouts of crying and screaming. Exhausted and irritated, I ask my wife whether we should give our baby up for adoption. At first my wife, assuming I am joking, plays along. "It would make our nights quieter. We could rest. We could go out at night." And I continue, "Yes, and we'd travel a lot. We'd have more time to work. On the other hand, we'd miss her. But I think we'd get over it in time." And suddenly it becomes clear to her that I am serious. This changes things (to put it mildly). What looked like a good joke turns out to reveal (what most of us would regard as) a clear deficiency in my relationship to my child. There is a difference between genuine critique and pantomime, even when it's difficult to detect in practice.

As the example illustrates, what matters is not whether the agent thinks about the value's justificatory status. The person with sacred values may be perfectly happy to take philosophy classes, to engage in detached skeptical reflection about the values, and so forth. But these values serve as fixed points for him; he is not willing to let them go. So what matters is not whether the agent reflects, but whether the agent stakes his commitment to the value on the outcome of this reflection.

I will treat this as the third essential feature of sacred values. It is not that proponents of sacred values are unable or unwilling to engage in justificatory reasoning about their values. Rather, it is that the degree of commitment to the value does not hinge on the outcome of this justificatory reasoning. The commitment to the value is *dialectically invulnerable*:

Dialectically Invulnerable: The agent insulates her commitment to the value from the effects of justificatory reasoning. That is, while the agent may think about the value's justification, consider objections to the value, consider alternatives to the value, engage in thought experiments with respect to the value, and so on, the agent does not stake her commitment to the value on the outcome of this justificatory reasoning. There is no dialectical move that would disrupt the agent's commitment to value.

In other words, an agent with a sacred value will remain committed to that value regardless of the degree of justification that she takes the value to enjoy. In some cases, she will think that she has a decisive justification for the sacred value. But in more interesting cases, or in counterfactual cases, her degree of commitment to the value will greatly exceed her degree of belief in her having an adequate justification for it.

Let me offer four clarificatory remarks on this notion of dialectical invulnerability and the way in which it relates to more familiar philosophical topics. First, dialectical invulnerability is a claim about the maintenance or sustaining of a commitment rather than the origination or production of the commitment. Few of our commitments are acquired through justificatory reasoning: many of our commitments arise through acculturation, habit, and so on. What distinguishes sacred values from ordinary values is not whether they originate from justificatory reasoning (few values do), but whether they are *responsive* to justificatory reasoning.[14]

Second, a few words on how the Incontestability of sacred values relates to their Dialectical Invulnerability. Incontestability concerns contemplated tradeoffs or exchanges of values, whereas Dialectical Invulnerability concerns justificatory reasoning. These are conceptually distinct: it's conceivable that someone could exempt a value from the effects of justificatory reflection and nonetheless be willing to seriously consider compromising it for other values; just so, it's possible that someone will refuse to consider compromising a value but be willing to modify his commitment to it if justificatory reflection undermines it. For this reason, I've listed the points separately.

Third, dialectical invulnerability is distinct from (standard forms of) self-deception and willful ignorance. The person with dialectically invulnerable beliefs needn't be self-deceived: she may acknowledge that her commitment is impervious to ordinary justificatory standards, that it is not disrupted by contrary evidence, that it is inconsistent with other claims that she accepts, and so forth.

---

[14] For this reason, I think Lisa Tessman's otherwise illuminating discussion of sacred values (Tessman 2014) goes astray. Tessman associates sacred values with "intuitive moral judgments," which she defines as follows "intuitive moral judgments differ from reasoned moral judgments in that they are not based on any *justifying reasons*—though one might engage in reasoning *post hoc* in order to produce reasons that do justify the judgment" (2014: 74). This suggests that Tessman sees sacred values as requiring a certain etiology: if I acquire a value as a result of engaging in justificatory reasoning, then it will not qualify as sacred. But this is too restrictive: as I point out above, sacralization refers to the way in which a value is maintained rather than to the way in which it originates. Relatedly, Tessman suggests that sacred values are experienced "as normative or prescriptive regardless of the fact that they come without justifying reasons" (2014: 75). Again, this seems too strong: what matters is not whether the agent can locate justifying reasons for his sacred values, but whether he allows his commitment to the value to be affected by justificatory reasoning. For yet a third example, Tessman writes "any search for justification suggests that the value in question would be abandoned if justification were not found. But abandoning or sacrificing a value is unthinkable if the value has been sacralized" (2014: 96). While the last sentence can be read as endorsing what I am calling Dialectical Invulnerability, the first sentence in this quotation again seems overly restrictive: while a search for justification *can* indicate that the agent will abandon the value if justification isn't found, it doesn't have to indicate this. A great deal of theological reflection, for example, strives to find justifications for belief in God's existence but doesn't genuinely seem to stake belief in God on the discovery of these justifications. In sum: while Tessman provides an extremely insightful discussion of the role of sacred values in ethical life, her analysis of the connection between sacred values and justificatory reasoning is flawed.

So, too, dialectical invulnerability is distinct from willful ignorance. To simplify a bit, some philosophers understand willful ignorance as a case in which (i) I suspect that p is true and (ii) I could determine whether p is true by performing actions that have little cost, but (iii) I decline to perform these actions (see Lynch 2016 for a somewhat more complex version of this account). Dialectical invulnerability differs: the agent might well consider this evidence, engage in critical scrutiny of the belief, and so forth, but these acts have no effect on his certainty. His credence in p simply doesn't track his thoughts about p's degree of justification.[15]

Fourth, it is important to distinguish Dialectical Invulnerability from the more familiar phenomenon of motivated reasoning. In general, motivated reasoning occurs when reasoning processes (or their precursors) are impacted to an unusual degree by a person's motivations and goals. There is a massive literature in empirical psychology investigating the way in which memory, information selection, attitude formation, judgment, decision making, perceptual salience, attention, and so on are influenced by people's emotions, desires, attitudes, habits, feelings of cognitive dissonance, and other factors.[16] The key point for our purposes is that motivated reasoning can lead a person to be biased in their reasoning, such that they become more likely than a neutral party to see their commitments as justified. For example, imagine that Andy is politically conservative and has an exceptionally strong desire to retain her belief that tax cuts are always beneficial. Her desires are so strong that they lead her to ignore contrary evidence, to discount good arguments, to excessively weight considerations that support her view, and so on. It might begin to look as if Andy's belief is invulnerable to critique. Would this count as a case of Dialectical Invulnerability?

It depends. We have to distinguish two possibilities. Suppose Andy is presented with evidence that in certain circumstances tax cuts are harmful; and suppose she takes this evidence to be well founded and decisive. If she abandons or reduces her credence in the claim that tax cuts are always beneficial, this would show that the belief is dialectically vulnerable. If she maintains the belief despite regarding it as lacking warrant, the belief would be Dialectically Invulnerable. (In the latter case, we could imagine that she maintains the belief

---

[15] Some philosophers argue that a necessary feature of beliefs is that they are responsive to considerations bearing on their truth. So, for example, if I believe that p, when I come across evidence that *not p* my belief will tend to dissipate. To the extent that this relationship does not obtain, the mental state in question will not be a belief but will be some other attitude such as a hope, a wish, or what is sometimes called an *alief*. (Railton 1997 and Velleman 2000 offer influential defenses of this claim. For an interesting argument against the claim, see Viedge 2018.) If we accept this account, it will follow that beliefs cannot be dialectically invulnerable. Nothing in my argument hinges on whether we label the dialectically invulnerable attitudes *beliefs*; those who are tempted by these accounts of belief can treat the dialectically invulnerable attitudes as something other than beliefs, such as aliefs (see Gendler 2008 for this notion).

[16] For a quick overview, see Molden and Higgins 2012.

not because of its justificatory status, but because of its function as a marker of her identity or tribal affiliation.)

As this example illustrates, the distinction between motivated and non-motivated forms of reasoning does not coincide with the distinction between dialectically vulnerable and dialectically invulnerable commitments. Motivated reasoning concerns the extent to which various motives influence justificatory reasoning; dialectical invulnerability concerns the extent to which justificatory reasoning influences commitments. (In fact, we might expect dialectically invulnerable commitments to be less likely to involve motivated reasoning: motivated reasoning can be seen as an attempt to preserve commitments in the face of justificatory reflection, which is unnecessary if the commitments are unaffected by justificatory reflection.)

2.4 The Emotional Concomitants of Sacred Values

At this point, I've argued that sacred values have three core features: they are Inviolable, Incontestable, and Dialectically Invulnerable. I think these are the only essential features. However, in the following sections, I will discuss additional features that have been associated with sacred values.

Some writers have argued that there is a distinctive repertoire of affective responses that are associated with sacred values. Let's address this by thinking about how sacred values are lived. Sacred values prohibit tradeoffs and contemplation of tradeoffs. Of course, life does sometimes force us to perform or at least contemplate these tradeoffs. What then?

Here's one common reaction: we draw a distinction between avowed and actual commitments. People *profess* commitment to sacred values. But, when push comes to shove, they are willing to compromise these values. We *say* that human life is inviolable, but we don't take every possible step toward preserving human life. We don't lower the speed limit to 25mph; we don't spend all of our GDP on healthcare; we don't spend very much at all on attempts to alleviate dire poverty. So, while we may avow commitment to sacred values, our actions reveal a different set of preferences altogether. In the language of economics: sacred values are *avowed values,* rather than *revealed ones.*

Tempting as that reductive move might be, I think it is misguided. Our behavior doesn't straightforwardly express our values. True, if the world forces me to choose between X and Y, I may choose Y. But this doesn't show that I value Y more than I value X. After all, I may have deep regret; I may wish the world were other than it is; and so on.

So what does happen when people are forced to contemplate—or, worse yet, to engage in—tradeoffs between sacred values and non-sacred values? Well, one thing that happens is that agents are deeply troubled and in some cases traumatized. As Skitka puts it, one of the most widely replicated findings in social psychology is that fair procedures (e.g., procedures free from bias, that provide opportunities for constituency voice, or that treat involved parties with appropriate dignity and respect), generally lead people to accept non-preferred outcomes... An equally widely replicated finding, however, is that the fair process effect *does not emerge* when people have a moral stake in outcomes...

(Skitka 2010: 274, emphasis added)

In the above passage, Skitka is defining "moral stakes" in roughly the way that I am defining sacred values: they are commitments or values that the person is unwilling to compromise. As she emphasizes, agents tend to persevere in these sacred values even when procedurally fair mechanisms require their violation. In particular, agents tend to experience feelings of anger, disgust, anxiety, and contamination when sacred values are compromised. And this brings us to another feature that is frequently discussed in the psychological literature on sacred values: their connections with particular emotions.

Some psychologists draw very tight connections between sacred values and particular types of emotions. For example, Haidt associates sacredness with feelings of disgust, degradation, horror, and repugnance; moreover, he claims that without the capacity for these emotions, we would be unable to experience commitments as sacred (Haidt 2012: 118–22, 170–9). Other psychologists focus on the way in which agents will find these situations of choice between sacred values highly aversive and thus engage in behavior designed to avoid them. Baron and Spranca highlight what they call "agent relativity" of sacred values: the agent contemplating tradeoffs cares about the participation of the decision maker, rather than simply caring about the consequences of the action. In other words, what's important is not just what happens, but what the agent does. Thus, when a sacred value must be compromised, agents seek to avoid their own participation in this. One way of doing so is by trying to foist responsibility for the choice on another party. Another way of doing so is by denying that there is a tradeoff. In particular, agents often seek rhetorical reframings of choices, so that what's originally presented as a situation in which a sacred value must be compromised gets reconfigured as a balancing of mundane values. Finally, agents experience anger when forced to contemplate these tradeoffs (Baron and Spranca 1997).

Philosophers have sometimes touched on this point. David Wiggins writes that our moral sentiments regarding "the utterly forbidden" concern something the violation of which "menaces the very fabric of the ethical by threatening to destroy the basis of the ethical in solidarity" (Wiggins 2006: 248). Stuart Hampshire writes "I believe that critical reflection may leave the notion of absolutely forbidden, because absolutely repugnant, conduct untouched. [...] [There] may be reflective reasons, in the sense that one is able to say why the conduct is impossible as destroying the ideal of a way of life that one aspires to and respects, as being, for example, utterly unjust or cruel or treacherous or corruptly dishonest." (Hampshire 1983: 90).[17]

Notice the language, here. The utterly forbidden *menaces, threatens to destroy;* the absolutely forbidden is absolutely forbidden because it is absolutely *repugnant.* It's no accident that this decidedly purple prose emerges. Thoughts of violating sacred values tend to bring with them feelings of contamination.

Examples could be multiplied, but the basic point should be clear: sacred values are typically associated with feelings of reverence, respect, honor, and awe. Potential violations of sacred values typically elicit feelings or horror, disgust, and anger. These emotions arise not only when actual violations occur but even when agents merely contemplate their violation. Thus, we might add an additional point to our analysis of sacred values. If V is a sacred value, then:

Emotional concomitants: V is typically associated with feelings of reverence, honor, and awe; violations or contemplated violations are associated with disgust and other purity-related emotion.

Notice that I've phrased this point in terms of what's *typically* the case. These are not essential features of sacred values.[18] What's essential—what makes something a sacred value—is the prohibition on action and deliberation expressed in Inviolable and Incontestable, together with the particular form of dogmatism expressed by Dialectically Invulnerable. According that status to a value exempts it from the effects of deliberative weighing and justificatory responsiveness that all other values undergo. Conversely, commitments that are associated with feelings of reverence, awe, and so forth are probably more likely to be exempted in this way. So the feelings could come first. But the feelings alone aren't sufficient: I can be reverential toward things that I do not regard as having sacred value. I feel awe at the Grand Canyon and in front of an old redwood, but I don't treat their value as sacred; I would accept their loss for ordinary values, if the ordinary values were sufficiently weighty. And I have no problem whatsoever contemplating such tradeoffs and comparisons.

Another reason for declining to treat these emotions as essential is that there's massive variance across individuals and cultures in the emotions associated with sacred values. Consider some examples. Catholics who accept the ideas concerning the sacredness of human life might experience any number of emotions: some

---

[17] Or take Kant: Kantian respect is arguably in this vein. Pure practical reason "*strikes down* self-conceit, that is, humiliates it" (Kant 1788/1996: 5:73).

[18] This is controversial. Haidt and others deny it, arguing that the sacred bears an essential connection to certain emotions. "If we had no sense of disgust, I believe we would also have no sense of the sacred" (Haidt 2012: 173–4). But I will put the point this way: if Haidt is right, that would be a substantial additional argument. It would show that Inviolability, Incontestability, and Dialectical Invulnerability either necessitate or are necessitated by these emotions. I am not aware of any good argument of that form.

will feel reverence and respect towards human life; others won't experience those sentiments with any regularity, but will feel revulsion and disgust at those who they perceive as failing to treat life as sacred (those who have abortions, let's say); others, still, won't experience revulsion and disgust, but will feel deeply saddened and experience grief when witnessing violations of this value; others, still, will feel awed by human life; others, still, will be emotionally cool, experiencing no intense emotions when witnessing violations of these values, but will nevertheless struggle mightily to preserve them. Having one of these reactions instead of the others wouldn't disqualify one from having a sacred value.

So there are certain emotions that tend to figure in the experience of sacred values. But these emotions aren't necessary. It's possible (albeit unusual) to have a sacred value without experiencing any of the emotions on this list. Moreover, the emotions on the list aren't universally associated with sacred values.

2.5 Subjective Significance, Import, and Meaningfulness

Another notable feature of sacred values is that they seem to be associated with *significance, import,* and *meaningfulness.* There seems to be a tight connection between treating something as sacred and seeing it as meaningful. When we look at the candidate sacred values—Christian views about the sacredness of human life, Palestinian views about territorial integrity, and so on—it's clear that their adherents see these values as more meaningful, important, or significant than many other values.

What is this connection? It's not one of identity: treating something as sacred is not *identical* to treating it as subjectively meaningful or important. After all, I can see things as meaningful and important without seeing them as inviolable, incontestable, and dialectically invulnerable. I take certain works of literature, athletic accomplishments, philosophical profundity, and so forth as quite meaningful and important, but I don't see them as sacred. So a sense of importance or meaningfulness doesn't require sacred values.

The entailment might seem to run the other way: if V is a sacred value—that is, if V is treated as inviolable, incontestable, and dialectically invulnerable—then V tends to have subjective importance, significance, or meaning. Although I am wary of treating this as a strict entailment, I do think it is highly unusual for an individual who has sacred values and raises questions about meaning, import, or significance not to answer these questions in part by thinking about her sacred values. After all, if an agent has a sacred value she will be committed to the valued object (or person, or state of affairs, or relationship, or goal) in a special way: she will tend to experience intense aversions to violating the commitment; she will refuse to treat the commitment as fungible; she will decline to allow the commitment to be affected by justificatory reasoning; she will be likely to treat the object of commitment with reverence and respect. And this does seem to put us in the conceptual territory of the meaningful, or the significant, or the important. But this is a very complex point; I will address it in Chapter 4 and, in a different way, in Chapters 6 through 8.

2.6 Sacred Values and Inarticulacy

There's one final difference between sacred values and ordinary values. Many sacred values are inchoate or difficult to articulate fully. This isn't a necessary feature of sacred values: sometimes we are completely articulate about them. But it is a very common feature.

Consider some examples. There are a number of religious and political views which claim that human beings possess *dignity*. I've discussed the way in which this claim appears in the German constitution, in the Universal Declaration of Human Rights, in Kant's ethical theory, and in various philosophical works. But this is a notoriously obscure claim. What is it for a human being to have dignity? How should this notion be understood? In religious contexts it is often associated with the idea that human beings bear a special relationship to the divine; in political contexts it is associated with claims about protecting the rights of human beings; in ethical contexts it is sometimes linked to claims about autonomy and self-direction (e.g. in Raz 1986). But what's interesting about this term is that despite its widespread use, there's no agreed upon definition (see Rosen 2018).

Or take some of the nationalist movements that have gripped the US and parts of Europe. Trump's rhetoric of making American "great again" harkens to some hazily imagined form of past glory and, at the same time, conjures up imagined threats: witness his inauguration speech, which made reference to "carnage" and protecting the US from the "ravages of other countries".[19] Or we might consider Viktor Orbán, the prime minister of Hungary, who in 2017 said that Hungary would block the immigration of refugees but would "let in true refugees: Germans, Dutch, French, and Italians, terrified politicians and journalists who here in Hungary want to find the Europe they have lost in their homelands."[20] Again, we have a call to return to some lost utopian realm. And we have vague threats: "Here there are large predators swimming in the water, and this is the transnational empire of George Soros."[21] What exactly this means—what these "large

---

[19] https://www.politico.com/story/2017/01/full-text-donald-trump-inauguration-speech-transcript-233907.
[20] https://web.archive.org/web/20190626230140/https://www.kormany.hu/en/the-prime-minister/news/this-year-we-must-defend-ourselves-against-five-major-attacks.
[21] https://web.archive.org/web/20190626230140/https://www.kormany.hu/en/the-prime-minister/news/this-year-we-must-defend-ourselves-against-five-major-attacks.

predators" are, how they are linked to Soros, how immigration threatens Europe, and so forth are left vague and unarticulated.

In these cases, the politicians identify certain concerns (what to do about the refugee crisis, how to mitigate economic losses) but seem to derive much of their power and attraction from something much hazier and more diffuse than these problems: there is an imagined realm to which we can return, or which we can achieve. Aside from that, many of these politicians actively resist concrete, determinate proposals.

Let's distinguish *degree of commitment to a claim* with *degree of articulacy about the claim*. A Trump supporter can be completely and unequivocally committed to the idea that we must make American great again without being able to say anything determinate about what this means. Or, to take an example from the opposite end of the political spectrum, a vocal environmentalist can be absolutely firm in her belief that the biome has intrinsic value, without being able to explain in a non-circular, informative fashion what this value is or why it should be prioritized over others.

With the distinction between degree of commitment and degree of articulacy at hand, we can make two points: a descriptive point and a normative one. First, the descriptive claim: many of our sacred values are opaque and seem actively to resist clarification; we don't want to look too closely at them. (This isn't a necessary feature of sacred values but, as the examples above suggest, it is a very common one.) Second, a normative claim: this makes sense, it is something we should do. I will argue for both claims, though in this Chapter I focus on the former.

What might explain the pervasive forms of obscurity about sacred values? Why do we tend to be inarticulate about our deepest commitments? No doubt there are many possible explanations, but here is one. Today, there is widespread agreement that we should be able to provide some justification of our commitments. We ought to be able to explain to others why we hold these commitments; asking for reasons is viewed as appropriate. But in the typical cases we justify our commitments by relating them to other, more fundamental commitments. So, I justify my attraction to a certain political candidate by pointing to the way in which her proposals conform to my sense of what is just; or, I justify my being a philosopher by pointing to the value that I place on intellectual inquiry. But when we ask about the person's deepest commitments—about the value of equality, or intellectual inquiry, or some other relatively fundamental value—we can't justify them in the same way. We can't point to something deeper which justifies them, at least not to the exclusion of their competitors. And we often struggle to articulate what these values really are.[22] So if we were to justify them in the standard way we'd need to

---

[22] Talbot Brewer argues that many of our most basic commitments have a deepening structure. They involve "activity whose value cannot be grasped with perfect lucidity from the outset, but must be progressively clarified via engagement in the activity itself" (Brewer 2009: 39). They thus have a "self-

do two things—to make them explicit and to relate them to more fundamental concerns. But neither works.

But it's not just that justifying one's sacred values is more difficult. Suppose these deep commitments are dialectically invulnerable. One way of ensuring invulnerability is by making something opaque. By keeping something inchoate, imprecise, by enabling shifting definitions, we can make it irrefutable. Everyone who has had arguments about philosophical or political topics recognizes this point: some people can't be argued with because they can't be pinned down. They're not precise and careful enough to be refuted. If you press them on one point they shift to another.

Insofar as we want *both* dialectical invulnerability *and* an appearance of apportioning all of our commitments to the results of critical reflection, and insofar as there are good objections to our commitments, one way of resolving this is by keeping our basic commitments somewhat inarticulate or hazy. I can't be refuted if I am not precise enough to be refuted. I can't discover that my commitment is unjustified if it is too inchoate to permit of justification.

I think this is why sacred values tend to be imprecise. Imprecision promotes dialectical invulnerability. And imprecision is often coupled with an aura of mystery and ineffability. I will return to this point in Chapter 9.

2.7 The Full Definition of Sacred Values

We are now in a position to offer a full account of sacred values.

(**Sacred value**) Let V1 be a value or normative commitment. Then V1 counts as sacred iff:

1. **Inviolable**:   if V2 is an ordinary value, then it is prohibited to sacrifice V1 for V2, regardless of the quantities of V1 and V2.

2. **Incontestable**:   It is prohibited to *contemplate* trading or sacrificing V1 for most or all other values.

3. **Dialectically Invulnerable**:   The agent insulates her commitment to V1 from the effects of justificatory reasoning. That is, while the agent may think about V1's justification, consider objections to V1, consider alternatives to V1, engage in thought experiments with respect to V1, and so on, the agent does not stake her commitment to V1 on the outcome of this justificatory reasoning. There is no dialectical move that would disrupt the agent's commitment to V1.

---

unveiling character, in the sense that each successive engagement yields a further stretch of understanding of the goods internal to the activity, hence of what would count as a proper engagement in it" (2009: 37).

Features (1)–(3) are necessary. The following features are not necessary, but merely typical:

4. Emotional concomitants: V1 is typically associated with feelings of reverence, honor, and awe; violations or contemplated violations are associated with disgust and other purity-related emotions.

5. Subjective import: V1 is often taken as subjectively important or meaningful

6. Inarticulacy: the agent often resists clear, perspicuous, fully articulate specifications of V1.

Notice that this isn't just a haphazard list of dissociated features. These features actually possess a certain unity; it's unsurprising that they tend to occur together, for they are mutually reinforcing. Suppose some value is subjectively important (feature 5). Then I may be reluctant to trade it against competing goods (feature 1). If it's dear to me, I may be reluctant even to contemplate these tradeoffs (feature 2). To the extent that I genuinely treat the value as meaningful, I will at the very least be resistant to arguments purporting to undermine its value; and this may set me on the path to feature 3. I will have strong feelings associated with it (feature 4). None of these are strict entailments; it's possible to resist any of them. But I do think that there are clear connections here; exhibiting feature 5 makes it more likely that one will exhibit features 1–4. (As well as 6, but this point is more complex; see Chapter 9.)

Likewise, suppose you have some value that exhibits features 1 and 2. If you're not even willing to entertain the possibility of compromising this value, it will be marked off as distinct from the many values that you treat as fungible. This alone will mark it off as having a special significance or meaning (feature 5).

Similar points can be made about each of these features. They tend to be mutually reinforcing, in the sense that high degrees of commitment to any one of them will make it more likely that the others also show up.

2.8 Concluding Remarks

I end this chapter with an observation. Some philosophers have incorporated elements of sacred values into their ethical theorizing, though often without treating sacred values as having all of the features that I have enumerated above. Kant is a good example. He distinguishes between two kinds of value that a thing can have: dignity and price (*Würde* and *Preis*). What has price can be replaced, exchanged, and traded against other things that have value; what has dignity cannot. As he puts it: "In the kingdom of ends everything has either a price or a dignity. What has a price can be replaced by something else as its equivalent; what on the other hand is raised above all price and therefore admits of no equivalent has a dignity" (*Groundwork* 4:434). In short, things with price are fungible, whereas things with dignity are not. Kant claims that humanity has dignity. And this claim does a great deal of work in Kant's theory: many of his arguments in *The Metaphysics of Morals* and elsewhere rely on the claim that humanity has dignity, as opposed to mere price. The Kantian notion of dignity seems very close to, and perhaps identical to, Inviolability. But Kant does not seem to me to incorporate Incontestability into his argument. And he certainly denies Dialectical Invulnerability, for he takes the dignity of humanity to be securely established through rational argumentation.

Or take Raimond Gaita. In an oft-quoted passage, he writes of his experiences with patients in a psychiatric ward. He claims that the ward's staff included many well-intentioned people who professed belief in the dignity and equality of the severely incapacitated patients. However, one day a nun came into the ward and interacted with these patients. And

> everything in her demeanour towards them – the way she spoke to them, her facial expressions, the inflexions of her body – contrasted with and showed up the behaviour of those noble psychiatrists. She showed that they were, despite their best efforts, condescending, as I too had been. She thereby revealed that even such patients were, as the psychiatrists and I had sincerely and generously professed, the equals of those who wanted to help them; but she also revealed that in our hearts we did not believe this. (Gaita 1999: 18–19)

So the nun illustrates a commitment to the dignity and equality of the patients. But Gaita continues:

> If I am asked what I mean when I say that even such people as were patients in that ward are fully our equals, I can only say that the quality of her love proved that they are rightly the objects of our non-condescending treatment, that we should do all in our power to respond in that way. But if someone were now to ask me what informs my sense that they are rightly the objects of such treatment, I can appeal only to the purity of her love. For me, the purity of the love proved the reality of what it revealed... From the point of view of the speculative intelligence, however, I am going round in ever darkening circles, because I allow for no independent justification of her attitude. (Gaita 1999: 21–2)

Here Gaita claims that his valuation of human equality is not something that can be independently justified. At best, he can appeal to "the purity of [the nun's] love," but from a standard point of view this is no justification at all: for we would have to ask what justifies the nun's love, and no answer presents itself. Although these passages raise interpretive difficulties, I suspect that Gaita is treating his valuation of human equality as Dialectically Invulnerable: despite the fact that he takes himself to have no independent justification for it, his commitment to valuation persists.

And examples could be multiplied. Kantian-inflected discussions of the value of humanity (e.g. Setiya 2014, Korsgaard 1996, Anderson 1995, Rosen 2018) often make space for Inviolable values. Iris Murdoch and those influenced by her often speak of a type of moral vision that seems exempted from justificatory considerations and hence might be regarded as issuing Dialectically Invulnerable commitments (Murdoch 1970, Setiya 2014). Elizabeth Anderson (1995), Susan Wolf (2010) and Bernard Williams (Smart and Williams 1973) treat certain values as not to be compared with others—more on this in Chapter 4—and hence as potentially Incontestable.

So we find features of sacred values playing central roles in many areas of philosophy. But, as my examples indicate, these philosophers often discuss only *one* aspect of sacred values. Arguably, they fail to see that the values that they are discussing also exhibit the other features. The Kantian value of humanity, for example, seems to be a prime example of something that is not only Inviolable but also Incontestable and Dialectically Invulnerable. To the extent that we miss these additional features of the values under discussion, we may be led astray.

3
Resisting Comparisons of Comparable Items

The previous chapter was largely descriptive. I provided an analysis of the core features of sacred values. But I said nothing about whether holding sacred values is defensible. And indeed, much of what I have said about these sacred values might make them look deeply problematic. After all, the person with a sacred value refuses even to contemplate tradeoffs and declines to stake his degree of commitment to a value on the value's justificatory standing. Aren't these obvious forms of irrationality?

I am going to argue that it can be rational to hold certain kinds of sacred values. In essence, I will argue that certain goods, including certain forms of commitment, are available only when we sacralize our values. This gives us reason to adopt sacred values instead of contenting ourselves with ordinary values.

But let me straightaway qualify this claim in two ways. First, it is obvious that some sacred values can be ruled out on epistemic or moral grounds. For example, if a neo-Nazi treats racial purity as a sacred value, we can criticize him on moral grounds: his valuation of racial purity is morally criticizable in that it conflicts with our commitment to equality. But in cases like this it is the *content* of the agent's value that is criticized, rather than the fact that the agent treats this content as a sacred value. When valuing some content is already problematic, sacralizing that value will inherit and potentially exacerbate the problems.

I want to set aside cases of this form, focusing instead on contents that are not objectionable when treated as ordinary values. Restricting our attention to cases in which it would be unobjectionable to treat some content (e.g., a person, relationship, state of affairs, goal, etc.) as valuable, we can ask whether it would also be unobjectionable to treat this content as having sacred value. For example: assuming that it is unobjectionable to treat equality as valuable, would it also be unobjectionable to treat equality as having sacred value? Or, even more strongly: might there be good reasons to treat equality as a sacred value rather than just as an ordinary value? I will argue that there are a number of cases in which the answer is yes.

But this brings me to the second qualification. In an important range of cases, it is perfectly fine to treat some content as valuable, but objectionable to treat this content as having sacred value. For example, we could imagine a case in which it is reasonable to value territorial integrity, but objectionable to treat this as a sacred value. Or, for a more controversial example: perhaps it's reasonable to value gun ownership, but unreasonable to treat this as a sacred value. In these kinds of cases, treating certain contents as valuable is perfectly fine, perhaps even reasonable, but treating these contents as sacred values is problematic. I am going to investigate these kinds of cases at length in Chapter 7, but for now I set them aside.

My goal, then, will be to argue for a qualified claim: while certain sacred values are problematic, the mere fact that a value is sacralized is not in itself a ground for criticism. On the contrary, we have good and sufficient reasons for adopting certain sacred values. And not only that: in certain cases, treating a content as possessing ordinary rather than sacred value constitutes a moral failure.

Recall that sacred values have three distinguishing features: they are Inviolable, Incontestable, and Dialectically Invulnerable. So another way of putting my point is this: it can be rational to treat certain values as Inviolable, Incontestable, and Dialectically Invulnerable. But I approach this piecemeal. In this chapter, I examine the way in which it can be rational to have values that are Inviolable and Incontestable. I defer consideration of Dialectical Invulnerability until the next chapter.

The plan of the chapter is as follows. In Section 3.1, I clarify the way in which the Inviolability and Incontestability of sacred values conflicts with some widely held views in moral philosophy. In particular, sacred values conflict with views according to which every normative consideration can be assigned a weight (you're forbidden to weigh or even entertain the idea of weighing sacred values). Moreover, sacred values conflict with views according to which every normative commitment is potentially defeasible (they're not defeasible; at best they're sacrificed). In Section 3.2, I argue that we have reason to reject this widely held view. Instead, I argue that it can be rational to hold certain sacred values. In particular, I argue that in order to preserve valuable forms of commitment—which themselves enable the appreciation or realization of certain otherwise inaccessible goods—we will need to exempt certain commitments from weighing and from evaluative comparison. In short: we have good reason to adopt certain sacred values. In some cases, this is because the irrationality of holding sacred values is outweighed by the rationality of some larger process that is enabled by holding sacred values (local irrationality promotes a more global form of rationality). But in other, more interesting cases, a failure to adopt sacred values would involve a pernicious form of devaluation, in which we fail to be appropriately moved by important values.

3.1 Weighing Reasons

A number of philosophers believe that normative entities always have weights. The idea is intuitive enough: normative theories will treat some things (saving lives, preventing extreme suffering, etc.) as to be promoted at the expense of others (securing mild pleasures, watching a good movie, etc.). Intuitively, there's reason to do all of these things, but there's more reason to do the former. So the reasons in favor of the former seem *weightier* than the reasons in favor of the latter.

In order to account for this phenomenon, it seems that, as Errol Lord and Barry Maguire put it, "any decent [normative] theory needs to have at least one *weighted* notion in its normative toolkit" (Lord and Maguire 2016: 3). That much is relatively uncontroversial. But does this mean that every normative entity will be weighable? We can distinguish two claims:

i. For some normative commitments, there is a scale on which they can be weighed.
ii. For any two normative commitments, there is a scale on which they can be weighed.

Claim (i) is plausible. Extreme particularists might deny it, but almost everyone else accepts it. I will assume that it is true.

But what about (ii)? It has an initial appeal. After all, life daily forces us to weigh disparate valued options against one another. Should I do more work or take a nap? Should we preserve historic charm of a neighborhood or maximize the amount of housing? Should we allow some environmental damage in order to produce a significant economic benefit? Should I choose the career that does the most good or brings me the most joy? We do in fact make these sorts of decisions, and it's tempting to assume that we thereby assign weights to valued options.

Moreover, there's a straightforward argument that might seem to indicate that (ii) is true. Whenever it looks like one commitment cannot be weighed against another, we can in fact find some scale on which they can be weighed if we imagine counterfactual scenarios. Variants of this argument are widespread in the literature, but Ralph Wedgwood's presentation of it is particularly clear. First, he begins with an observation:

> *everything that matters in life comes in degrees.* The factors on which both reasons and values – including both moral and non-moral reasons and values – are grounded seem to be capable of varying in arbitrarily small increments from one case to another. For example, an act can be morally bad because it causes harm, but causing harm is a factor that can vary by tiny increments. For example, even if one harm is greater than a second, the degree to which the first harm is greater than the second may be extremely small. Indeed it is not clear that there is any limit to how small the difference between a greater and a lesser harm can be; harms seem to be capable of varying by arbitrarily small increments.
>
> (Wedgwood 2013: 49)

Good enough so far. These points seem like truisms. Of course factors on which reasons and values are grounded can vary; of course harms can be greater and lesser; of course the difference between harms can be extremely slight.

In light of this, Wedgwood thinks we can produce an argument for (ii). The rejection of (ii) would entail that there are some values or reasons that are discontinuous: they cannot be weighed on the same scale. Wedgwood writes:

> We can explore the problems with these discontinuity claims by imagining the following spectrum of cases, $C_1, \ldots C_n$. In each case C_i, there are two options available to you, A_i and B_i. There is at least one case C_k in which there is indisputably both a moral reason in favour of A_k and a non-moral reason in favour of B_k; and throughout this spectrum, the factors on which these reasons depend in C_k vary only very slightly between each case and its successor. But intuitively in the first case C_1 the moral reasons in favour of A_1 seem overriding, while in the last case C_n, the non-moral reason in favour of B_n seems clearly *not* to be overridden by any countervailing moral reason. (Wedgwood 2013: 49)

Let's fill this out with a more concrete example. In the first case, C_1, you have reason to keep your promise to meet a friend despite the fact that doing so will cause an extremely minor harm (say, it will make you slightly tired). In case C_2, the magnitude of the harm increases very slightly (you'll be a little more tired). We continue increasing the magnitude of the harm. At some point, Wedgwood believes, the balance of reason will tip: the harms will be great enough that you are no longer required to keep your promise (you've been up for fifty hours and are at risk of illness if you delay sleeping).[1]

Wedgwood is focusing on moral reasons as a potential case of discontinuity: some philosophers think that if you have a moral reason to A, and a non-moral reason not to A, then you're required to A. In other words, some philosophers think that there are no cases in which non-moral reasons can outweigh moral reasons. But arguments of the above sort would show this to be false. Moral reasons might be very weighty, but they are continuous with non-moral reasons. And analogously with any other values that we might want to consider.

If we accept a global version of this point, we get something like the following picture, which is defended by Garrett Cullity:

---

[1] Of course, there are objections we can raise to this sort of argument. One peculiarity of Wedgwood's presentation is his idea that we can always create a spectrum of cases of this form, where each one will count as the *same type* of case. Arguably when we vary the magnitudes enough, we actually get fundamentally different types of cases. (Is the case in which you keep a promise and sacrifice a quick nap just a less intense version of the case in which you keep a promise at the cost of severe bodily damage?) Another peculiarity is the idea that *everything* comes in degrees. *Breaking Bad* is better than *Mad Men*, I think; but is there a degree to which it's better? Is there any sense to the idea that we could keep making *Mad Men* slightly better, increment by increment, until it surpasses the goodness of *Breaking Bad*? It's an odd thought.

There are only two directions a reason for action can have: either for or against. But the magnitude has no such restriction; it can vary just as much as physical weights can. The weights of the reasons for and against an action can be summed, and this determines how strongly supported the action is, overall, by the reasons that bear on it, for and against. The reasons for doing something are sufficient when no other action is more strongly supported, overall, and decisive when this action is most strongly supported (Parfit 2011: 32–3) – then you ought to do it. You ought to perform the action with the greatest net balance of reasons in favour over reasons against: the one there is most reason to perform...

(Cullity 2018: 423)

Call this the Global Weighing Picture.[2]

But notice that sacred values wouldn't fit into this picture. Suppose we have a case of the following form:

The agent has a reason R1 to A, where R1 derives from a non-sacred value.

The agent has a reason R2 *not* to A, where R2 derives from a sacred value.

The agent would be prohibited from A-ing, regardless of how weighty the reasons to A are. Moreover, even contemplating these tradeoffs would be prohibited.

Again, there are real cases of this. The Palestinian and Israeli examples from Chapter 1 show that some individuals are willing to increase human suffering to arbitrarily high levels in order to avoid compromising a sacred value (territorial integrity). Analogous cases abound: Rawls and others take considerations of justice to override arbitrarily high levels of (for example) pleasure and pain; Sultana, Abase, and Begum thought that considerations of honor and religious commitment mandated extreme sacrifice and violence; Hill thought that environmental preservation should outweigh any economic considerations.

Is this mere irrationality, something that should be overturned upon reflection? Aren't there good reasons for thinking that everything than *can be* weighed, compared, and measured *should be* weighed, compared, and measured? I will address that below.

3.2 Can Prohibitions on Comparisons Be Justified?

On certain views, the refusal to entertain comparisons will look like rank irrationality. But it's easy to spot a flaw with this objection: it presumes that any

---

[2] The strongest version of the Global Weighing Picture would deny the existence of incomparable values. A slightly weaker version would hold that there may be some incomparable values, but that all other values can be weighed against one another. Cullity thinks there are local exceptions to the Global Weighing Picture, such as incomparable values. He therefore accepts the weaker version.

distinctions in permissible ways of valuing must be grounded in the nature of the valued object. And that assumption is dispensable.

To see this, consider the following argument:

(1) The value of X is comparable to the value of Y.
(2) Therefore, it is irrational to prohibit comparisons of the value of X to the value of Y.

There's a suppressed premise here. The argument assumes that if the value of X is comparable to the value of Y, then there will be circumstances in which rationality requires that we weigh the value of X against the value of Y. But no argument for this claim has been given. And, in fact, we can find good reasons for rejecting it.

I will consider three types of scenarios in which comparing X and Y is problematic:

(a) Comparing X and Y would lead to an error.
(b) Comparing X and Y would create some kind of harm.
(c) Comparing X and Y would lead to devaluation.

In cases of type (a), comparing X and Y would lead to some kind of error or mistake. This is a point that often appears in discussions of utilitarianism. Suppose that deliberating about the expected utility of certain scenarios involves too many variables, is too complex, takes too long, invites self-deception, and so on. Then it might be better if the agent simply forgoes the deliberation and acts in the way that seem intuitively correct to him. John Stuart Mill makes this point, writing that generations of accumulated moral wisdom have instilled in us intuitive reactions that tend to track the truth in straightforward cases (Mill 1861/1998: chapter 2). And Henry Sidgwick agrees, writing that expected utility may be maximized by hiding the truth of utilitarianism from the masses and inviting them, instead, to rely on their intuitive reactions (Sidgwick 1981: 489–90). For example: rather than encouraging individuals to deliberate about whether stealing is permissible in particular circumstances, it might be better to promote the idea that stealing is always wrong. Rather than encouraging individuals to think about whether murdering particular people would boost aggregate utility, it might be better to promote the idea that murder must always be avoided. And so on.

Cases of type (b) are a bit more complex. Here, it's not that deliberation would lead to the wrong answer, but that deliberation would generate some kind of harm. Let me give an example. There's debate about whether organ sales should be permissible. Given the current state of medical technology, the demand for organs far outstrips the supply. For example, in the US there are currently 93,000 people on the waiting list for kidney transplants. Most of these individuals will need to wait 4–5 years before moving to the front of the line; during this time, their health is negatively impacted and about 5% die. The majority of donated kidneys come from deceased donors. However, it is now fairly common for live, healthy donors to offer kidneys; about one-third of donations in the US now come from live donors. This requires surgery and carries some risk, but often has no significant long-term effects on the donor.

These donations are voluntary and uncompensated. Suppose there were a market for kidney sales. Some individuals who are unwilling to donate kidneys would be willing to sell them at an appropriate price. This price might be quite high indeed: a 2009 study found that kidneys were selling for $160,000 on the black market. This raises grave ethical concerns: the people selling these organs are often impoverished; they typically receive insufficient care; they typically receive only a fraction of the sale-price, with most of the money going to middlemen; they are often coerced. But some individuals argue that these problems could be avoided, and the supply of organs greatly increased, if there were a tightly regulated market for organs. (There are models for this; Iran, for example, has such a market.) Ignoring the vast complexities involved in setting up such a market, we could ask: if it were possible to produce a non-exploitative, fully voluntary, tightly regulated market for selling kidneys, ought we to do so?

Some say yes (see, for example, Brennan and Jaworksi 2015). After all, we could imagine individuals being lifted out of poverty by selling their kidneys to wealthy individuals. If I am in need of food and basic medical care for my family, and can secure it by selling an organ and undergoing a brief recovery period, then it might be rational for me to do so. It would certainly be reasonable for some people to take this option once presented.

But an opponent can argue that these options should not be present. *A person who would reasonably take an option once presented could still have a reason to reject the presentation of that option and to prefer a prohibition.* Although that might seem odd as first glance, there are many examples. I will give two.

First, consider recent discussions of torturing suspected terrorists in the United States. Let's just grant a very controversial premise: let's suppose that there are some cases in which torturing a suspect would prevent otherwise unavoidable mass casualties. Even if this were true, we might prefer to avoid having government officials deliberating about whether it's permissible to torture particular individuals. For, once those questions are genuinely opened, we will have at least some cases in which innocents are tortured, in which torture reveals no useful information, in which dehumanizing attitudes toward prisoners are cultivated, in which there is a tendency for torture to become increasingly mainstream, and so on. An absolute prohibition on torture might be preferable to allowing government officials to deliberate on this matter.[3]

---

[3] For interesting reflections on these points, see "Three Kinds of Moral Imagination" in Chappell 2017.

Or take a less consequential example. Many competitive sports enforce prohibitions on performance-enhancing drugs. It's easy to see why: allowing performance-enhancing drugs would create an arms-race, with each player incentivized to take as many of these drugs in as great a quantity as possible. Assuming that these drugs actually do enhance performance, players who didn't take them would be at a disadvantage. We could imagine players faced with a choice: either take these drugs or lose their jobs to others who were willing to take the drugs. While it might be rational to take the drugs in a scenario like this, we can see why many players would prefer not to be presented with this choice. An absolute prohibition on performance-enhancing drugs makes sense, even though it would be rational to choose to take these drugs if they weren't prohibited (see Beck 2013 for a clear discussion of this case).

As these examples indicate, there are cases with the following form:

> It can be rational to prohibit X, even though we would choose X, and be rational in doing so, if X were an option.

But there are different reasons for this. Some of these cases arise simply because if X were an option, everyone would take it, and each person would then be worse off than before. Consider familiar tragedy of the commons cases: it is reasonable for me to exploit the commons if I am allowed to do so; but if everyone exploits the commons, then it will collapse, and no one will be able to use it at all. So it's in my interest to accept prohibitions. Other cases, as in the torturing and sports examples, are different: the presentation of the choice creates a situation in which participants are (arguably) worse off no matter what they choose.

Finally, let's consider cases of type (c). In these cases, merely considering trading X against Y—merely making this a legitimate possibility—undermines the value of X. I will call this *devaluation*. This is the more interesting argument for our purposes.

Let me start with an anecdote. A very famous philosopher with consequentialist tendencies once asked a friend of mine, who has multiple children, whether he'd considered aborting some of his children or, failing that, at least giving some of them up for adoption. This was asked with complete seriousness, not in a way intended to produce offense or to shock. And my friend and I have no objections to abortion or adoption. But the question seemed to me to reveal a severe impoverishment in the appreciation of value. It asked the father to weigh the value of his children against abstract concerns about overpopulation and resource distribution. (Imagine the father going home and saying, "Sorry, Tommy, but I've been convinced by my conversation with philosopher X that I am ethically required to give you up for adoption. Let me help you pack your things." Even contemplating this as a serious possibility is absurd.)

But why is this? I entirely agree that, in the abstract, people should be discouraged from having children; that it would be better if people gave their children up for adoption if this prevented others from having children; and so on. But, in asking for this kind of overt comparison, the questioner is asking the father to do something with quite different significance: she was asking him to relate to his children in a detached, impersonal way; to take seriously the possibility of giving them away in order to realize marginal gains in environmental and social justice. To relate to one's children in this way—to treat one's commitment to them as contingent upon the belief that it does not raise even the slightest of moral qualms—is to fail to value them in the right way.

Examples of this form are legion. Consider a few more:

Family: Ralph is a construction worker who sometimes takes on projects that involve sustained absences from his family. If offered a job that requires a month of absence but pays $10,000, he would take it without hesitation. But if an eccentric billionaire offers Ralph $10,000 not to work but simply to stay away from his family for a month, Ralph would decline the offer. So Ralph is willing to trade paid work for time away from his family, but he is not willing to trade equivalent monetary payments for the same amount of time away from his family.[4]

Why not? Because of what these choices say about Ralph's valuation of his family. Ralph thinks it is perfectly acceptable to take compensated work at the expense of family time; that's a necessity in the modern world and doesn't reflect poorly on his relationships. But taking a directly monetary payment for time away would signify something different: it would require weighing family against money quite directly. And this would express a different stance: not just that work and family must be balanced, but that family time is valuable only insofar as it doesn't interfere with other valued goods. (And notice that in cases like this, our first inclination is to reach for ways to re-describe the situation, to reframe it so that the choice doesn't look quite so bad.)

Prostitution: many people believe that although sex for pleasure is perfectly fine, sex for money is objectionable. Suppose Angie is at a bar and has been talking with Bill. He's hitting on her; she's attracted to him and considers going home with him. But then, before she makes a decision about whether to leave with him, Bill offers her a thousand dollars to come home with him. This immediately transforms the significance of her choice. She's disgusted with Bill and declines.

In a way, this looks irrational. Angie was wavering about leaving with Bill. Adding a thousand dollars should sweeten the pot, making her more inclined to do so. But it has the opposite effect. And the reasoning is obvious: deciding whether or not to have sex with someone for pleasure seems fine; deciding whether to have sex with someone for money is something that signifies a willingness to engage in

---

[4] I take this case from Raz 1986.

prostitution. (Of course, there are also other factors, including what the monetary offer would say about Bill's view of Angie and of sex more generally.)

Human rights: suppose we can violate one individual's rights to secure benefits for others. There's been a terrorist attack inflicting mass casualties; governmental officials can't find the responsible party, but do have one individual who has been involved in disreputable activities and whom they could easily frame for the crime. Doing so would relieve anxiety and make millions of people feel safer. Should we consider violating one individual's rights so as to assuage widespread fear?

Endangered species: suppose a wealthy individual makes a donation of a million dollars to an environmental conservation group in exchange for the right to hunt and kill one endangered animal. The money would be used to save several endangered animals that would otherwise likely perish.

Friendship: suppose Zed is offered a monetary payment if he cuts off all communication with a friend for one year. After a year, he can tell the friend why he's done this. Zed could really use the money and isn't the best at keeping in touch with friends anyway.

And so on. In each of these cases, the decisions are perceived as revealing something about the way in which one values the involved objects and persons. Even when substantial benefits arise from treating the valued object in a certain way, individuals—some individuals, at any rate—will experience profound reservations about making these choices.

These comparisons are ruled out because they are seen as undermining either the value of one's relationship to the object or the value of the object itself. If we merely consider the straightforward consequences of these acts, this might look irrational. Angie has inconsistent preferences when it comes to sex, pleasure, and money; Ralph has inconsistent preferences concerning family time, money, and work; and so on. And indeed, this is how some philosophers view these cases. In the introduction, I quoted Peter Singer's claim that "only a rump of hard-core, know-nothing religious fundamentalists" would hold on to these kinds of irrational beliefs about the inviolability of certain things (Singer 2009; see also Brennan and Jaworski 2015). So, Singer presents himself as a champion of clear, rational thinking, being willing to subject everything to critique and rational scrutiny, not ruling out any comparisons, letting reason lead him where it will.

But making these comparisons does in fact generate a different kind of relationship to the objects in question. And, insofar as prohibiting comparisons and exchanges is necessary for valuing the object in a certain way, those who follow Singer are thereby barred from these kinds of relationship.

To illustrate this, let me give a longer and more detailed example. In a 2003 *New York Times Magazine* article, the disability rights lawyer Harriet McBryde Johnson reflects on a debate that she had with Peter Singer. McBryde Johnson was born with a degenerative neuromuscular disease. At the time of her encounter with Singer, she weighed 70 pounds; needed to use a wheelchair; had a severely twisted spine; described herself as looking like a "jumble of bones in a floppy bag of skin"; and required assistance for most tasks. McBryde Johnson takes Singer to be committed to the view that it would be better if she had not been born.[5] As she puts it,

> He insists he doesn't want to kill me. He simply thinks it would have been better, all things considered, to have given my parents the option of killing the baby I once was, and to let other parents kill similar babies as they come along and thereby avoid the suffering that comes with lives like mine and satisfy the reasonable preferences of parents for a different kind of child. It has nothing to do with me. I should not feel threatened. (McBryde Johnson 2003)

And she continues:

> In the lecture hall that afternoon, Singer lays it all out. The "illogic" of allowing abortion but not infanticide, of allowing withdrawal of life support but not active killing. Applying the basic assumptions of preference utilitarianism, he spins out his bone-chilling argument for letting parents kill disabled babies and replace them with nondisabled babies who have a greater chance at happiness.
> (McBryde Johnson 2003)

McBryde Johnson appears deeply ambivalent about Singer's position. On the one hand, she describes his view as "bone-chilling," she is "horrified by what he says," and she is initially reluctant even to shake hands with him; on the other, she praises his "clear and lucid counterarguments" and describes him as engaged in "a grand, heroic undertaking" (McBryde Johnson 2003).

Why does Singer's conclusion seem "bone-chilling" but logical or sensible? Notice that Singer is committed to the view that it is irrational to refuse to compare values that are in fact comparable. And it might seem that human lives *are* in certain respects evaluatively comparable. In particular, it is widely believed that we can compare lives in terms of the degree of well-being that they exhibit. For example, a life full of misery and misfortune ranks lower on the scale of well-being than a life replete with happiness and joy. A life of chronic pain would, all else being equal, rank lower than a life in which this pain is absent.

Suppose that's right. Then we could ask whether the lives of severely disabled people tend to exhibit less well-being than the lives of non-disabled people. Singer thinks they do: while he acknowledges that there can be exceptions, he claims that in general non-disabled people tend to enjoy greater well-being than severely

---

[5] Singer argues that infanticide could be justified in cases where the infant suffers from a disability that is serious enough to affect her quality of life and her future prospects (see Singer and Kuhse 2002). McBryde Johnson takes this to apply to her; Singer seems to agree with her assessment.

disabled people.[6] So Singer invites us to consider a comparison: suppose you can produce one non-disabled life by eliminating one disabled life. Here is one of his early examples (originally published in 1979): parents learn shortly after the birth of their child that the child will be severely disabled. They still want a child, but prefer to raise a non-disabled child. Singer claims that in a case of this sort, it would be justifiable for the parents to "kill the defective infant and go ahead with another pregnancy" (Singer and Kuhse 2002: 120). In other words, Singer takes infanticide to be justified in this case because the loss of well-being for the first infant is outweighed by the gain of even greater well-being for the second. Singer presents this as a courageous result of logical thinking: while it is "shocking," while we have emotional and cultural resistance to drawing this conclusion, he claims that refusing to draw it for that reason would be irrational (Singer and Kuhse 2002: 120–1). So Singer is going "to puncture comfortable beliefs" and show us where logic leads us (Singer and Kuhse 2002: 5).

But this has implications that some find abhorrent. In treating lives (or at least infant lives) as fungible, it asks us to relate to persons in the same way that we relate to coins, trinkets, and cars: we willingly exchange one for another, straightforwardly measure them against one another, and have no qualms about doing so.

Of course it *is* possible to do this; and, if we accept certain versions of utilitarianism, doing so will be eminently rational. But consider McBryde Johnson's response to Singer. While she sometimes contests particular factual claims that Singer is relying upon,[7] her central claim is simply this: "We should not make disabled lives subject to debate" (McBryde Johnson 2003). She sometimes suggests that, in refusing to entertain these comparisons of disabled and non-disabled lives, she is departing from the impartial purity and logical rigor of Singer's vision. But there is another way of understanding McBryde Johnson's response. McBryde Johnson is treating human life as possessing sacred value. Accordingly, she is refusing to entertain certain comparisons.

This need not be a sign of irrationality. In the terminology that I have introduced, Singer's comparisons lead to *devaluation* of human lives. For, once parents are viewed as appropriate arbiters of the existence of their newborn children, certain justificatory demands will arise. Did you make the right choice in not killing this child? Would another child have been better? Rather than accepting the child as given, as something that simply must be cared for, as something that possesses an inviolable and incomparable value, we would be burdened with these justificatory questions. Something precious to us, something that we exempt from exchanges and comparisons, would become a fungible good like any other—more valuable than most things, perhaps, but still something that ought to be weighed.

---

[6] Obviously this is contestable, but my goal is not to assess this premise.
[7] For example, she takes Singer to be relying on the claim that disabilities necessarily reduce one's well-being, and she denies this claim.

Much of the power of McBryde Johnson's article lies in her moving portrayals of the costs of devaluation, the costs of entertaining comparisons of disabled and non-disabled lives. Her article is peppered with lovely examples of the way in which legitimizing these sorts of comparisons devalues the lives of disabled people. She emphasizes the way in which Singer overlooks the "profoundly beautiful" relations that severely disabled people can enter into with others: she describes the intimate ways in which her assistant, Carmen, cares for her; or a moment when she requires Singer himself to move her wrist forward an inch; or a day at the beach as a child. In all of these cases, the contrast between Singer's highly simplified and abstracted cases ("imagine a disabled child at a beach, watching the other children play") and the lived reality of McBryde Johnson brings home the way in which barring certain kinds of comparisons makes possible forms of appreciation and interaction that might otherwise prove inaccessible. So the problem is not just that if Singer's vision were enacted, these forms of relationship would disappear (though of course that's true). The problem is that in treating human lives as fungible, Singer arguably blinds himself to the very possibility of these relationships; his evaluative world is poorer than that of McBryde Johnson.[8] He is like the construction worker who sees no difference between the work-related absences and the direct payments for staying away.

It's tempting to think that prohibitions on evaluative comparisons are an imperfection, something dogmatic or irrational: a fully rational agent would be willing to entertain any comparisons whatsoever. The thought is that values and commitments are in fact comparable; and a refusal to entertain these comparisons therefore looks like willful and self-imposed blindness. But this is a mistake. Our refusal to entertain certain kinds of comparisons is what determines the normative structure of these options. This need not be seen as an attempt to get at some deeper truth or to discern some respect in which these values are in fact incomparable. The refusal to compare them *constitutes* their incomparability. In the normative domain, some truth depends on the agent's—or the culture's—beliefs.[9]

So one reason for resisting certain comparisons is that doing so enables a different form of relationship to the valued object. But we can also offer a mixed justification of these prohibitions, combining claims about the symbolic significance of certain acts with claims about the utility of maintaining that

---

[8] As Hopwood 2016 perceptively notes, one thing that McBryde Johnson is trying to do is get Singer to adopt a different perspective on these matters, to see something that he could not have seen from his impartial standpoint.

[9] Note that a refusal to entertain comparisons can take two forms. I might view myself as unwilling to entertain comparisons while recognizing that this merely expresses a personal preference; or I might view myself as unwilling to entertain comparisons while treating this as something that all people (or all similarly situated people) should do. It is only in the latter case that we treat values as Incontestable.

symbolic significance. Consider Emile Durkheim on a case involving violations of human rights:[10]

> [Violations of individual rights] cannot rest unpunished without putting national existence in jeopardy. It is indeed impossible that they should be freely allowed to occur without weakening the sentiments they violate; and as these sentiments are all that we have in common, they cannot be weakened without disturbing the cohesion of society. A religion which tolerates acts of sacrilege abdicates any sway over men's minds. The religion of the individual can therefore allow itself to be flouted without resistance only on penalty of ruining its credit; since it is the sole link which binds us to one another, such a weakening cannot take place without the onset of social dissolution. Thus the individualist, who defends the rights of the individual, defends at the same time the vital interests of society.
> (Durkheim 1975: 69)

Durkheim thinks that prohibiting certain tradeoffs (and, by extension, certain comparisons) is necessary if particular "sentiments" are to be preserved. He claims that these sentiments are necessary for social cohesion. If something like this is right—if maintaining certain sacred values is necessary for a form of moral or social stability—then we would have an additional reason for thinking that it can be rational to prohibit comparisons of comparables. The next chapter argues in favor of a version of this.

So there are certain commitments whose nature depends upon the existence of prohibitions on comparisons. (Not all comparisons are ruled out. Ralph can weigh family time against work, but not against direct monetary payments; Angie can weigh sex against other forms of pleasure, but not against money.) Insofar as it is rational to preserve commitments of this form, we have reason to reject the following claim: if a commitment requires prohibiting comparisons of things that are in fact comparable, then the commitment is irrational. Instead, we should accept the following claim:

- It can be rational to prohibit comparisons of things that are in fact comparable.

As the examples indicate, it can be perfectly rational to maintain commitments of this form. So the mere fact that sacred values prohibit comparisons of

---

[10] Durkheim is writing about the Dreyfus affair: in 1894, a French artillery officer, Alfred Dreyfus, was accused of passing military secrets to the Germans and was sentenced to life imprisonment. In 1896, high ranking French military officers became aware that Dreyfus was innocent and that another individual, Major Esterhazy, had committed the crime. Nonetheless, this evidence was suppressed and army officials produced forged documents supposedly establishing Dreyfus' involvement. The fact that the army had framed Dreyfus came to light in 1897, eventually resulting in public outcry and new trials; he was freed (by pardon) in 1899 and exonerated in 1906.

comparables is not a sign of their irrationality. Moreover, I've suggested that certain ways of valuing and certain forms of relationship are available only if we refuse these comparisons.

3.3 Conclusion

This chapter has argued that it can be rational to prohibit certain kinds of tradeoffs and comparisons. Even when two goods can be weighed or compared, it can make sense to prohibit these weighings and comparisons. The fact that sacred values involve prohibitions on tradeoffs and contemplated comparisons is thus not a mark against them. On the contrary, prohibiting certain comparisons enables valuable forms of relationships that would otherwise be impossible or inaccessible. The person who treats all values as to be compared lives in a poorer world than does the person who prohibits certain comparisons. In short: we enrich and deepen our evaluative lives by refusing to compare certain comparables.

4
Devotion and Dialectical Invulnerability

The previous chapter argued that prohibitions on certain kinds of comparisons—and more generally prohibitions on deliberation about certain topics—can be rational. If this is right, then the first two features of sacred values can be justified in certain contexts. But we haven't yet examined the third feature: dialectical invulnerability. Sacred values are immune to the effects of justificatory critique. This is, I think, the aspect of sacred values that will look most problematic to philosophers.

This chapter argues that it can be rational to treat certain commitments as dialectically invulnerable. It does so by introducing a concept that I think is crucial yet mostly overlooked by philosophers: devotion. I will explicate this concept, arguing that devotion consists in having a commitment; treating this commitment as dialectically invulnerable; and aiming to maintain the dialectical invulnerability of this commitment. With this notion in place, I argue that it can be rational to manifest devotion. If it can be rational to devote oneself to things, and if doing so requires treating one's commitment to these things as dialectically invulnerable, then it can be rational to render certain commitments dialectically invulnerable.

* * *

To get there, we will need to make a few preliminary clarifications. Sometimes, even the most central commitments in our lives are dialectically *vulnerable:* we maintain the commitment only because and to the extent that we think there is a defensible justification for doing so. For example, I think that certain forms of egalitarianism are valuable; I think that progressive taxation is one way of achieving egalitarian outcomes; hence, I am committed to supporting progressive taxation. But if you showed me a convincing argument that progressive taxation imperils egalitarianism, I would readily abandon my commitment to it. So that's a case of a dialectically vulnerable commitment. Or, to use a more consequential example: I know someone who was deeply committed to her religious faith, taking it not only as a practice that informed her life but also as an object of academic study; she was a passionate student of religion, conceiving of this as one of her most central commitments; she chanced into taking a philosophy class and gradually became convinced that the value she had formerly attributed to the academic study of religion was in fact present to a much higher degree in the study of philosophy; and, as a result, she gave up her commitment to the academic study of religion, switching to philosophy instead. So again, we have a very deep commitment that is nonetheless dialectically vulnerable. There are countless examples of this form.

Philosophy of Devotion: The Longing for Invulnerable Ideals. Paul Katsafanas, Oxford University Press.
© Paul Katsafanas 2022. DOI: 10.1093/oso/9780192867674.003.0004

Although there are many cases in which our commitments depend on these kinds of judgments, I want to focus on cases where this connection is broken. Politics, religion, and personal relationships are fertile grounds for cases in which the strength of the person's commitments often seems resistant to justificatory reflection. We need no list of examples, no studies, no intricate arguments to see that people's judgments about what is justified tend to founder against these commitments. A quotation from Proust makes the point nicely:

> It is life that, little by little, case by case, enables us to observe that what is most important to our hearts or to our minds is taught us not by reasoning but by other powers. And then it is the intelligence itself which, acknowledging their superiority, abdicates to them through reasoning and consents to become their collaborator and their servant.   (Proust 2003: Vol. V, p. 569)

Proust is using the notion of importance to pick out something like my concept of devotion. The point, here, is that many of our deepest commitments neither originate from nor are affected by justificatory reasoning. And not only that: once we come to regard something as important (or, I will argue, as an object of devotion), our critical and justificatory reasoning about that thing begins to operate in a non-standard way. Proust suggests that in these cases, reasoning abdicates its typical powers. I will be making a similar argument.

The goal of this chapter is to clarify the concept of devotion by examining the way in which it involves a dissociation from rational responsiveness to justificatory considerations. I will suggest that devotion is a species of commitment. In particular, devotion to an object, end, or person arises when the relevant commitment is rendered dialectically invulnerable *and* the agent aims to maintain this invulnerability. Moreover, I will argue that it can be rational to have commitments that are in this way unresponsive to justificatory reflection. This is not to say that every instance of devotion is praiseworthy; on the contrary, many instances of devotion will be criticizable in terms of their content, their effects, and so on. My point, instead, is that the mere fact that a commitment takes the form of devotion is not an objection to the commitment and can, instead, be a mark in its favor.

The structure of the chapter is as follows. Section 4.1 introduces the notion of devotion, distinguishing it from intention and other forms of commitment. Section 4.2 investigates the relationship between commitments and justificatory reflection. There, I draw on Bernard Williams' and Susan Wolf's discussions of the idea that certain types of ethical reflection involve "one thought too many." Although Williams' discussion is often read as suggesting that excessive reflection on our commitments can be problematic, I argue that what is at issue is not the *quantity* of reflection but whether the commitment's standing is staked on the outcome of justificatory reflection. In particular, I claim that Williams shows that insulating certain commitments from the effects of justificatory reflection can be laudable. Developing some ideas from Williams and Wolf, I offer an analysis of devotion. Section 4.3 clarifies the way in which devotion involves dialectical invulnerability. Section 4.4 explains how devotion relates to having sacred values. Section 4.5 discusses the relationship between devotion, alienation, and identification. Finally, Section 4.6 considers a potential objection: isn't it perverse to identify devotion with commitments that resist justificatory reflection? I argue that it is not; it can be rational to have and maintain dialectically invulnerable commitments.

4.1 Distinguishing Devotion from Commitment

Devotion is a species of commitment, so let's begin by considering what it is to be committed to something. Intuitively, it seems that we use the term "commitment" to pick out cases in which an agent sticks with an end despite encountering things that might sway others from that end. Suppose we consider two students: Lisa is committed to her studies but Frank is not. Part of what this means is that Lisa will persevere in the face of obstacles, difficulties, distractions, and temptations, whereas Frank will not. So, as they both settle in to the library to study for tomorrow's test, Lisa will turn off her phone and focus on her work while Frank keeps checking his texts, posting on social media, and chatting with friends. And we will see the same pattern over time: Lisa consistently rejects courses of action that would interfere with her studies, whereas Frank does not. It is in cases of this sort that we tend to speak of commitment. The same structure emerges in interpersonal commitments: we say that a person is in a *committed* relationship when they persevere in the face of difficulties, when they resist temptations to engage in activities that they see as harmful to the relationship, and so on.

In general, we speak of commitment when we are considering relatively long-term goals, activities, or relationships that require some degree of perseverance in order to be achieved or maintained successfully. It would be odd to say that I am committed to getting a cup of coffee if all that this requires is effortlessly walking to my kitchen; it would be somewhat more natural to speak of a commitment to getting coffee if this requires a more arduous, long-term process, such as walking through a snowstorm to the local coffee shop. So commitment seems to involve a willingness to pursue an end despite obstacles. These obstacles can take many different forms: difficulties, boredom, disengagement, distraction, objections, the recognition of other appealing options, and so on.

Commitment comes in degrees. If we compare my commitment to being on time for my office hours to my commitment to promoting my child's welfare, the latter is *much* more robust. Although I am committed to being on time, I can imagine many circumstances in which I would abandon this commitment: if the weather is really disastrous, or if I have a cold, or even if I run into a friend who

I haven't seen in many years, I might be a bit late for my office hours or even cancel them. Not so with the commitment to my child's welfare: I wouldn't imperil her welfare on these grounds.

Because commitments vary in degree, there will be borderline cases in which it is unclear whether the person really has a commitment at all. Suppose a disengaged student like Frank, above, claims to be committed to studying, and will in fact study when there are no other appealing options, but will abandon studying whenever something moderately enticing presents itself. In this case it's tempting to say that he either is not committed at all or displays only the most modest degree of commitment.

Just as we can sort a particular person's commitments into those that are held very robustly and those that seem more tenuous, we can distinguish variances across people. Some people are very good at sticking to their goals in general: they display a general disposition to persevere in the face of obstacles, difficulties, distractions, competing goods, and so on.[1] We can count on these people: if they commit to something, we can be sure they will do it. Others lack this disposition: they give up at the first hint of difficulty, get distracted by the first thing that catches their eye. When we consider commitments, then, it's clear that there are variances both within individual agents and between agents. Commitment is degreed.

4.1.1 Analyzing Commitment

Let's make this notion of commitment more precise. We can begin by asking how being committed to some end differs from intending that end. After all, intentions also involve some degree of willingness to withstand obstacles and contrary pressures: if I claim that I intend to run a marathon, but give up at the first hint of difficulty or the first temptation to do something else, we might be skeptical of the claim that I genuinely intended to run the marathon—perhaps I merely wished or desired to do so.[2] So intentions seem to share certain features with commitments.

Although I won't pause here to offer any detailed account of intention, I think Cheshire Calhoun's account of the relationship between commitment and intention is illuminating. I will rely on it. Calhoun argues that commitments can be understood as a type of intention (cf. Calhoun 2018: 93). They differ in that commitments involve both an intention *and* a disposition to maintain the intention. As Calhoun puts it,

---

[1] See Morton and Paul 2019.   [2] See for example Bratman 2012.

> Constitutive of any commitment is a stance of being prepared to sustain the commitment. That is, a commitment is both an intention to engage with something (a person, relationship, goal, activity, identity, etc.) and a preparedness to see to it that that intention to engage persists. (Calhoun 2018: 95)

So commitment is a type of intention. But, whereas commitment involves a disposition to sustain one's intention, other intentions lack that feature. Return to my example of fetching a cup of coffee. Suppose I start to head out for a cup of coffee, put on my boots and coat, make it out the door, but then notice that it's really very chilly indeed; I reconsider, and decide to stay at home. I did intend to get a cup of coffee, but I reconsidered that intention and abandoned it. In a case like this, we can say that I have an intention but lack a disposition to ensure that the intention persists. I hence lack a commitment to getting the coffee. Analogous points apply to the two students: Lisa and Frank both intend to study, but Lisa is committed to studying and Frank isn't.

Of course, the disposition to sustain the intention comes in degrees: I am willing to undertake some difficulties in order to sustain my intention to hold my office hours on time, but I am willing to undertake many more in order to sustain my intention to promote my child's welfare. So, as Calhoun writes,

> We measure depth of commitment by what a person is prepared to do or to resist in order to see to it that the intention to engage persists. Someone prepared to do very little to see to it that her intention to engage persists has made only a shallow commitment or a "commitment" more accurately described as a *mere intention* or a *provisional plan*, rather than a commitment. (Calhoun 2018: 95)

I am committed to holding my office hours on time, but if I have a cold or my car breaks down I probably won't look for other possible ways of holding them; I will just cancel. Not so with my commitment to my child: if her welfare would be affected by my failure to be present at a given time, I would go despite illness or car trouble or other inconveniences. I would be disposed to find alternative solutions in a way that I wouldn't with my office hours. I am committed to both of these things, but my disposition to sustain and preserve the intention is much stronger in the one case than in the other.

So far, we've merely said that commitments are intentions coupled with a disposition to sustain the intention. But there's also another important feature: a commitment to some end, E, involves intentions to follow through on E-ing in the face of circumstances that, in the absence of the commitment, would make it rational to give up the intention to E. Calhoun puts it this way:

> I take it that what distinguishes commitments from mere intentions, as well as from provisional plans, is that commitments are intentions to follow through

despite or in the face of developments that would, in the absence of commitment, make it rational to reconsider one's mere intentions or provisional plans... In short, to be committed, one must be prepared to weather circumstantial and informational changes that would provide sufficient reason to alter mere intentions and provisional plans. (Calhoun 2018: 96–7)

Suppose we consider an activity such as *learning French*. The relevant difference between *intending* to learn French and *committing* to learning French is that the latter involves (1) a disposition to sustain the intention to learn French; and (2) intentions to follow through on learning French in circumstances where, absent the commitment, it would be rational to give up the aim of learning French. So, if I merely intend to learn French, it might be rational to give up this intention when I see how long it will take, how arduous it will be, how many other valued activities I will have to abandon or postpone in order to carry it out. After all, while it would be nice to be fluent in French, doing so would take a great deal of effort over many months and years, and that is time that I will no longer have available to spend on other valued pursuits. These seem to me to be good reasons for abandoning an intention to learn French: they are not decisive, but they are sufficient reasons for abandoning the intention. But if I am *committed* to learning French, then I will persevere in learning French despite my recognition that there are sufficient reasons for abandoning the pursuit.[3]

4.1.2 Devotion

I think Calhoun's analysis of commitment is illuminating and I will adopt it in what follows. I am going to argue that just as commitment is a species of intention, so too devotion is a species of commitment. To establish this point, I need to introduce a distinction between two types of reasons for abandoning a commitment.

First, there can be reasons that arise from motivational problems: you believe that you have good reason to maintain your commitment, but find yourself incapable of sticking to it. You want to maintain your commitment to learning French, you see good reasons for doing so, but you simply can't muster the energy; your affective engagement with this goal fails. Whenever you settle down to study, a moment later you're distracted. It's a struggle and you come to think that the struggle just isn't worth it. Sometimes, in the face of these repeated motivational

---

[3] Although I've focused on Calhoun's account of commitment, other accounts are available. Holton 2009 and Andreou 2022 provide insightful analyses of "resoluteness," which in some ways mirrors Calhoun's notion of commitment. Bratman 2018 argues for a concept of planning agency according to which it can be rational for an agent to adhere to a plan even if she finds that her present evaluative perspective warrants abandoning it.

failures, it can be rational to give up the commitment: you learn by experience that the commitment just isn't for you. It's not motivationally tenable; it's harder for you than you imagined, and the rewards don't repay the efforts. So you move on. You might still have a wish or a desire to learn French; but the commitment is gone.

Second, there can be reasons that arise from epistemic considerations: you come to think that maintaining the commitment is unjustifiable ("I can't justify spending all this time learning French at the expense of other valued goals!"), or that you have reason to abandon it ("I can just use translations"), or that it makes sense to revise it ("If I am going to learn a new language, I should really learn Mandarin instead"). Of course, these sorts of reflections can sometimes be manifestations of irrationality; I might be engaged in self-deception. But they don't have to be. As Calhoun points out, commitments involve a willingness to stick to some end despite considerations that, in the absence of the commitment, would make it rational to give up the end. So genuine questions about whether it makes sense to maintain the commitment can arise.

Although the reasons arising from motivational problems are quite interesting, in this chapter, I am going to focus on the reasons arising from epistemic considerations. Here's a way of putting the point: typically, when we come to think either that some commitment is unjustifiable or that we have good reasons to abandon it, this erodes our degree of commitment. So, for example, if I come to think that I lack sufficient reason for maintaining my commitment to learning French, this would typically lead me to abandon or modify the commitment.

In this sense, commitments tend to be responsive to justificatory reasoning. To be clear, this is not to say that they *originate* through justificatory reasoning: many of our commitments are adopted haphazardly, with little reflection, sometimes through acculturation or social influence, sometimes just on a whim. But many of our commitments are *responsive* to justificatory reasoning: if I come to think that there's a good reason to abandon a commitment, this typically has some impact on the commitment. Or, at least, it does so insofar as I am rational. For commitments are what are sometimes referred to as judgment-sensitive attitudes. Scanlon defines judgment-sensitive attitudes as follows: "attitudes that, insofar as we are rational, will be responsive to our assessments of the reasons for them" (Scanlon 2007: 90; cf. Scanlon 1998: 20–4). This is, after all, what we should expect: intentions are judgment-sensitive attitudes, and commitments are a species of intention.

But there is a particular type of commitment that *doesn't* seem to be in this way judgment-sensitive. I will call this type of commitment *devotion*. Devotion is impervious to justificatory reasoning. This doesn't mean that we cannot reflect on devotion or its objects. I might be devoted to promoting my child's welfare but perfectly happy to reflect at length on the nature of my commitment, on the child herself, on parent–child relations in general, and so on. I might reflect on whether my devotion to her welfare is warranted, whether it is subject to criticism, whether there are reasons for and against it, and so on. But what will be crucial is that this justificatory reflection has no effect on the commitment itself: even if I were to become convinced that my devotion to my child's welfare were unjustifiable, that there were decisive reasons against it, I would remain committed.

Love, of both the parental and the romantic varieties, is a fertile ground for devotion.[4] But devotion extends far beyond this realm. I think that many of our deepest political, philosophical, and religious commitments are instances of devotion. It's a truism of folk psychology that we shouldn't expect to argue people out of their political and religious commitments; it's an axiom of the old newspaper manners columns that the attentive host avoids these conversations at the dinner party; a google search on "arguing about politics and religion" will turn up pages of advice on how to avoid hurt feelings, damaged relationships; and so on. There's something to this. Certain commitments don't respond to justificatory reasoning in the standard way.

Commitments could be impervious to justificatory reflection in two ways. First, the agent might decline to engage in justificatory reflection about certain matters. Second, the agent might be willing to engage in justificatory reflection, perhaps spending countless hours thinking about the justificatory status of certain commitments; but this reflection might have no effect on the commitment. For now, I just want to mark this distinction. In Section 4.2, I am going to argue that it is the second form of resistance to justificatory reflection—which I call dialectical invulnerability—that characterizes devotion.

Notice that devotion involves both a practical and an epistemic side. Someone who claims to be devoted to learning French, but who finds himself swayed whenever a more attractive activity presents itself, is not a good case of devotion. Given the frailties of human psychology, even devotion will be compatible with some degree of lapse; but systematic or regular lapses will call the purported devotion into question. In this respect, though, I think devotion is analogous to ordinary commitment: it is not the *practical* or *motivational* side that distinguishes devotion from commitment. A commitment can be extremely robust, motivationally speaking, without being an instance of devotion. Indeed, we can make the commitment arbitrarily strong: it overpowers every competing urge, it occupies the person's attention and emotional energies, she never wavers from manifesting it; and yet, were she to come to regard it as unjustifiable, she would abandon it.

It is the epistemic side that distinguishes devotion from commitment. Whereas commitment is judgment-sensitive, devotion is not. As I will explain below, devotion manifests a particular form of dialectical invulnerability.

---

[4] Of course, love involves more than just devotion. I am claiming that devotion often arises in cases of love, not that love is reducible to devotion. More on this below.

Before proceeding, one clarificatory note. Notice that I am not claiming that my analysis of devotion corresponds to every use of the word "devotion" in ordinary language. We sometimes speak of devoted agents in order to pick out a high degree of motivational investment in some end. What I am saying is that it is *philosophically useful* to use the term in the way that I am suggesting. In effect, it helps us to distinguish ordinary commitments from sacralized commitments. To see why this notion is philosophically useful, I want to examine a classic debate that was initiated by Bernard Williams.

4.2 The Importance of Dialectically Invulnerable Attitudes

Bernard Williams famously argues that certain ways of thinking about morality provide the agent with "one thought too many." In Section 4.2.1, I will review his argument as well as Susan Wolf's response to it. Williams and Wolf agree that it can be praiseworthy to maintain certain commitments while refusing to reflect on their justificatory status. In Section 4.2.2, I will argue that Williams' and Wolf's points can be sharpened: it is not the *quantity* but the *effect* of reflection that matters. In Section 4.2.3, I introduce the notion of Dialectical Invulnerability and argue that it can be laudable to have Dialectically Invulnerable commitments. In short: it can be laudable to manifest devotion.

4.2.1 Williams and Wolf on the Refusal to Reflect on Certain Commitments

Although Williams' claims about having "one thought too many" will be familiar to many readers, it will be useful to recall the details. Williams is responding to an argument from Charles Fried, who imagines a scenario in which a man on a boat could save one of two people in equal peril; one is his wife and one is a stranger. Fried says that so long as the man is not acting in some official capacity ("captain of a ship, public health official or the like"), it would be absurd to insist that he flip a coin in order to determine who to save. The man is morally permitted to be partial, here, and save his wife (Fried 1980: 227). But why?

Williams thinks that most readers will say that there is some "moral principle [that] can legitimate his preference, yielding the conclusion that in situations of this kind it is at least all right (morally permissible) to save one's wife" (Williams 1981a: 18). However, Williams claims that

> this construction provides the agent with one thought too many: it might have been hoped by some (for instance, by his wife) that his motivating thought, fully

spelled out, would be the thought that it was his wife, not that it was his wife and that in situations of this kind it is permissible to save one's wife.

(Williams 1981a: 18)

Williams' basic claim is clear enough: there's something problematic about reflecting on whether it's permissible to save one's wife instead of a stranger. What is the problem supposed to be?

I will draw on an illuminating discussion by Susan Wolf (2012). Wolf notes that many readers agree with Williams that there would be something amiss with the man who sees his wife and a stranger in the water and wonders who to save. According to the most common reading of this passage—Wolf calls it *The Standard View*—what's problematic is that the rescuer *pauses*, at the moment of action, and deliberates about whether morality allows saving his wife rather than a stranger. There are, after all, several potential problems: we might think that the answer should be so obvious as to render deliberation pointless; or we might think that pausing to deliberate in a crisis is absurd—one should just act; or we might think that the pause reveals an odd detachment from the wife; or that he is too cold, too calculating, too passionless. No doubt there are other variants. But the core idea, here, is that what's problematic about the rescuer is *what he does at the moment of action*. And so, according to the Standard View, there would be nothing inappropriate about the rescuer saving his wife and *later* wondering whether he acted in a morally permissible way. For, "according to the Standard View, the ideal moral agent is the one who always does the moral (that is, the morally permissible) thing, but who does not always have to think about it" (Wolf 2012: 79). So what's standard about The Standard View is the focus on the moment of action.

Wolf rejects the Standard View. The problem is this: the Standard View takes Williams to be focused on whether the rescuer does something wrong during the moment of action. But, Wolf points out, Williams' discussion actually does not focus on what happens at the moment of action. He is concerned with broader questions about the relationship between "deep attachments" and morality. After all, having given the example, Williams then says: "the point is that somewhere... one reaches the necessity that such things as deep attachments to other persons will express themselves in the world in ways which cannot at the same time embody the impartial view, and that they also run the risk of offending against it." And, he continues, "Life has to have substance if anything is to have sense, including adherence to the impartial system; but if it has substance, then it cannot grant supreme importance to the impartial system" (Williams 1981a: 18). Williams' conclusions aren't restricted to what happens at moments of deliberation and action; they concern, more broadly, the relationship between morality and the agent's deepest attachments and concerns.

What the rescuer does at the moment of action is problematic, but it's clear that Williams is taking it as symptomatic of some deeper problem that does not itself concern the time of action. But what is this problem? In an attempt to clarify Williams' intent, Wolf asks us to imagine a variety of additional scenarios that we might see as involving objectionable extra thoughts. One of her examples involves a person thinking counterfactually about a variety of lifeboat cases. Although not actually facing any real decisions, he wonders whether he would save his wife or the stranger; and then wonders what would happen if it were a choice between his wife and two strangers, or fifty, and so on (Wolf 2012: 76–7). Wolf says that if "the agent subjects himself to these various thought experiments unprovoked," this "puts me off, even before hearing what substantive answers he would come to about whom he would save and under what conditions" (Wolf 2012: 77). She describes such an agent as "obsessive" in wanting to assure himself "that in all possible situations his behavior will be morally justified" (2012: 77).

But what's wrong with worrying about the moral justifiability of your actions? Isn't that what we should want? Or, even if we don't want people to contemplate all of these scenarios, don't we want their actions to be responsive to moral considerations, so that they refrain from immoral acts and perform moral ones?

Wolf answers negatively. She writes:

Reflecting on the circumstances in which I would prefer that my husband not consult morality (nor want to) before rushing in to save me, my preference does not seem to me to be captured by the hope that considerations of moral permissibility be guiding him, but subconsciously; my hope is rather that he not care so much about the rulings of morality (in these instances) at all. More generally, what strikes me as unpalatable about the Standard View is not that its ideal agent is so willing to think about morality; it is that he is so unconditionally committed to morality—that is, that he is unconditionally committed to acting according to morality's demands. (Wolf 2012: 80)

As she clarifies, her "distaste is for an *absolute and unconditional* commitment to morality—not for a commitment of a more usual sort. Of course I want people, myself and my partner included, to care very much about morality, and for this concern to guide and constrain their (and our) behavior in many ways" (2012: 80). She doesn't want her partner to go about thieving and murdering whenever the fancy strikes him; but she also doesn't want morality to be an absolute, unconditional requirement for him.

In short, Wolf claims that there is something problematic about the person who is so unconditionally committed to morality that he would overrule all other interests for it. This unconditional commitment is revealed by incessant unprovoked reflection on cases, thinking through counterfactual scenarios, having "one thought too many" while he watches his wife flounder in the water, and so on.

But this might seem odd, given that many philosophers think morality should be absolutely and unconditionally overriding. Wolf disputes that claim, arguing in other works that there are non-moral considerations (e.g. of meaningfulness) that can override moral considerations (Wolf 2010). If we are moved by these concerns, we can see why someone might be disturbed by the scenarios that Wolf mentions. She writes:

> The wife who hopes that her husband would not consult or care about morality when faced with the need to choose between rescuing either her or a stranger hopes more concretely that he will not be concerned about impartiality either. What she wants, we might imagine, is that the sight or sound of his wife in danger would—in these circumstances—so fill up his consciousness that it leaves no room for thought or care about morality or the impartial point of view. But that is not all—for the subjunctive realization of that hope would only establish that the man would not think about or be motivated by considerations of moral permissibility (or impartiality) at the moment of action. What the woman must also hope is that her husband be comfortable with these deliberative and motivational dispositions (or perhaps that the husband would be comfortable with them if he had occasion to notice and reflect on them). Recognizing that he would respond to the rescuing situation in this way, he does not feel the need, or perhaps even any interest, in finding out counterfactually whether his response would be permitted by one who adopts an impartial point of view.
>
> (Wolf 2012: 84).

So she wants her partner not to treat morality as overriding and to be committed to not treating it as overriding.

4.2.2 Does the Quantity of Reflection Matter?

As these passages indicate, Wolf rejects both of the following:

(1) Moral commitments should override all competing commitments.
(2) We should reflect on each case of potential conflict between moral commitments and other commitments.

She claims that we should reject (2) because of its connection to (1): her suggestion is that (1) and (2) tend to stand or fall together, in that each suggests (though does not strictly entail) the other.

Wolf's rejection of claim (1) is controversial. But we can set it aside, for what concerns us is not restricted to conflicts between morality and other interests. Williams and Wolf construct cases in which a commitment conflicts with morality; we take morality to be something that provides good reasons; so we take there to be a good reason to abandon or modify the commitment, or at least to worry about whether we should do so. But the point is really independent of *morality*. It's about conflicts between commitments in general. We could imagine cases where what conflicts isn't commitment to wife and commitment to morality, but commitment to wife and commitment to career, or commitment to wife and commitment to art (as in Williams' famous Gauguin case [Williams 1981b]), and so on. The content of the conflict isn't essential. So we gain clarity by setting aside morality and thinking instead about practical reflection generally.

Let's then rewrite (2) as follows:

(2') We should reflect on each case of potential conflict between our commitments.

This brings us to the central point of Wolf's discussion:

(3) Certain commitments will be sustained by the agent's refusal to engage in critical reflection.

Wolf focuses on the idea that some non-moral commitments are sustained by the agent's refusal to engage in critical reflection. She wants her husband not to reflect, either at the moment of action or retrospectively, on whether his commitment to rescuing her would be morally permissible. For, she assumes, this kind of deliberation would be premised on the idea that morality is (or could be) overriding. (3) states this point in a way that is independent of specifically moral concerns.

With this in mind, I want to point out that it is not really the mere *occurrence* of reflection that is at issue here. Notice that someone could *agree* with Wolf that morality is not overriding, and yet still engage in reflective scrutiny of his commitments. Indeed, this could be a reason to *increase* reflection: precisely because morality is one source of concern among others, I might be motivated to reflect all the more. What matters isn't the sheer quantity of reflection but the relation between *reflective critique of the commitment and its persistence*. What we want in these cases is not for the agent to refuse to think about the commitments; what we want is a commitment that will be held regardless of the results of critical reflection. So, even if the agent were to conclude that morality requires saving the stranger, he wouldn't be moved by this. Insofar as we're doing autobiography, this is what I would want: even if my wife concluded that a commitment to saving me over a stranger were immoral, I would want her to set morality aside.

So we can clarify what's at issue by setting aside mere engagement in critical reflection and focusing instead on *staking commitment on critical reflection*. In other words: whereas Wolf's phrasings suggest that we should distinguish between the agent who engages in critical reflection and the agent who doesn't,

I suggest that we should distinguish between the agent who stakes her commitments on the outcome of critical reflection and the agent who doesn't. (To be clear, I think Wolf would agree with this point. While Wolf's phrasings suggest that the propensity to engage in reflection is what's relevant, I am suggesting that the deeper issue to which Wolf's examples draw attention is the question of whether we should stake all of our commitments on the outcome of critical reflection.)

Certain commitments are insulated from the effects of critical reflection. We may not reflect on these commitments or on their justifications; we may do so only with reluctance; or we may do so happily and persistently. What matters is that the commitments are impervious to the verdicts of this critical reflection: even if we find the commitment unjustified, the commitment does not slacken. So, regardless of whether the agent finds his commitment to his wife to conflict with impartial morality, career, art, or whatever, his commitment remains.

4.2.3 Dialectically Invulnerable Commitments

Drawing on our terminology from Chapter 2, let's say a commitment or attitude is *dialectically invulnerable* when it is in this way insulated from the effects of justificatory critique. In particular:

> A commitment or attitude is *dialectically invulnerable* when there is no argument, distinction, clarification, or other dialectical move that would dislodge it or cause it to dissipate. Showing the commitment or attitude to be irrational, inconsistent with other commitments, in conflict with moral principles, lacking adequate justification, and so forth has no effect.

To be clear: other, non-dialectical approaches might cause the commitment or attitude to dissipate. A bump on the head, inflamed rhetoric, or striking up new emotions might cause it to change or dissipate. What is ruled out is simply dialectical approaches.

Consider Williams' rescuer: he might treat commitment to saving his wife as dialectically invulnerable. If he does, then considering counterexamples, making fine distinctions, contemplating moral principles, and so forth is pointless: regardless of his conclusions, the commitment won't budge. Or imagine what happens all the time in philosophical discussions: we see that some of our firmly held convictions are subject to counterarguments and cannot be sustained by any non-question begging arguments; nonetheless, the commitment remains as firm as ever. And of course there are problematic cases as well: witness the neo-Nazi who believes that there is an attack on whiteness, and who maintains this commitment regardless of evidence, arguments, and other dialectical moves. His commitment, too, is dialectically invulnerable.[5]

The fact that there are problematic cases should not distract us from the deeper point to which Williams and Wolf are drawing attention. It seems not just permissible but *laudable* when certain commitments are dialectically invulnerable. There is something defective about the person who fails to do this, who stakes each commitment on his ability to justify it impartially.[6]

4.2.4 Devotion and Dialectical Invulnerability

So far, I have introduced the idea that certain attitudes and commitments are dialectically invulnerable, and I have suggested that this can be laudable. But now I want to link this notion of dialectical invulnerability to devotion. I suggest that this kind of *un*responsiveness to judgment is criterial for manifesting devotion. In particular:

(**Devotion**) An agent is devoted to a person, state of affairs, value, or goal iff (i) she is committed to engaging in the relevant ways with that person, state of affairs, value, or goal, (ii) this commitment is dialectically invulnerable and (iii) she is disposed to maintain the dialectical invulnerability of this commitment.[7]

If we examine paradigmatic cases of devotion, I think we find this structure. Take political commitments which are unresponsive to judgment and which are, in many cases, scarcely articulable; or religious commitments; or familial

---

[5] And notice that we should distinguish two cases: a case in which the agent actually considers various arguments against an attitude, comes to conclude that the attitude is unwarranted, and maintains it nonetheless; and a case in which the agent doesn't consider arguments, but would, in counterfactual scenarios, conclude that it was unwarranted and maintain it nonetheless. No doubt the former is rarer than the latter. More on this below.

[6] Let me flag a complication that I will address in the next chapter. I have suggested that the Williams and Wolf cases involve agents with dialectically invulnerable commitments. But another interpretation might seem to be available: perhaps these commitments (to one's spouse, for example) are not *directly* vulnerable to justificatory considerations, but are parts of some broader ethos that *is* responsive to justificatory considerations. For example, perhaps Wolf's commitment to her spouse appears to be dialectically invulnerable only because it is a constituent of a broader ethical view, namely that familial commitments justifiably override considerations of impartiality; and perhaps this broader ethical view is responsive to justificatory considerations. In short: perhaps by moving from more particular to more general commitments, we will reveal that the commitments are in fact responsive to justificatory considerations. While this move might seem tempting, Chapter 5 argues that it is a dead end: the more general or fundamental commitments are *especially* likely to exhibit dialectical invulnerability.

[7] Commitment comes in several forms: you can be committed to maintaining a relationship with some person, to respecting a person, to promoting the welfare of a person, to bringing about some state of affairs, to respecting and promoting some value or ideal, to achieving some goal, and so on. I follow Calhoun in using the general term "engagement" to pick out these disparate ways of interacting with the objects of commitment.

commitments. As I mentioned in Section 4.1, it's exceedingly common for these commitments to be resistant to critique: offering arguments for and against the commitments seems to have no effect.[8] And this supports the claim that paradigmatic cases of devotion are those that do not yield to reason.[9]

A few clarifications. First, notice that Devotion requires more than merely having a dialectically invulnerable commitment. In addition, it requires *being disposed to maintain* this invulnerability. To see why this second condition is important, consider an example. Maria has a habit: whenever she uses salt, she is committed to throwing a bit of it over her shoulder. This habit isn't responsive to justificatory critique: Maria will freely admit that there's absolutely no good reason to engage in this practice; she doesn't think it actually accomplishes anything; she just regards it as a quirk with which she's satisfied. And she can cite good reasons for abandoning this habit: it annoys her roommate; it makes a mess; it is wasteful; her cat has begun licking up the salt. At first, these considerations have no effect whatsoever on Maria's habit: although she acknowledges that these are all good and sufficient reasons for giving up the habit, she remains firmly committed to throwing salt over her shoulder. She's committed to the habit, and the commitment is dialectically invulnerable. But is this a case of devotion?[10]

To answer that question, we have to assess whether Maria is disposed to maintain the dialectical invulnerability of the commitment. If she's disposed to maintain the dialectical invulnerability of her commitment, then she would count as devoted; if not, she wouldn't. So let's suppose that from time to time justificatory considerations arise. We can imagine that on some occasions, as she's about to throw the salt, she hesitates, gripped by the thought that she really shouldn't be

---

[8] As I pointed out earlier, the notion of dialectical invulnerability is meant to pick out commitments that are *completely* unresponsive to justificatory reasoning. Responsiveness to justification comes in degrees. We can imagine a spectrum, with commitments that immediately respond to justificatory considerations at one end and commitments that are dialectically invulnerable at the other. In between, we will find commitments that display varying degrees of resistance. It's easiest to see this by contrasting different types of commitments. It seems to me that my philosophical commitments are more responsive to justification than my political commitments, at least in the sense that I see justificatory considerations affecting the former much more frequently, and to a much greater extent, than they affect the latter. We are especially likely to find some degree of resistance to justificatory considerations in the commitments with which we are emotionally invested, the commitments that we see as meaningful or important, and the commitments that we see as constituents of our identity (more on this in Chapters 6–9). But this resistance does not have to go all the way to invulnerability.

[9] As I mentioned earlier, there's a great deal of psychological research on related topics. For example, there's a body of work by D.M. Kahan and others which shows that arguing against certain political commitments is counterproductive: rather than weakening the commitments, the critiques cause them to become ever more deeply entrenched. The mechanism which Kahan posits is this: individuals subconsciously reject factual information that conflicts with their central values (see, for example, Kahan 2013). The large literature on sacred values, which I discussed in Chapter 2, also tends to associated sacred values with some form of dialectical invulnerability; see Chapter 2, Section 2.3 for discussion.

[10] Notice that being devoted to something does not entail treating it as a sacred value: you can be devoted to X without X qualifying as a sacred value, for X needn't exhibit Inviolability and Incomparability. So the fact that the habit is something trivial doesn't entail that it can't be an instance of devotion. More on this in the next section.

doing this. We can imagine two possibilities. First, she might decide to stop. The commitment, which was formerly dialectically invulnerable, has become susceptible to justificatory considerations; and perhaps it dissipates. Perhaps she lets it go, or at least doesn't make any effort to sustain it. This would indicate that we have a case of mere commitment rather than devotion.

The second possibility is that she resists. Seeing that her habit is becoming responsive to considerations of its justificatory standing, she refuses to yield. She tells herself: yes, there are good reasons not to do this, but I don't care; I will persevere. She might try to stop thinking about whether throwing the salt is justified; or she might continue to dwell on it but take steps to block its effects, recommitting to the habit despite its admitted lack of justificatory standing. If so, this would indicate that Maria is disposed to maintain the dialectical invulnerability of her commitment. This would be a case of devotion.

It might strike the reader as odd to focus on a trivial example—who cares whether I throw salt over my shoulder? Why be devoted to *that*? But I actually think that these trivial cases pervade our lives: many of our quirks, habits, and customs display this form of dialectical invulnerability. Nonetheless, we can also consider more consequential examples. Imagine an adherent of a particular religion. Madeline is a devout Catholic; she is devoted to this faith. At a certain point, she begins to doubt: while she's always been aware of the conceptual possibility of questioning certain tenets of her faith, she begins to feel these questions eroding her faith. We can consider two possibilities: she allows this to proceed; or she is disposed to resist the corrosive effects of justificatory reflection. In the former case, she is committed but not devoted to Catholicism; in the latter case, she is devoted.

This brings us to the second clarificatory point. Each of our attitudes typically depends upon a host of presuppositions. Sometimes, the falsification of a presupposition will render the attitude untenable, and this will be true even of dialectically invulnerable attitudes. Consider cases of romantic love. Sam's love for Beatrice might be invulnerable to her dismissive, brusque attitudes; but is it invulnerable to the idea that she's human instead of a cleverly disguised robot? Is it invulnerable to the idea that she's dead? Of course not—of course the love would dissipate if a sufficient number of factual beliefs were altered. But this isn't an objection to my account of devotion. On the contrary, this actually supports my account. True, the commitment would dissolve in this kind of case, but this is a case in which we would be inclined to say that he is no longer devoted to the relationship with Beatrice (in part because he would no longer regard that relationship as *possible*).

Third, devotion and overridingness come apart. Treating a commitment as dialectically invulnerable does not require treating it as overriding all other concerns or placing it highest in a lexical priority ranking. My commitment to environmental preservation might be dialectically invulnerable yet outweighed by my commitment to my own life. Or my commitment to equality might be dialectically invulnerable yet outweighed by my commitment to my child's welfare. Dialectical invulnerability concerns not the *degree* or *lexical status* of the value that something has, but the effects of justificatory reflection on whatever value the thing has.

Finally, according to my account of devotion, it doesn't matter whether the person actually reflects on and critiques her attitudes. What matters is what would happen if the person did reflect and find justification lacking. If she were to conclude that an attitude lacked rational support, would the attitude dissipate? Or would it remain as forceful and entrenched as before the reflection? If it would remain, then it fulfills this condition.

With this in mind, here's another way of putting the central point. Consider what it is to have a commitment that is dialectically *vulnerable*—that is, a commitment which you're willing to abandon or modify if you find reasons against it. What might those reasons be? Perhaps the commitment is inconsistent with other things that you accept; perhaps other values, goals, or aspirations conflict with it; perhaps it is premised on factual claims that you now discover to be erroneous. But it's tempting to say that if I am willing to abandon X because it is inconsistent with Y, this reveals that I am more deeply committed to Y than to X. After all, to see how committed you are to something, you can determine what you are willing to give up in order to preserve it. In the ultimate case, the agent is willing to give up rationality, coherence, and so forth in order to preserve the commitment. These are the cases in which we speak of devotion.

And this is one way of thinking about why dialectical invulnerability is connected to devotion. Dialectic can reveal that X is inconsistent with other things that I accept; that X conflicts with some moral principle that I accept; that X is not in my self-interest; and so on. But if I genuinely stake my acceptance of X on its compatibility with these things, then my acceptance of X is conditional. Dialectically invulnerable commitments are unconditional: no dialectical moves can dislodge them.[11] They are our firmest commitments. As Pascal puts it, with an eye as always towards his religious commitments: "We have an incapacity for proof that can be conquered by no dogmatism. We have an idea of the truth that can be conquered by no skepticism" (*Pensées* 395).

---

[11] Although, as I point out above, there is a complication. Some dialectically invulnerable attitudes depend on the possibility of their object continuing to exist. For example, in the love case the dialectically invulnerable attitude concerns a relationship; if the relationship is no longer possible, for example because the beloved dies, the attitude can no longer persist in the same form. Or, for another example, consider the Palestinian and Israeli case discussed in Chapters 1 and 2: a sizeable percentage of Israelis treat territorial integrity as a sacred value. If a terrible earthquake were to send all of Israel and Palestine under the sea, sacralized claims about territorial integrity would be moot, for the territory would no longer exist as a possible object of sacralization. In this limited sense, even dialectically invulnerable attitudes respond to facts about the world. My point, above, is simply that dialectically invulnerable attitudes don't respond to *justificatory reasoning* in the same way that standard attitudes do.

4.3 Clarifying the Notion of Dialectical Invulnerability

Introducing the concept of dialectically invulnerable commitments helps us to analyze a widespread feature of ethical life. But two points need clarification. First, different kinds of justificatory questions apply to different kinds of commitments. Second, commitments tend to be holistically intertwined, and this can make it difficult to determine which element in a cluster of commitments is dialectically invulnerable. I address these points below.

4.3.1 Do All Commitments Invite the Same Kinds of Justificatory Questions?

I have been investigating the way that we insulate certain commitments from the effects of justificatory reasoning. But consider the range of objects to which we can be committed: a person, a relationship, an ideal, a goal, a habit, a political position, a religious outlook, a philosophical view, an ethical theory, and so on. Justificatory considerations pertain to these things in different ways. It's one thing to request a justification for a person's political views; it's quite another to request a justification for a person's commitment to their child. After all, consider the reactions we might have to these cases. If a person's political commitments are impervious to justificatory considerations, we might regard this as objectionable; whereas if a person's commitment to their child is impervious to justificatory considerations, we might regard this as admirable.

Consider a few contexts in which justificatory questions arise. One important context is *commitments that involve choice between competing alternatives*: you can be committed either to X or to Y, but not both. For example: I can be committed to progressive taxation or I can be committed to flat taxation, but not both. In supporting the one, I am committed to rejecting the other. So a proponent of the alternative view can ask me to justify my commitment.

Another important context is *commitments that demand compliance from others*. In some cases, a commitment to X entails acceptance of the claim that others can be compelled to value or respect or be bound by X. For example: in being committed to progressive taxation, I accept the idea that everyone in my country should be taxed in this way. By contrast, in being committed to a purely personal pursuit such as scuba diving, there is no pressure to think that everyone else should engage in diving, value diving, or have any particular attitude toward it. Demands for justification are more likely to arise in the first kind of case than in the second.

Yet another important context is *being committed to something solely because it has a particular feature*: you are committed to X because it has feature F. Suppose other things have F to a greater degree, and choosing one of these other things is a live option. For example, you are committed to buying this car solely because it gets excellent safety ratings. But then someone points out that a comparable car gets even better safety ratings. Or, you are committed to running solely because it promotes health and produces pleasant feelings; but then someone argues that cycling is even better at promoting health and is more pleasant. Requests for justification seem appropriate here.

I have listed three contexts in which justificatory questions frequently arise. This list isn't meant to be exhaustive: there are many other contexts that invite these questions. But keeping these common justificatory contexts in mind will be helpful.

For some objects of commitment, those contexts arise regularly. For example, political views often involve a choice between competing alternatives, impose costs on others, and are chosen because they are seen as maximizing some desirable feature. So justificatory questions are very likely to arise for political values. For other valued objects, these contexts arise only in exceptional circumstances. Consider a parent who is committed to his child's welfare. Only in the most outlandish cases would a parent be faced with a choice between being committed to and not being committed to his child's welfare, or to demanding that others be committed to his child's welfare in a non-standard way, or to choosing between the welfare of his own child and the welfare of some other child that exhibits more valuable features than his own child. I don't think these contexts are impossible to generate: if the child is a sociopathic mass murderer, questions concerning whether it is appropriate to continue being committed to the child's welfare might arise; if promoting the child's welfare places unusually high burdens on others, questions as to whether this is justifiable can arise; and so on. But those contexts are rare. So questions about the justification for political commitments will be routine, whereas questions about the justification for parental commitments will be rare. Nonetheless, I take it that questions of this form are appropriate in certain contexts. Commitments, whether in the parental or political case, are something for which justificatory considerations are relevant.

A commitment is dialectically invulnerable when it is insulated from the typical effects of justificatory reasoning. Dialectical invulnerability will be easiest to detect when we consider commitments that involve choices between competing alternatives, that demand compliance from others, and that arise solely because the object of commitment has some particular feature. But even when we consider commitments of other types—such as parental commitments—we can distinguish between dialectically invulnerable and dialectically vulnerable commitments by considering counterfactual scenarios.

4.3.2 Identifying Dialectically Invulnerable Commitments

Finally, let's consider a complication: in real cases, it can be difficult to pinpoint exactly which elements in a person's set of beliefs, values, and commitments are dialectically invulnerable. After all, beliefs, values, and commitments are holistically intertwined. Consider political values. I am committed to various liberal values. I value equality, dignity, respect, tolerance. I believe that people should be treated equally. I am committed to movements that promote equality. I suspect that something in this constellation of commitments and values is dialectically invulnerable, for reasons that I will explain more fully in the next chapter. But I have trouble knowing what exactly it is. Is it the idea of dignity? Or equality? Or human rights? Or autonomy? Or tolerance? Or some combination of these things? Would I budge on my commitments to autonomy if I could preserve my commitments to equality? Or is autonomy really the fixed point? These kinds of questions can be difficult to resolve.

Just so, it can be difficult to distinguish cases in which a person's *commitment* is dialectically invulnerable and cases in which the person's *perceived justification* for the commitment is dialectically invulnerable. To see how these come apart, consider two cases.

First, suppose Antonio is committed to driving an SUV but regards this as unjustifiable: he is completely convinced that there are decisive environmental reasons for driving smaller, more fuel-efficient cars; he does not think that the pleasure he derives from driving the SUV outweighs the environmental costs; and so on. He freely admits that his commitment is unjustifiable, yet his commitment is unaffected by this reasoning. Antonio has a commitment that is dialectically invulnerable.

Second, suppose Saul used to be an atheist but has a conversion experience: one day, on the road to Damascus, he believes that he hears the voice of God. This convinces him to accept the Christian religion. And let's indeed grant that if one were to hear the voice of the Christian God, this would be a decisive justification for accepting the Christian religion. Saul's experience, were it veridical, would justify his commitment to Christianity. Of course, we could raise doubts about Saul's experience: perhaps he was hallucinating or daydreaming. But suppose Saul is completely unwilling to let these kinds of doubts have any impact. In a case like this, we might want to say that Saul's religious commitment itself is dialectically responsive, but that the perceived justification for this commitment is dialectically invulnerable. For the commitment *is* responsive to justificatory considerations; but the particular consideration to which it responds (the belief that he has had an experience of divine revelation) is dialectically invulnerable.

As these considerations indicate, it can be very difficult to identify the particular elements in a person's psychology that are dialectically invulnerable. For some, it will be a particular belief or experience; for others, a particular valuation; for others, still, it can be broader swathes of political, religious, or evaluative beliefs. Fortunately, none of my arguments turn on identifying the particular elements in individuals' psychologies that exhibit this feature.

Relatedly, it will often be difficult to determine whether an agent's commitments really are dialectically invulnerable. It can be hard to tell whether an agent genuinely thinks that an objection is decisive and nonetheless renders his commitment immune to its effects, or whether he is uncertain about the cogency of the objection. For example, does the person in Williams' scenario (a) think that he has more reason to act on the demands of morality than on love of his wife, but set this aside and act on love anyway; or does he (b) think that in certain cases there is more reason to act on the demands of love than on the demands of morality? Only in (a) do we have a potential case of dialectical invulnerability; but, to distinguish (a) and (b), we would need to know quite a bit about the person's psychology. While I acknowledge the difficulty, it doesn't matter: hard as it may be to prise these apart in practice, they are conceptually distinct.

4.4 The Relationship between Sacred Values and Devotion

We are now in a position to analyze the relationship between valuing something, treating something as having sacred value, and being devoted to something. The first thing to note is that these are all different. Devotion is a species of intention, but values (sacred or otherwise) aren't reducible to intentions. Devotion can involve judging that certain things are valuable or possess sacred value, but merely judging that something has value—even sacred value—won't just by itself constitute devotion. So we need to clarify the connections between these phenomena.

We can start with values in general. In recent years, it has become common to distinguish *believing that something is valuable* and *valuing that thing*. To see why, consider an example: I believe that opera is valuable, but I don't value opera. I am basically indifferent to opera. I don't experience enjoyment, respect, admiration, or awe when listening to opera. I don't seek out occasions to listen to opera or contribute to funding opera. I don't read about it. I barely think about it. So there's no interesting sense in which I can be said to value opera. Nonetheless, I readily assent to the proposition that opera is valuable. So here we have a case in which I judge something to be valuable but don't value it.

By contrast, consider my relationship toward philosophy. I seek out occasions to participate in philosophical inquiry; I devote large portions of my life to reading, writing, and thinking about philosophy; I admire skilled philosophical writing; I am in awe of insightful philosophical points; and so on. I regard these emotions as merited by features of the objects to which I'm responding. And I take various considerations pertaining to philosophy as reasons for action, as when I note that a book looks philosophically rich and take that as a reason to study it. So this seems to be a case in which I not only judge that philosophy is valuable but also value it.

These examples indicate that we should distinguish between believing valuable and valuing. Valuing involves a much wider range of attitudes, intentions, and dispositions than does believing valuable. Samuel Scheffler puts it this way:

> Valuing, in my view, comprises a complex syndrome of interrelated attitudes and dispositions, which includes but is not limited to a belief that the valued item is valuable. Valuing something normally involves, in addition to such a belief, at least the following elements: a susceptibility to experience a range of context-dependent emotions concerning the valued item, a disposition to experience those emotions as being merited or deserved, and a disposition to treat certain kinds of considerations pertaining to the valued item as reasons for action in relevant deliberative contexts. Thus, valuing is an attitudinal phenomenon that has doxastic, deliberative, motivational, and emotional dimensions.   (Scheffler 2013: 16–17)

While a full analysis of the distinction between *judging valuable* and *valuing* would require more detail, this should be sufficient for our purposes. The point I want to focus upon is this: whereas judging valuable sometimes involves nothing more than having an isolated belief that is disconnected from attitudes, intentions, and dispositions, valuing will involve (i) a disposition to experience certain emotions pertaining to the valued item; (ii) a disposition to experience those emotions as merited; and (iii) a disposition to treat certain considerations pertaining to the valued item as reasons for action.

Let's now consider the relationship between valuing and commitment. Insofar as I value something, I have relatively stable and enduring dispositions to engage with it in the relevant ways. For example, if I value my dog, I will have relatively stable and enduring dispositions to feed her, care for her, and so on. These disposition will involve regularly exhibiting various intentions: to feed her when she's hungry, to take her for walks, and so on.

Recall that commitment is intention plus a disposition to maintain the intention. As Scheffler defines valuing, it does not necessarily share this feature: it's conceptually possible to value something without being disposed to maintain the relevant intentions over time. But notice how odd this would be. Would we really speak of someone valuing philosophy if, when the dispositions to engage with philosophy slacken, he takes no steps to restore them? I think we wouldn't. A person who lets the relevant forms of engagement with the valued object fade is someone who is ceasing to value the object.

If that's right, then valuing involves not just a disposition to have certain intentions, but a disposition to have certain commitments. Again, the nature of these commitments will vary. If I value philosophy, I will be committed to engaging with it when the opportunity arises, promoting it when I can do so, and so on; if I value my dog, I will be committed to caring for her, to promoting her welfare, and so on. But in each case of valuing, we will find that valuing involves having commitments. (The reverse direction does not hold: I can be committed to something without valuing it. For example, I might be committed to playing a game that I regard as worthless.)

"Sacred value" is usually used as a noun rather than a verb, but let's introduce the rather clunky phrase *sacredly-valuing*. Recall that sacred values differ from ordinary values in the former are Inviolable, Incontestable, and Dialectically Invulnerable. So, in sacredly-valuing (for example) human dignity, I will be disposed to treat all violations of human dignity as anathema; I will be opposed to any comparisons of human dignity with other goods; and my valuation of human dignity will be impervious to dialectical reasoning.

It follows that if I sacredly-value X, I will be *devoted* to X. Recall the definition of devotion:

> (Devotion) An agent is devoted to a person, state of affairs, value, or goal iff (i) she is committed to engaging in the relevant ways with that person, state of affairs, value, or goal, (ii) this commitment is dialectically invulnerable and (iii) she is disposed to maintain the dialectical invulnerability of this commitment.

In sacredly-valuing human dignity, I will be committed to engaging in the relevant ways with human dignity (e.g. by respecting it, treating its value as non-fungible, opposing violations of it, and so on). In addition, this commitment will be dialectically invulnerable. Finally, I will be disposed to maintain the dialectical invulnerability of this commitment. If I detect a slackening in the dialectical invulnerability of my commitment, I will take steps to address this.

Put simply, then: just as valuing entails a disposition to manifest ordinary commitment, so too sacredly-valuing entails a disposition to manifest devotion (the sacralized version of commitment).

But notice that the converse doesn't follow. Just as you can be committed to something without valuing it, you can be devoted to something without sacredly valuing it. After all, you can be devoted to something that you perceive as either worthless or having merely ordinarily value. As an example of the former, consider salt-throwing Maria. As an example of the latter: I am devoted to philosophy, but I do not treat philosophy as having sacred value.

To sum up, then: values entail commitment. Sacred values entail the sacralized version of commitment, which I have called devotion. But devotion does not entail sacred values.

4.5 Devotion, Alienation, and Identification

I have argued that devotion involves commitments that are dialectically invulnerable and that the agent is disposed to maintain as dialectically invulnerable. But consider a potential objection: if an attitude is dialectically invulnerable, won't this be pathological? And doubly so to the extent that the agent strives to maintain this dialectical invulnerability?

There are two ways of understanding this objection. On the one hand, we might think that the agent will experience herself as *alienated* from commitments that have these features. I will explore this possibility in Section 4.5.1 and offer a response in 4.5.2. On the other hand, we might think that devoted agents are in some sense irrational. I will discuss this point in Section 4.6.

4.5.1 Alienation and Rational Responsiveness

We can pose the first objection by considering Richard Moran's work on alienation and identification. Though he uses different terminology, Moran in effect claims that when an attitude manifests dialectical invulnerability, we experience ourselves as alienated from that attitude. If this is right, it will be a problem for my account of devotion; for it seems puzzling to say that we will be alienated from our own devotion. On the contrary, devotion seems like it should be something with which we tend to identify.

Adopting Harry Frankfurt's terminology, Moran claims that I am *identified* with an attitude when (a) the attitude is a possible product of practical reasoning, and (b) if I lost justification for the beliefs on which the attitude depends, the attitude would tend to dissipate (Moran 2017: 145). In other words, Moran thinks the questions of identification and alienation arise only for states that are judgment-sensitive; these states are "possible products of practical reasoning." Moran's view is that such states are typically responsive to judgments: when the agent takes himself to lack justification for the beliefs on which the attitude depends, the attitude tends to dissipate. Alienation arises when the agent has a judgment-sensitive attitude which does *not* respond in this way to the agent's beliefs about justification. As Moran puts it,

> Being alienated from [a desire] *means* that [the agent] does not take his desire to be subject to his thinking about what is good to be pursued. The desire itself, as an empirical fact about what drives him, does not adjust itself in the light of his own considerations of what's worth pursuing. It is not an expression of his thinking or his other attitudes, but is rather experienced by him as a facticity that his thinking and other attitudes must somehow accommodate.
> (Moran 2017: 145)

For Moran, the desires from which I am alienated, the ones that I am passive with respect to, are the ones that are the right types of states to be judgment-sensitive, but in this particular case are not responsive to my judgments. They are type- but not token- judgment-sensitive. Analogous points apply to commitments: commitment is judgment-sensitive. A commitment that wasn't judgment-sensitive would be a commitment from which the agent is alienated. It would be experienced as a pathological compulsion.

4.5.2 Dialectical Invulnerability as the Relevant Form of Unresponsiveness to Reasons

I think Moran's proposal is insightful, but ultimately flawed. It's not just possible, but *routine*, for people to be identified with attitudes that are type but not token judgment-sensitive. The attitudes involved in romantic love are an obvious example, and I will work with those first.[12]

Consider the narrator of *In Search of Lost Time*. As a young man, his love is both that with which he is most deeply identified and that which is completely resistant to his judgments as to its merits. For some time he is "so madly in love with Gilberte that if, on our way, I caught sight of their old butler taking the dog out, my emotion would bring me to a standstill and I would gaze at his white whiskers with eyes filled with passion" (Proust 2003: Vol. 1, p. 451). Every day is arranged around the hopes of meeting her; every absence is regretted. But Gilberte is more distant than he'd like, lacking the same obsessive attention to him. Eventually discovering, due to her butler's remark, that Gilberte finds him tiresome and "importunate", the narrator decides that he "must cease for the present to attempt to see Gilberte" (2003: Vol. 1, p. 657). He expects her to write to him urging a meeting; when no letter arrives, he waits, every day, not daring to leave the house; "there was no longer a single minute in the day during which I was not in that state of anxiety"—for "instead of the acceptance, pure and simple, of that suffering, [there was] the hope, at every moment, of seeing it come to an end" (2003: Vol. 1, p. 634). Ultimately, he sees that Gilberte will not write him, "and I renounced Gilberte for ever," though still hoping that "when, better than by mere words, by a course of action indefinitely repeated, I should have proved to her that

---

[12] I am assuming that love is a judgment-sensitive attitude. Recall that judgment-sensitive attitudes are "attitudes that, insofar as we are rational, will be responsive to our assessments of the reasons for them" (Scanlon 2007: 90). Thus, I am assuming that we can ask questions such as "What, if anything, justifies my love for this particular person?," and that a fully rational agent's love would be responsive to cases in which the love was regarded as wholly inappropriate or otherwise unjustified. This is relatively uncontroversial, for it is widely accepted that there can be reasons for love (though see Frankfurt 1998, Frankfurt 2006, and Zangwill 2013 for some counterarguments). There are debates about what form these reasons for love take. According to the qualities view, the qualities of the beloved make love appropriate or inappropriate (examples include Abramson and Leite 2011, 2018; Jollimore 2011; Keller 2000). Another possible view is that the reasons for love are grounded in facts about the relationship between the lover and the beloved (e.g. Kolodny 2003). Others defend the view that the beloved's rational nature (Velleman 1999) or humanity (Setiya 2014) grounds the reasons for love. But what's common to all of these views is the idea that love is a judgment-sensitive attitude.

I had no inclination to see her, perhaps she would discover once again an inclination to see me" (2003: Vol. 1, p. 634). But in time he recognizes that his love, which up to now had been the very *center* of his life, that around which he arranged all his plans, hopes, and desires, is fading:

> What was perhaps the most cruel thing about it was that I myself was its architect, unconscious, wilful, merciless and patient. The one thing that mattered to me was my relationship with Gilberte, and it was I who was labouring to make it impossible by gradually creating out of this prolonged separation from my beloved, not indeed her indifference, but what would come to the same thing in the end, my own. It was to a slow and painful suicide of that self which loved Gilberte that I was goading myself with untiring energy, with a clear sense not only of what I was doing in the present but of what must result from it in the future: I knew not only that after a certain time I should cease to love Gilberte, but also that she herself would regret it and that the attempts which she would then make to see me would be as vain as those that she was making now, no longer because I loved her too much but because I should certainly be in love with some other woman whom I should continue to desire, to wait for, through hours of which I should not dare to divert a single particle of a second to Gilberte who would be nothing to me then. (Proust 2003: Vol. I, p. 657)

He watches his love for Gilberte dissipate (just as, much later, he watches his love for Albertine fade after her absence and death). The narrator is deeply identified with this love, to the extent that he describes its passing as the suicide of his self and the emergence of a new self. There is no interesting sense in which he is alienated from this love; he takes it as criterial of his identity; it is the right type of attitude to be judgment-sensitive; yet it fails to respond to judgment, fails to dissipate when regarded as unjustified; and partly for this reason the narrator takes it to be essential. Only indirect strategies—only the passage of time, the continuous refusal of meetings, and so forth—bring about the transformation of this attitude.

If this were an isolated or idiosyncratic example, it wouldn't matter. But what's powerful about Proust's descriptions is how recognizable they are, how they identify something common to experiences of the attitudes with which we identify. Some of our most important, central commitments are supported by attitudes that are *resistant* to judgment, and this very resistance is partly criterial for their import. A love that dissipates immediately upon being regarded as unjustified is no love at all. And analogous points apply to other forms of commitment: while we sometimes lament the unresponsiveness of commitments to justificatory considerations, at other times we welcome and encourage it.

I think this indicates that Moran's claim doesn't generalize. It is not true that we are alienated from attitudes (or constellations of attitudes, or patterns of action, or the commitments that are partly based upon these attitudes) that are type but not token judgment-sensitive. In the Proust case, this is especially clear: Proust's narrator is deeply identified with an attitude (and its attendant commitments) that is dialectically invulnerable. Indeed, he takes this attitude and the associated commitments to be definitive of or integral to his self.

Suppose I have some attitude that resists critical reflection. I refuse to submit it to critique precisely because it is central for me and I want to preserve it. Or, if I do critique it, this has no effect; the attitude persists, mute and unmoved by the critique, like a stone.

These are the right *types* of attitude to be judgment-sensitive; but I refuse to stake my commitment to them on the outcome of my judgments. They're type but not token judgment-sensitive. So, on Moran's account, they should be attitudes from which I am alienated. But they're not; they're paradigms of things I am identified with. Prior to his break with Gilberte, the narrator knows that his love for her is in many ways unjustified, that he derives no pleasure from it:

> For, although I now no longer thought of anything save not to let a single day pass without seeing Gilberte ... yet those moments which I spent in her company, for which I had waited so impatiently all night and morning, for which I had quivered with excitement, to which I would have sacrificed everything else in the world, were by no means happy moments; and well did I know it, for they were the only moments in my life on which I concentrated a scrupulous, unflagging attention, and yet could not discover in them one atom of pleasure.
>
> (Proust 2003: Vol. I, p. 433)

His unreciprocated love is a torment from which he cannot release himself. And yet it is so tightly bound up with his self that we cannot see him as alienated from it (at least until he begins trying to make it cease). As Proust writes about an analogous case, Swann's love for Odette: "And this malady which Swann's love had become had so proliferated, was so closely interwoven with all his habits, with all his actions, with his thoughts, his health, his sleep, his life, even with what he hoped for after his death, was so utterly inseparable from him, that it would have been impossible to eradicate it without almost entirely destroying him; as surgeons say, his love was no longer operable" (2003: Vol. I, p. 336).

These, I think, are the attitudes and commitments with which we are most deeply identified. And our identification with the attitude is indicated in part by the fact that we aim to maintain its dialectical invulnerability. When that stops—when we seek to have the commitments and associated affects respond to judgments of warrant—we've already begun to distance ourselves from them, as Proust's discussions so vividly illustrate.

I've dwelt on this literary case because it is a realistic illustration of the way in which our deepest attitudes and commitments tend to be dialectically invulnerable. Of course, most of Proust's remarks on these passages center on love, and love isn't reducible to devotion. So let's move past love, considered as an attitude, and focus more specifically on the narrator's devotion to Gilberte. Employing our definition of devotion from Section 4.2.4, the narrator will count as devoted to Gilberte iff (i) he is committed to engaging in the relevant ways with her; (ii) this commitment is dialectically invulnerable; and (iii) he is disposed to maintain the dialectical invulnerability of this commitment. The passages quoted above make it clear that these conditions are fulfilled. The narrator is devoted to Gilberte—in fact, I think it's even clearer that he is *devoted* to Gilberte than that he *loves* her.[13]

Now, Moran wanted to maintain that we are alienated from judgment-sensitive attitudes which are not properly responsive to judgment. I've disagreed, asserting something like the contrary position. There is a way for Moran to respond: being committed to these things and refusing to critique them could still be sensitive to some deeper judgment. Focus, for example, on Proust's narrator. Even before he contemplates a break with her, he thinks that Gilberte is in many respects defective, that she has fallen short in countless ways, that she doesn't deserve his love. These would typically be taken as judgments that undermine the justification for love, and for that reason I've interpreted his love as dialectically invulnerable. But these judgments aren't alone: the narrator also judges that a wondrous relationship with Gilberte would be possible if only she'd change certain things; if only she'd give up other relationships and focus exclusively on him. So we might see the narrator as wavering between two judgments: he remains committed to an ideal of love, while being more fickle and changeable with regard to the particular women who might serve as the objects of that love.[14] The attitude persists, and he remains identified with it, either because he hasn't reached a decisive verdict or because there is some deeper, more fundamental justification for it.

But such a response would miss the point. Proust writes that "love, even in its humblest beginnings, is a striking example of how little reality matters to us", and surely Gilberte is meant to illustrate this (Proust 2003: Volume V, p. 647). The narrator's vacillations aren't designed to show that he is valiantly struggling to reach some decisive verdict on the justificatory standing of his love; they are meant, instead, to show how his judgment is subordinated to his love, how it is the

---

[13] After all, we might resist describing the narrator's attitude as *love*. Jose Ortega y Gasset memorably remarks that *Swann's Way* shows us every kind of human feeling *except* love (Ortega y Gasset 1927: 263, quoted by Bersani 2013: 85). Perhaps the narrator exhibits mere attraction or infatuation rather than love. What's important for my purposes is not whether we deign to call the narrator's attitude love, but that it is (a) an attitude that he regards as type but not token judgment-sensitive, (b) an attitude that is dialectically invulnerable, and (c) an attitude with which he is identified.

[14] It's undeniable that he sometimes does this: witness his claim that his love persists while alternately taking as its object different members of the "little band" of girls at Balbec, so that one day it is directed at Albertine, another at Giselle, and so on (Proust 2003: Vol. 2).

passage of time, rather than the work of judgment, that will cause the love to dissipate.

And there are other examples of the phenomenon. The basic strategy that Moran needs to employ is this: when presented with an example of a judgment-sensitive attitude with which the agent is identified but which is not responsive to judgment, find some explanation of why alienation doesn't arise. For example, find some deeper judgment to which the attitude *is* responsive; or treat the agent as defective or confused. Proust on love is one example of how this fails, but there are others. Suppose I judge that I want to live according to some religious text; I see that the religious text mandates faith in certain dogmas; so I refuse to critique these dogmas. In one way my belief in the dogmas isn't judgment-sensitive, as I won't critique them directly. But in another way it is judgment-sensitive: it is derived from or based upon a commitment that could itself be judgment sensitive, namely my commitment to the religion as a whole. But then we can simply ask whether that ground-level judgment, that basic commitment to a particular religion, really is judgment-sensitive. And it seems that this just pushes the problem back. In a range of familiar cases, no justification for these ground-level commitments is available. We can make up reasons for it, we can fish about for justifications, but the commitment doesn't actually depend on them: if these reasons were abandoned, the agent would just find some alternative justification.

So I think Moran is right that the possibility of identification and alienation arises only for judgment sensitive attitudes; but it does not follow, and is not true, that identification and alienation track whether the attitude is properly responsive to judgment. We can be identified with commitments and associated attitudes that are unresponsive to our judgments about reasons. And when we strive to preserve these commitments and attitudes as unresponsive to judgment, as dialectically invulnerable, we manifest devotion.

In sum: Moran argues that attitudes with which we are identified, including commitments, will be judgment-sensitive attitudes; these judgment-sensitive attitudes may not be under direct voluntary control, but will nonetheless be responsive to judgment; when they are not responsive to judgment, we will be alienated from them. I've argued that many of our core commitments are judgment-sensitive attitudes but are *not* responsive to judgment; nonetheless, they are attitudes with which we identify.

4.6 Can We Have Good Reason to Be Devoted?

So far, I've argued that a commitment constitutes devotion if it is dialectically invulnerable and we aim to maintain this dialectical invulnerability. But this might look problematic. If we put the point into Moran's terminology, I am saying that being devoted to something is having attitudes toward it that are of the right type to be judgment sensitive, but which are in fact unresponsive to judgment. Worse still, I am saying that being devoted to something involves actively striving to maintain this unresponsiveness. Even if I am right that the agent needn't experience herself as alienated from these commitments, she might nonetheless look paradigmatically irrational.

Of course, in any given case, I might have dialectically invulnerable attitudes that happen to align with (what I take to be) the balance of reasons. Then critical reflection won't undermine the attitudes. But this can only be accidental; in counterfactual scenarios in which critical reflection shows the attitudes to be unwarranted, they would nonetheless persist and I would be committed to this persistence. If the judgments change, the attitudes don't. So again, we seem to have irrationality. Isn't it perverse to associate this form of irrationality with devotion? Or, looking at this from the other direction: if this is what devotion is, isn't devotion something we have good reason to reject?

As a first response, let's distinguish several different ways in which a commitment can fail to be aligned with the balance of reasons.

The most problematic case will look like this: an agent has certain commitments which he treats as dialectically invulnerable but which can be shown to be irrational from premises that he wholeheartedly accepts; moreover, the agent recognizes and openly acknowledges this irrationality. For example, suppose we can offer a good, compelling argument against racism from premises that everyone should accept. Yet Ted is a racist and he treats his racist commitments as dialectically invulnerable. To make matters even worse, let's say that Ted *knows* this: he sees that there are good arguments against racism, he acknowledges their force, and yet his commitments remain intact and he aims to maintain them. So this is a case in which an agent has commitments that he openly acknowledges as irrational, but which he nonetheless sustains.

I don't think there's anything particularly surprising about cases like this. If rationality, consistency, or coherence aren't especially important for certain people, then we should expect to find some of their central commitments diverging from their judgments of rationality.

In fact, variants of this case are widespread: many of us maintain commitments that are irrational on the basis of premises that we accept. For example, you might be committed to exploring haute cuisine or driving SUVs or going on fancy vacations to distant lands, but think there is no way of justifying these pursuits given rampant inequality, dire poverty, environmental damage, and so forth. Or, you are committed to saving your wife over the stranger, but think this can't be justified. Here, the agent holds certain commitments while acknowledging decisive objections to them. His commitments are more important to him than consistency, coherence, adherence to morality, and so forth. In this kind of case, I think it makes sense to speak of devotion.

So the phenomenon I am investigating is widespread. But it might also appear problematic, involving irrationality, inconsistency, or akrasia. Are there any cases of devotion that look more appealing?

I think there are. I will present a simple argument for the rationality of having dialectically invulnerable commitments. First:

1. Reflective individuals can usually find reasonable grounds for rejecting or attenuating their commitments.

Imagine a case in which Kelly has a dialectically invulnerable commitment which *cannot* be shown to be irrational from premises that she accepts, but which *can* be shown irrational from premises that she regards as reasonable. Let's say Kelly is a Kantian and the dialectically invulnerable attitude is a belief that we have no direct duties to non-human animals. She sees that there are other reasonable starting points, such as the ones articulated by classical utilitarianism, which reach the opposite conclusion. Moreover, she isn't dogmatic and uncritical: she recognizes that many of the central arguments for Kantianism are disputable and she sees how, in light of this, one might find utilitarianism tempting. Nonetheless, her belief that we have no direct duties to non-human animals is secure; she treats it as dialectically invulnerable, and she's committed to doing so, regardless of the fact that she acknowledges cogent objections.

Or consider another example of the same type of case. Rob is a principled libertarian who strongly desires to minimize the role of government in our lives, and for that reason objects to some proposal for progressive taxation. Yet he sees that others could legitimately disagree; he doesn't think people are irrational when they endorse these conflicting proposals, though his own core commitments rule them out. The fact that he acknowledges these other views and the force of their potential objections has absolutely no effect on his desire, though; it remains as forceful as ever.

I think most of our commitments fall into this category: there are few (if any) that can be established on the basis of theory-neutral starting points. There are multiple reasonable yet inconsistent conceptions of the good life, and these will yield contrary verdicts about particular cases. So, as (1) asserts, in many cases reflective individuals can find grounds for dismissing or attenuating their commitments. (I will offer an argument for this claim in the next chapter; for now, I just ask the reader to grant it.)

Of course, it's not irrational to maintain attitudes and commitments that are susceptible to objections from reasonable premises that we don't accept. If it were, then almost all of our attitudes and commitments would be irrational, for almost all of our commitments are disputable from alternative reasonable premises.

There's no particular problem with having commitments that are open to objections from alternative starting points. But recall that my account of devotion does something more: it says that the agent will treat certain commitments as dialectically invulnerable. It's not irrational to hold commitments that are susceptible to legitimate objections. But is it problematic to treat these rationally optional commitments as dialectically invulnerable?

It's not. I submit that the following is true:

> 2. Certain types of projects and relationships require firm commitments. Call these *resolute* projects and relationships.

Suppose I alter my degree of commitment to X based on the degree of justification that I believe I have for X. If I think there are good, but not fully persuasive, grounds for being just, then I am only somewhat just. If I think there are good, but not fully persuasive, grounds for being partial toward my children, then I am only somewhat partial toward them. If I recognize reasonable grounds for not loving my wife, then I attenuate my love. This would be strange, perhaps pathological; it would, at any rate, differ from the person who has resolute projects and relationships.

In general, we do not think it is always appropriate to apportion degree of commitment to degree of justification. Certain projects and relationships demand a degree of commitment that cannot be justified by critical reflection, and yet the person who for that reason rejects these projects and relationships seems impoverished.

> 3. Maintaining resolute projects and relationships requires insulating the relevant commitments from the effects of (1).

By way of illustration, imagine a politician who works tirelessly to combat inequality while recognizing that there are reasonable starting points (certain versions of libertarianism, for instance) entailing that inequality doesn't matter. What exactly is she supposed to do with that recognition? The mere fact that her commitment is disputable doesn't have any practical consequences for her. Engaging in justificatory reflection and staking her commitment on its outcome (by genuinely allowing doubts, critiques, and so forth to alter the degree of her commitment) would undermine the commitment. So it makes sense for her to insulate the commitment from the results of critical reflection. And it makes sense for her to be committed to this insulation: absent it, her central projects, around which her life has been organized, would collapse or at least become attenuated.

If it makes sense to insulate rationally optional commitments from the effects of dialectic, we can see how an extension is tempting. The case I've described involves acknowledging that legitimate objections to my commitments exist, though I myself don't accept the premises on which they depend. But it's a short step from there to acknowledging objections from premises that I *do* accept.

After all, most of us aren't absolutely certain about these premises. Take a philosophical example: a reflective individual could be torn between Kantian and utilitarian premises, tempted by each, leaning first one way and then another. But she has to act, she has to make decisions, and in doing so she will sometimes make judgments that conflict with one theory and accord with the other. Her commitment to her attitudes outstrips what she takes to be her rational warrant for them. And if this continues to a sufficient degree—if her commitment is sufficiently strong—then the commitment will be dialectically invulnerable. If the commitment involves factors that she takes as definitive of her identity or as otherwise central to her, she may strive to maintain this dialectical invulnerability. Regardless of the fact that she recognizes objections to her commitment, she will persevere in it.

While I don't intend (1)–(3) to be taken as a watertight argument in favor of dialectically invulnerable commitments, I do hope (1)–(3) give an indication of why having dialectically invulnerable commitments can be rational. Of course, objections can be raised. Here's one: there are plenty of cases in which devotion in particular and dialectical invulnerability in general are pernicious. The neo-Nazi might be devoted to Aryan dominance; the terrorist might be devoted to inflicting severe suffering on perceived enemies; the evangelical might be devoted to imposing his religious norms on his society. There are (I believe) compelling arguments against each of these activities and goals, so it would be better if these particular commitments were dialectically *vulnerable*.

But can we move from the fact that certain dialectically invulnerable commitments are reprehensible to the idea that all dialectically invulnerable commitments are problematic? We can't. We need to distinguish two things: (a) whether devotion as such is problematic and (b) whether being devoted to certain ends, activities, values, or relationships is problematic. These come apart. We can freely admit that many particular instances of devotion are problematic; but what makes them problematic is not the mere fact that they are instances of devotion. What makes them problematic is, instead, the particular end, activity, value, or relationship that the devotion is directed upon. In short: devotion as such isn't problematic but certain objects of devotion can be problematic.

Yet there is a complication. Certain objects will be problematic regardless of whether we are devoted to them or merely committed to them. Others will be problematic only when we are devoted to them, but not when we are merely committed to them. To see this, contrast two cases: being committed to Aryan dominance and being devoted to Aryan dominance are both bad, though the latter is worse; being committed to gun rights is arguably unobjectionable, whereas being devoted to gun rights is arguably problematic. After all, what distinguishes devotion from commitment is dialectical invulnerability: if an agent is devoted to something, then his commitment to this thing is dialectically invulnerable and he is disposed to maintain the dialectical invulnerability of the commitment. It's bad to be committed to Aryan dominance, but it's even worse if this commitment is dialectically invulnerable, and worse still if the agent is disposed to maintain the dialectical invulnerability of the commitment. It's fine to be committed to gun rights, but it's arguably problematic if this commitment is dialectically invulnerable.

Still, the larger point stands. The fact that there are *certain cases* in which devotion is problematic does not entail that devotion *in general* is problematic. And indeed, we can see this by considering the kinds of cases I have been discussing above. For example, it's arguably *better* to be devoted to your child's welfare than to be merely committed to your child's welfare.

Let's consider one final objection. I've suggested that maintaining resolute commitments requires rendering these commitments dialectically invulnerable. But isn't there another option? Rather than trying to make my commitments impervious to justificatory considerations, can't I simply decline to engage in justificatory reasoning in the first place? The politician in my example above is resolutely committed to fighting inequality. Suppose she is aware that there are objections to her views, but she simply ignores them or gives them only the most cursory examination. Then her commitment to combating inequality would be secure. It would be unaffected by justificatory reasoning precisely because, as a matter of fact, she doesn't engage in justificatory reflection about it. And we can assume further that this is not a case of dialectical invulnerability: we can stipulate that in a counterfactual scenario in which the politician did engage in justificatory reasoning, she would experience an attenuation of her commitment. In short: here we seem to have a case of resolute commitment without dialectical invulnerability.

I agree that this is possible. People who aren't prone to engaging in justificatory reasoning about their commitments won't face an attenuation these commitments and hence won't need to render the commitments dialectically invulnerable. My argument is intended to be restricted to those who do engage in justificatory reasoning about their commitments. However, in the next chapter, I am going to suggest that the class of people who fit this description is very wide indeed. For, I argue, even within everyday deliberation about perfectly ordinary matters, there are pressures toward justificatory reasoning about core commitments. This is not to say that every deliberating person will in fact experience and respond to these pressures; but I will suggest that the phenomenon is sufficiently widespread to be a matter of concern.

4.7 Conclusion

I've been trying to draw attention to the way in which many of our central commitments are insulated from the effects of justificatory reflection. I began by focusing on Bernard Williams' argument that certain commitments are deeper than moral commitments, and thus don't need to be validated by checking to see whether they are morally permissible. I've extended this point, arguing that certain commitments are deeper even than a commitment to rationality. Using an example of Proust on love, I've tried to show that there are cases in which the agent is so deeply committed to something that it becomes dialectically invulnerable; no dialectical move will disrupt it. When agents have dialectically invulnerable commitments and aim to maintain this dialectical invulnerability, they are devoted.

In sum, I've argued that devotion should be understood as having a commitment, insulating the commitment from the effects of critical reflection, and being committed to this insulation. This, I think, is the real lesson of the examples from Williams and Wolf. An unconditional commitment to apportioning all commitments to the results of critical reflection would result in an attenuation of most or all commitments. In the face of that recognition, it is not irrational to maintain commitments despite one's lack of justification for them. And it is a short step from there to treating one's commitments as dialectically invulnerable.

With that, we can return to the broader topic: is it irrational to have dialectically invulnerable commitments? We can now see that the answer is no. First, having resolute commitments requires that they be dialectically invulnerable. Second, it can be rational to have resolute commitments. So it can be rational to manifest devotion.

So, at this stage, we have the following claims: sacred values are inviolable, incontestable, and dialectically invulnerable. I've argued that all three features can be warranted. Indeed, they don't just seem warranted: they seem crucial for the preservation of central features of ethical life. So sacred values are not irrational. In the next chapter, I will bolster this conclusion by examining another important role that sacred values play in ethical life.

5
Nihilism and the Abundance of Values

The previous chapters have explored the important roles that sacred values and devotion play in ethical life. I noted that certain types of human relationships—in particular, those demanding resolute commitments—require sacred values. In addition, I argued that one of the features of sacred values, dialectical invulnerability, is linked to the manifestation of devotion.

But there is one objection that I haven't yet addressed. My arguments have all hinged on the idea that we need to treat certain commitments as fixed and immutable. One way of treating commitments as fixed is by immunizing them from critique, in the ways that I've examined. But another way would be by decisively establishing these commitments through ordinary rational argumentation. Suppose for example that Kant's ethical theory were successful: we begin with some undeniable facts about agency and then somehow show that an analogue of enlightenment values follow from them. If this worked, then we could do away with the dialectical invulnerability component of sacred values: we wouldn't need to treat the values as dialectically invulnerable, because dialectic would decisively establish them.

I think this strategy has no hope of success. In this chapter I explain why. My central argument is simple enough: reasonable agents can always find good grounds for questioning their commitments. But to make this more precise and to show just how problematic it can be, I investigate the way in which disagreement about values can give rise to a form of nihilism. I suggest that having sacred values is one way—perhaps the only sustainable way—of preventing the relevant form of nihilism.

* * *

Nihilism occupies a puzzling position in moral philosophy. A few immensely insightful writers, including Nietzsche and several existentialists, treat nihilism as an object of tremendous concern: they take it to be among the deepest and most pressing of ethical problems. But nihilism as it is typically defined seems inconsequential and easily dismissed; recent treatments of nihilism emphasize the way in which it is rests on dubious assumptions, or is confused, or is unlivable, or all three. One possible conclusion to draw is that Nietzsche and others were simply mistaken in thinking that nihilism poses any deep or intractable philosophical problems. Another possible conclusion is that we have misunderstood the philosophical problem that these thinkers were trying to articulate. In this chapter I will

Philosophy of Devotion: The Longing for Invulnerable Ideals. Paul Katsafanas, Oxford University Press.
© Paul Katsafanas 2022. DOI: 10.1093/oso/9780192867674.003.0005

suggest that the latter possibility is actual. I argue that there is a type of nihilism that poses grave problems for ethical theory. Nihilism is a view not about the *absence* of values but about the *abundance* of values; the nihilist worries not that there are no values, but that there are all too many. Faced with a variety of competing and potentially incompatible normative claims, the nihilist finds herself unable to articulate an acceptable justification for prioritizing one claim over the others; she thereby finds herself unable to reach determinate verdicts within practical deliberation; and, as a result, she suffers from a motivational problem that I will call Normative Dissipation. Although I think this form of nihilism is suggested by Nietzsche and perhaps Camus, my goals are not at all exegetical: I articulate and defend the relevant form of nihilism without reliance on specific texts. My focus will be on the philosophical argument rather than its historical provenance.

The chapter proceeds as follows. Section 5.1 reviews the problems and prospects for the familiar forms of nihilism. Section 5.2 introduces an alternative conception of nihilism, which links nihilism to the perceived inability to justify weightings or lexical orderings of competing normative claims. Sections 5.3 and 5.4 make this more precise. In particular, Section 5.3 argues that reaching an all-things-considered ought judgment about what is to be done in a particular case typically requires assigning relative weights to competing normative claims. Section 5.4 argues that the nihilist endorses *Normative Weighting Skepticism*, which asserts that we lack sufficient justification for assigning these relative weights and thus are unable to reach all-things-considered ought judgments. Sections 5.5 and 5.6 argue that although Normative Weighting Skepticism rests on certain assumptions about moral uncertainty, it is a reasonable philosophical position. Sections 5.7 and 5.8 defend the claim that agents who accept Normative Weighting Skepticism will experience a motivational problem that I label Normative Dissipation: roughly, they will find that normative entities (reasons, values, or principles) formerly treated as overriding cease to function as overriding. Section 5.9 explains why Normative Dissipation cannot arise for sacred values. Section 5.10 concludes.

5.1 The Familiar Versions of Nihilism

In popular culture, the nihilist is the one who has no values or views all normative claims as false. Nothing is really good or bad, right or wrong, required or prohibited. In recent moral philosophy, nihilism is typically defined in analogous ways. For example, Jamie Dreier writes that "Nihilism is the view that there are no moral facts. It says that nothing is right or wrong, or morally good or bad" (Dreier 2006: 240). Nihilism is typically associated with error theory, à la Mackie: in moral discourse, we try to state facts, but fail to do so. So moral discourse involves claims that are systematically false. One way of understanding this is that it assumes an absolutist conception of value:

> Nihilism recognizes that common-sense moral concepts are absolutist concepts: our moral thoughts are 'as of' a single, independently existing moral order... But [the nihilist] regrets to inform ordinary thought that it is based on a mistake. There is nothing in the world that answers to the ordinary language of morals.
> (Dreier 2006: 260)

The nihilist is the one who looks at normative claims in the same way as the atheist looks at theological claims about the attributes and actions of God: they're systematically false in that they presume the existence of something that does not exist.

According to this understanding of nihilism, the nihilist eschews all moral claims. He may desire certain things; he may have various preferences; he may prioritize some ends over others; he may even value some ends; but he doesn't have any *moral* values. (Just what this means will depend on what we take morality to be. For example, if moral claims are defined as universally valid normative claims, then the nihilist denies the existence of universally valid normative claims but might accept other normative claims.)

How does nihilism, so defined, fare? As many discussants mention, nihilism so defined is an *extremely* counterintuitive position. For example, Dreier claims that it is "violently contrary to common sense... it says that every positive moral judgment is false" (2006: 241). For this reason, many writers find it hard to imagine actually living this theory.[1] After all, our actions are pervasively informed by our sense of what's good, what's bad, what's right, what's wrong in some purportedly universal sense. This point is familiar enough to show up in popular portrayals of nihilism. Consider the nihilists in *The Big Lebowski,* who claim "We believe in nothing, Lebowski. *Nothing."* Yet, a bit later, we get this dialogue:

NIHILIST 1: "His girlfriend gave up her toe!"
NIHILIST 2: "She thought we'd be getting a million dollars!"
NIHILIST 1: "Is not fair!"
WALTER: "*Fair?* Who's the fucking nihilist here?"

The self-proclaimed nihilists fail to live their nihilism, reverting to claims about fairness.

So nihilists are often presented as either confused, insincere, or unreflective: nihilists harbor obvious inconsistencies, asserting that there are no moral facts in one breath while relying on the idea that there are moral facts in the next. Perhaps

---

[1] See, for example, Dreier 2006, Hare 1972, and Shafer Landau 2017: 306–10.

for this reason, Dreier presents nihilism as an unlivable doctrine: people may claim to be nihilists, but (almost) no one actually is.

I think these characterizations should give us pause. It's certainly possible that nihilism, like many other philosophical views, will turn out to be problematic or even self-contradictory upon extended reflection. However, given that a number of skilled philosophers have treated nihilism as deeply concerning, we have reason to avoid analyzing nihilism in a way that makes its problems so glaringly obvious that the account would lack any initial appeal for thoughtful individuals.

One response to this worry is to argue that nihilism actually is more livable than Dreier suggests. Is it really so hard to live with the idea that there are no moral facts? Many error theorists believe that we can insulate ourselves from the consequences of error theory: although there are no moral facts, morality's falsity needn't undermine its practical employment. For example, Richard Joyce argues that we should reject moral facts in reflective, philosophical contexts while nonetheless retaining a version of them in everyday contexts (2001: 175–231; see also Olson 2014: 151–98). If we can, as Joyce and others suggest, insulate the theoretical acceptance of error theory from any significant practical consequences, then Dreier's claim that nihilism (construed as some version of error theory) is unlivable would be undermined. But this comes at a cost: to the extent that Joyce is right that error theory needn't have significant practical consequences, we might wonder whether it merits the label "nihilism," which has connotations of something momentous.

Rather than associating nihilism with the idea that there are no moral facts, we might understand nihilism differently. For a second popular understanding of nihilism is available. In the existentialist literature—especially in the works of Camus, but also in Sartre, de Beauvoir, and others—nihilism is the view that life has no meaning or no purpose. "The meaning of life is the most urgent of questions," writes Camus. "All the rest—whether or not the world has three dimensions, whether the mind has nine or twelve categories—comes afterwards. These are games; one must first answer" (Camus 1955: 3–4). And the nihilist is the one who answers this question negatively.

This version of nihilism is distinct from Dreier's version, in that it focuses on questions of *meaning* rather than *moral value*. While the connection between meaning and moral value is a matter of dispute, on many views they will come apart: you could assert that there are moral facts but find life meaningless; and, if some of the existentialists are correct, you could deny the existence of moral facts while finding life meaningful.[2] Thus, if we distinguish meaning and moral value, this existentialist notion of nihilism will differ from Dreier's version.

---

[2] Schopenhauer is perhaps an example of someone who accepts the idea of moral facts but finds life meaningless; Beauvoir and Sartre are examples of those who deny moral facts but find life (potentially) meaningful. Others treat questions of meaning as depending on the existence of moral facts; see, for example, Susan Wolf 2010.

This version of nihilism is certainly evocative. But it's not clear that it poses any novel philosophical problems. Although the details need not detain us, it's uncontroversial that Sartre and Beauvoir (Camus is a more complex case) intend to deny only a particular *kind* of meaning: a meaning that would obtain independently of our subjective motivations, goals, and projects. Sartre and Beauvoir are happy to say that I can *give* my life a meaning that it doesn't antecedently possess, by committing myself to projects or ideals through the making of "fundamental choices".[3] But if this is so, the version of nihilism often attributed to them (the denial of external or intrinsic meaning) has more limited significance and is less original than we might have thought. It involves a denial of views, like Susan Wolf's, that ground facts about meaning in facts about *external* reasons; but it would be compatible with most broadly internalist accounts of meaning.

5.2 Nihilism as the Loss of Higher Values

If the above suggestions are correct, there are potential problems with two traditional accounts of nihilism. Of course, responses are available: I don't take the brief discussions above to establish that these forms of nihilism are unimportant. Rather, I've simply indicated some challenges for these familiar forms of nihilism.

But I want to set these forms of nihilism aside. I am concerned with a rather different type of nihilism, which has been overlooked. This form of nihilism emerges from Nietzsche's texts. (Nietzsche's texts are notoriously complex, but my goals are not interpretive. Although I use Nietzsche to illustrate the view, nothing in this chapter hinges on exegetical claims.) Nietzsche describes nihilism as the loss of *highest values*: "what does nihilism mean?—*that the highest values devalue themselves*" (Nietzsche 2003: 146).[4] Notice that he focuses not on value in general, but *highest* values. So that raises a question: what are highest values? Elsewhere, I've argued that Nietzschean highest values are roughly equivalent to sacred values (Katsafanas 2015). Thus, a value qualifies as highest if it possesses a cluster of mutually reinforcing features: in particular, highest values are viewed as inviolable, incontestable, and dialectically invulnerable. They are inviolable in that it is seen as wrong to give up any quantity of the value so as to secure some other value. They are incontestable in that it is prohibited even to contemplate sacrificing or trading them for other values. And they are dialectically invulnerable in that they are insulated from the effects of justificatory critique. So the claim that a

---

[3] This point is made most explicitly in Sartre 1948 and Beauvoir 1976.

[4] Nietzsche discusses several additional varieties of nihilism. For example, he sometimes labels ethical theories nihilistic if they (according to his standards) produce a decline in human flourishing. I won't address these points here. For discussions of Nietzsche on nihilism, see Reginster 2006, Huddleston 2019, and Katsafanas 2015.

value is highest is a claim about the way in which it is treated within deliberation, rather than about its content.

In short, then, Nietzschean highest values are equivalent to sacred values. So he is associating the loss of sacred values with the emergence of nihilism. Why might that be? It seems like an idiosyncratic conception of nihilism. What might tempt us to accept it?

One thing that might tempt us to associate the loss of sacred values with nihilism is the idea that sacred values tend to confer meaning or significance on the activities that they structure. Sacred values aren't *defined* as especially significant or meaningful values; rather, they're defined as inviolable, incontestable, and dialectically invulnerable. However, Chapter 2 argued that sacred values are *typically* regarded as subjectively meaningful; and Chapter 4's examples support that argument. Insofar as sacred values tend to go along with a sense of subjective meaning or importance, the loss of sacred values could jeopardize a person's (or a culture's) sense of subjective meaning. If we accept some version of this claim, the Nietzschean version of nihilism will bear similarities to the existentialist account: it, too, will be concerned with the effects of a potential loss of meaning.

But I want to set aside questions of meaningfulness or importance and focus on the structural features of sacred values: the fact that they are inviolable, incontestable, and dialectically invulnerable. For these features alone, I will suggest, are enough to establish the connection between sacred values and nihilism.

We might picture the loss of sacred values as a kind of normative flatness: I have various normative commitments, but none of these commitments seem weightier than any others. None seem genuinely overriding. So, for example, I value good meals, engaging books, social justice, human life, and so forth, but when I look—when I *really* look—I don't see any reason to prioritize one of these over the others. I *may in fact* prioritize some of them: if I can trade a night of good reading for the promotion of social justice, of course I will do that. But when I step back and think about why I am doing this, I won't see a good way of justifying that prioritization. I won't be able to see it as anything more than a contingent matter of emotional attunement, desire, cultural pressure, and so on. So I assign weights to values, reasons, or normative principles within deliberation and action, treating some as outweighing others; but I don't see a way of *justifying* these weightings.

Put differently, nihilism can be understood as anomie: normative commitments break down, but not because I abandon them; rather, because they are all perceived as on par. None is perceived as overriding. (I think Camus may be portraying something similar with Meursault from *The Stranger*, but again my goals are not interpretive.)

Now anomie doesn't *directly* follow from the loss of sacred values. The fact that no value is *completely* or *unconditionally* inviolable and incontestable does not, by itself, entail that all values are on par. I might reject sacred values while still maintaining that human life is far more valuable than ice cream. So there is a lacuna in the argument. Having sacred values would be one way of avoiding anomie, but it is not the only way.

Or so it seems. But I am going to suggest that what looks like a lacuna is actually a deep insight. It is the point at which the Nietzschean theory of nihilism reveals something important about the relation between normative views and subjective concerns.

5.3 Practical Deliberation and All-Things-Considered Ought Judgments

So far, I've stated the Nietzschean form of nihilism in somewhat vague ways, merely trying to get the picture into view. In this section I will make the view more precise.

Suppose an agent is deliberating about whether she ought to perform some action X in circumstances C. Then:

1. In order to reach an all-things-considered ought judgment about whether to X in C, the agent must determine which normative claims apply to the case.

I take (1) to be a truism.

2. In typical cases of deliberation about whether to X in C, more than one set of normative claims can reasonably be taken to be applicable. Call these sets of normative claims $N_1, N_2, \ldots, N_n$.

Suppose I am trying to decide whether, given my current circumstances, I should book a vacation to some distant country. Here are some normative claims that I might reasonably take to be applicable: the norms of prudence, as when I consider whether I will spend too much money on the vacation. The norms of justice, as when I consider whether I have some obligation to spend this money on aid for refugees or victims of natural disasters. The norms of welfare, as when I consider whether going on the vacation will play some role in increasing my own happiness. I might also consider additional normative claims: those pertaining to the environmental impact of travel, the impact of tourism on the host country, and so on.

3. In typical cases, $N_1, N_2, \ldots, N_n$ taken in isolation will yield different ought judgments.

By way of illustration: if I consider my potential vacation only in terms of its effect on my welfare (and ignore all other applicable norms), I will arrive at the conclusion that I ought to go on vacation. If I consider my potential vacation only in terms of its environmental impact, I will reach a different conclusion: I ought not to go on vacation. And so on. In this case, I get different verdicts depending on whether I consider the potential action solely in terms of N_1, N_2, and so on.

Of course, not all cases have this form. There will be some cases in which all of the normative claims that can reasonably be taken to bear on the case yield the same verdict. For example, if I am considering whether, at no cost to myself, to pull back a child who is about to step in front of a speeding car, it's hard to imagine how we would get different verdicts.

Nonetheless, I take it that in *typical* cases, we do get different verdicts. That is, in typical cases of practical deliberation, there will be multiple reasons, normative principles, and other normative entities that can reasonably be taken to bear on the case, and some of these normative entities (when considered in isolation) will yield conflicting verdicts on what is to be done. For illustration, consider some simple cases. Suppose I am in a restaurant and I am trying to decide between the steak and the pasta. I can take as relevant only my own tastes; or I can consider animal welfare; or the environmental toll of meat consumption; and so on. Depending on which considerations I take to be applicable, I may get different conclusions: my tastes dictate the steak, whereas environmental concerns dictate the pasta. Or suppose my friend asks how he looks in his new shirt, which I find unappealing. The norms of kindness (when take in isolation) dictate one response, the norms of honesty another.

As these examples indicate, even when we're considering relatively straightforward and localized decisions, there tend to be multiple sets of normative claims that it would be reasonable to accept yet which, when taken in isolation, would yield conflicting verdicts. I think cases of this form are ubiquitous. I won't defend this assumption; I think it is widely accepted and consequently the burden of proof is on those who would want to deny it.

For simplicity, in the following steps I will consider a case in which only *two* sets of normative claims, N_1 and N_2, are taken to be applicable.

4. In order to reach an *all-things-considered* ought judgment about whether to X in C, the agent will have to assign relative weights to each of the different sets of normative claims. In a case where the relevant sets are N_1 and N_2, she will have to treat N_1 as outweighing N_2; or treat N_2 as outweighing N_1; or treat N_1 and N_2 as having equal weight; or treat N_1 and N_2 as incommensurable or incomparable.

Suppose N_1 considered in isolation yields the judgment that I ought to X, whereas N_2 considered in isolation yields the judgment that I ought to Y. Once I assign relative weights to N_1 and N_2, I may arrive at an all-things-considered judgment that I ought to X (for example, if I take N_1 to outweigh N_2 to the extent that N_2 has zero weight). Or I may arrive at an all-things-considered judgment that I ought either to X or Y (for example, if I take N_1 and N_2 to have incomparable weights). Or I may arrive at an all-things-considered judgment that I ought to perform some action Z that manages to fulfill both N_1 and N_2 to some extent (for example, if I judge that environmental concerns are weightier than concerns of taste, but still hold taste to have some weight, I may pick an entrée that is neither the tastiest nor the most environmentally sound, but that falls somewhere in between). And of course these are just a few of the possibilities. The important point, for our purposes, is simply this: what the agent believes she all-things-considered ought to do will depend on the relative weights that she assigns to N_1 and N_2.

I don't think any of the above steps are controversial; I state them merely for the sake of clarity. The next step is where the distinctiveness of the nihilist's position begins to emerge:

5. In typical cases of deliberating about whether to X in C, we lack sufficient justification for assigning relative weights to the applicable sets of normative claims N_1 and N_2. That is, in typical cases we lack sufficient justification for picking one of the four options (N_1 is weightier than N_2; N_2 is weightier than N_1; N_1 and N_2 have equal weight; N_1 and N_2 are incomparable or incommensurable) over the others.

Claim (5) is obviously controversial. I will say why the nihilist believes (5) in the next section. For now, let's grant (5) and consider what would follow from it.

What happens when I believe both that (a) reaching an all-things-considered ought judgment about whether to X requires assigning relative weights to N_1 and N_2 and (b) I lack sufficient justification for assigning relative weights to N_1 and N_2? Suppose, for example, that weighting N_1 over N_2 would entail that I ought all things considered to X, whereas weighting N_2 over N_1 would entail that I ought all things considered not to X. (I will ignore the other options for simplicity.) If I sincerely take myself to lack justification for assigning either of these relative weightings, then I will be unable to reach an all-things-considered ought judgment.

Now, if this happens only in a handful of cases, it's not particularly troublesome. But recall that claim (5) presents this as happening in *typical* cases. If these kinds of case are pervasive, they look much more worrisome.

The nihilist, in accepting (5), draws the following conclusion:

6. In typical cases of deliberating about whether to X in C, we lack justification for reaching an all-things-considered ought judgment.

That is, the nihilist takes (5) to entail a pervasive skepticism about our ability to reach justified all-things-considered ought judgments.

Does (6) follow from (1)–(5)? Not necessarily; there is a suppressed premise. Notice that claim (5) expresses a certain form of *moral uncertainty*. Recently, philosophers have begun explicitly discussing what we ought to do when we are uncertain about moral (or, more broadly, normative) facts.[5] This uncertainty can take different forms. For example, I might simply be uncertain about what the moral facts are. Claim (5) expresses a particular form of moral uncertainty: I take myself to know what the relevant normative facts are, but I take myself to be ignorant of how these facts should be weighed against one another (either in this particular case or in general). Philosophers have offered various responses to dealing with moral uncertainty: picking your favorite moral theory and going with whatever it entails (see Lockhart 2000 and MacAskill 2014 for critical discussions), maximizing expected moral value (Lockhart 2000; see Sepielli 2012 for a critique), considering the stakes of choosing one option over another (see MacAskill 2014), and so on. In general, these philosophers have tried to provide norms that would guide decision-making in cases such as those in (5). If we accept one of these norms, we could accept (5) and still reach an all-things-considered judgment about whether to X. So (6) wouldn't follow.

The nihilist, as I am defining her, doesn't find these discussions of moral uncertainty convincing. And for good reason. Any *particular* proposal about how to resolve moral uncertainty will be controversial; moreover, the particular proposals about how to resolve moral uncertainty often give *different* results.[6] In light of this, the nihilist is committed to accepting the following claim:

(5a) There are multiple mutually incompatible accounts of how to resolve moral uncertainty, and we lack sufficient justification for accepting one of these accounts over the others.

Of course, not everyone will accept (5a). But it is reasonable to accept it. And if we're tempted by (5), we're likely to accept (5a) as well.

If we accept (1)–(5) and (5a), then claim (6) follows. The nihilist, as I am defining her, is the one who endorses this argument. Again, I don't take this argument to be rationally mandated: steps (5) and (5a) are controversial. I've given some indication of why (5a) is reasonable. Let's now consider how we might support (5).

5.4 Normative Weighting Skepticism

Premise (5) expresses what we might call *normative weighting skepticism*. The proponent of (5) believes that we're justified in taking various normative

---

[5] Bykvist 2017 provides a helpful introduction to this literature. A few of the many other relevant works are: Christensen 2010, Harman 2015, Sepielli 2009 and 2014, Weatherson 2014, and Zimmerman 2014.

[6] Consider an example. Suppose I am deciding whether to lie to the murderer at the door who has asked where my friend is hiding. My favorite ethical theory is Kant's, which tells me that in this case I am prohibited from lying. But expected moral value is presumably maximized by lying (a lie is told, but a murder is avoided). So the proposals *use your favorite theory* and *maximize expected moral value* yield different results. The point generalizes.

considerations to bear on a case; but she believes that we *lack* justification for assigning relative weights to these considerations. What might make (5) tempting?

Before we begin, some expectation-setting. My goal is not to convince the reader to be a nihilist; I am after something more modest. I want to show that nihilism is a *reasonable* and *defensible* position. That is, I want to show that there are some good (though not invulnerable) arguments for nihilism and that the nihilist isn't making any obvious mistakes.

With that in mind, here are a few ways in which a commitment to (5) could arise. First, the agent might accept a normative view that contains competing fundamental principles and offers no way of adjudicating conflicts between these principles. For example, Sidgwick's ethical theory can be interpreted in this way. The principles "one ought to maximize one's own good" and "one ought to maximize aggregate good" are both, Sidgwick claims, derivable from self-evident truths, but clearly yield incompatible verdicts in many circumstances.[7] If we interpret Sidgwick as unable to offer a way of resolving conflicts between these principles, his theory would lead to a version of (5). In any given situation, one can assess the available options in terms of maximizing aggregate good or maximizing one's own good. Given plausible assumptions, these will typically diverge. There may be some cases in which they coincide (an isolated individual is shipwrecked on an island where his actions have no effects on others, etc.), but these will be rare.[8]

Second, the agent might be torn between competing comprehensive normative views, such as ethical theories, religious views, and political outlooks. Suppose the agent believes she has equally strong justifications for two ethical theories that yield incompatible verdicts. Suppose that these justifications aren't incontestable: we can see problems with them. But they seem roughly equal in their strengths. For example, we might imagine someone torn between utilitarian and Kantian ethics. The arguments for each theory have a number of compelling components, but also some premises or dialectical moves that are questionable. The person reflecting on these theories is unsure where to commit herself. She thinks that there are good reasons for being a Kantian and good reasons for being a utilitarian. Choosing to commit herself to either theory seems, to her, like it would be arbitrary; she might as well flip a coin. And that seems dissatisfying; she's not willing to let her endorsement of an ethical theory rest on such shoddy grounds. So she is led to a version of (5).

---

[7] See Sidgwick 1981: 420–1 and 508.
[8] Notice that I am *not* claiming that pluralistic ethical theories always lead to (5). That would be false. Take Ross' pluralistic theory: he claims that (i) there are multiple *prima facie* duties that might conflict; (ii) there is no general lexical ranking of these duties; but (iii) in any given case, one (or more) of these duties will take precedence over the others; this will be one's *duty proper*. In general, if an agent accepts a pluralistic theory that yields all-things-considered ought judgments, the agent won't accept (5).

But these conflicts don't have to arise only at the level of reflection on whole theories. Let's consider a third type of case, in which the agent is gripped by what David Wong calls "moral ambivalence."[9] Suppose I have several basic values, where these values are basic in the sense that they are not seen as derivable from or reducible to one another. And suppose further that I come to think that whereas I have struck a certain balance between these basic values, perhaps by prioritizing one over others, it would not be unreasonable to strike a difference balance. For example, I might see interpersonal duties and duties to myself as equally basic; and I might see that some people weight the former more heavily than the latter, whereas others do the opposite. Suppose I treat autonomy and familial duties as basic and weight the former over the latter; yet others, I think, might be justified in doing the opposite. In short, I see that while I have prioritized my basic values in one way, other reasonable agents might prioritize them in a different way. I needn't have a systematic ethical view in order to come to this conclusion; all I need to do is to think about my own basic values and their orderings.

In fact, the reflection doesn't even have to go that deep. Even without identifying basic values, the agent might simply think about her particular duties, principles, values, or reasons. For example, take the view that human life is sacred and inviolable and the view that it is merely extremely valuable. There are good arguments for treating human life as sacred but also for treating it as extremely valuable yet fungible. Someone might be genuinely torn between these views, wavering and unsure of which to accept. Or suppose someone accepts both that autonomy and beneficence are valuable, but is unsure what the relative weights of these values should be. Insofar as this kind of reflection continues, the agent could be led to (5).

In all four cases—reflection on ethical theories, on principles or values, on basic values, and on more particular cases—the agent is unable to find acceptable justifications for assigning relative weights to competing sets of normative claims. Of course, there is a question about what will happen next. Will the agent remain skeptical? Perhaps not: if a moral theory doesn't give you a way of adjudicating conflicts, you might abandon it; and if competing moral theories or particular normative principles yield different verdicts, you might continue trying to decide which one to pick. So, even if normative weighting skepticism arises, won't the agent soon move past it?

She might *try*. The question, though, is whether the agent will be able to find a satisfactory way of eliminating normative weighting skepticism. By hypothesis, we are considering an agent who, after careful reflection, takes herself to be unable to

---

[9] Wong says that moral ambivalence "consists in recognition of severe conflicts between important values and the possibility that reasonable people could take different paths in the face of these conflicts" (2006: xiv). As he later puts it, "moral ambivalence is the phenomenon of coming to understand and appreciate the other side's viewpoint to the extent that our sense of the unique rightness of our own judgment gets destabilized" (5).

find considerations that adequately justify weighting one normative claim over another. While she could resort to an act of arbitrary picking, she wouldn't be able to view herself as capable of justifying whichever option she picks. Thus, unless the agent either finds some new way of justifying her normative weightings or abandons her concern with doing so, she won't see herself as having a reasonable way of moving past normative weighting skepticism.

Note that normative weighting skepticism is thus different from mere recognition of value pluralism. Value pluralism, as I will use the term, is the claim that there are several different, mutually inconsistent sets of values that could be held by reasonable agents (Berlin 1990; Nagel 1979; Taylor 1982; Rawls 1993; Wong 2006).[10] Acceptance of value pluralism doesn't by itself lead to normative weighting skepticism. A committed Catholic can see that Jewish and Muslim people have substantive disagreements about particular values; a doctrinaire Baptist can see that liberal atheists have different views about abortion; and so on. In tolerant and openminded cases, those individuals could even hold that the incompatible views are legitimate for their proponents: although the Catholic doesn't see himself as required to perform ritual prayers or to make a pilgrimage to Mecca, he sees that the Muslim is so required; although the Muslim doesn't take himself to be committed to receiving the Eucharist or believing in the Trinity, he sees that the Catholic is so required.

Mere recognition of the existence of disparate normative views needn't lead to normative weighting skepticism; on the contrary, it might cement one more fully in one's original normative view. What generates normative weighting skepticism is the belief that one's adherence to a particular normative view is *problematized* by the existence of reasonable competing views. A person in this position not only recognizes that his Catholic normative view differs from Muslim and atheistic normative views; in addition, he worries that he has no good reason to remain committed to his original Catholic view. He may not give it up, but nonetheless something changes.

Using terminology from Sextus Empiricus, let's say that agents who accept normative weighting skepticism see competing sets of relevant normative claims as *equipollent*. Sextus articulates a form of skepticism that results from seeing that two conflicting principles can be equally well justified. The skeptic, so understood, may in fact be persuaded by one of these principles; she may in fact let one of these principles determine her action. But she is unable to decide which principle *ought*

---

[10] Value pluralism is sometimes understood merely as the denial of *monism*, which is the view that all values can be reduced to some fundamental value (such as happiness). So understood, pluralism would hold that there is more than one irreducible, fundamental value. But, unlike the view I am describing above, this version of pluralism needn't hold that the fundamental values are incompatible. See Chang 2014 for a discussion of this form of pluralism.

to determine her. The fact that one, rather than the other, determines her seems to her arbitrary and indefensible.[11]

I noted that Nietzsche associates nihilism with the loss of sacred values, and he suggests that this leads to anomie. The nihilist, so defined, isn't concerned about the validity of normative claims in general. She sees that subjective concerns, social customs, moral considerations, and so forth give us reasons for accepting certain normative claims. She accepts that people—herself included!—do in fact treat certain normative claims as outweighing others. But she worries that we cannot justify these weightings.

So the nihilist is not someone suffering from generalized doubts about whether normative claims are justifiable. She's not ignoring or refusing to see the arguments in favor of contractarianism, utilitarianism, Kantian ethics, and so on. She sees these arguments all too well. She believes that acceptance of any one of them, in preference to the others, would be unjustifiable. Of course, she may be more tempted by one of them than the others: perhaps utilitarianism seems, to her, more compelling than Kantianism. But, when she's honest with herself, she can't come up with any sufficiently compelling reasons for this preference. Or perhaps she's concerned with something more localized: she eschews high-level reflection on ethical theories and stays firmly at the level of particular principles. But she's at a loss: does environmental concern override economic development, or vice versa? She can't find acceptable answers for questions of this form.

The nihilist, then, is the person who treats competing relative weightings as equipollent. What for Sextus was an outcome toward which the skeptic strives, something won after a long struggle, is for the nihilist a condition to be lamented. Equipollence is her plight, rather than her goal.

5.5 Clarifications

Let me offer three clarifications. First, there is a difference between *having* a justification for some normative commitment and *being able to articulate* this justification. To borrow a case from Kyla Ebels-Duggan, imagine a person who reads a great deal of Shakespeare's work and comes to appreciate Shakespeare's literary greatness, but is unable to articulate a justification for the claim that Shakespeare's work exhibits literary greatness (2019: 2). Ebels-Duggan takes cases like this to illustrate that "It is quite possible, in fact absolutely ordinary, to have completely sufficient reasons for one's normative commitments while being fundamentally inarticulate about what these reasons are" (2019: 2). While

---

[11] As a recent commentator puts it, "The effect of equipollence on the skeptic does not consist in his being equally persuaded by both accounts, but in his being unable to determine by which account he ought to be persuaded, irrespective of which account *in fact* persuades him" (Svavarsson 2014: 356).

I would prefer to distinguish between *degrees* of articulacy rather than treating certain agents as totally inarticulate about their justifications, I do think Ebels-Duggan is right that we shouldn't identify articulacy about justification with possession of justification. And this suggests a potential response to normative weighting skepticism: could we say that in some cases the normative weighting skeptic actually does have a justification, but simply can't articulate it?

Of course. But the fact that this is true in some cases doesn't entail that it's true in all cases. In some cases, I will be unable to articulate a justification for my weighting of certain normative claims but will be reasonably confident either that I possess such a justification or that other people could articulate a justification. In other cases—the cases that I am focusing upon—I will be unable to articulate a justification for weighting certain normative claims and uncertain as to whether any such justification is available. While the former kind of case would forestall normative weighting skepticism, the latter wouldn't. (I will say more about articulacy in Chapter 9.)

This brings me a second, related point. Nihilism as I am defining it is primarily an *epistemological* problem: the agent doubts her ability to discover the correct weightings of normative claims (or, more radically, doubts her ability to discover whether there actually are any correct weightings of normative claims). But nihilism, as normative weighting skepticism, could also be motivated by a *metaphysical* claim: if the person denies the existence of all values, she will deny the existence of weightings of values. Normative weighting skepticism would then be a consequence of a more general philosophical thesis, such as error theory. Here, I focus on the more restricted, epistemological claim.

Third, given that my version of nihilism is principally focused on an epistemological problem (namely *uncertainty* about relative weights), does it merit the label nihilism? After all, nihilism is often interpreted as the claim that nothing really matters. But the agent suffering from normative weighting skepticism still thinks that things might matter: she just isn't sure *which* things matter and *how much* they matter.

In response, two points. First, my claim is not that this version of nihilism will capture all of the ordinary connotations of the term; as I pointed out in Section 5.1, there are several distinct views that have been called nihilism. Second and more importantly, I will argue in Sections 5.7 and 5.8 that normative weighting skepticism characteristically gives rise to a problematic psychological or motivational condition that I call Normative Dissipation. Insofar as normative weighting skepticism characteristically leads to a dissipation of the agent's commitments, there will be good reason for treating the view as a version of nihilism. Nihilism starts with uncertainty but doesn't end there.

5.6 Having Sufficient Justification for Normative Weightings

I've given some considerations that could lead an agent to accept (5). But notice that (5) says that we lack *sufficient* justification for assigning relative weights to competing normative claims. What counts as sufficient justification? Might the nihilist be operating with an overly demanding notion of sufficient justification?

To begin answering this question, notice that nihilism is not just a question about *justification in general*. Even if we can show that a normative commitment is justified, we might still worry about its prioritization over other claims. For example, I can believe that I am justified in holding that justice is to be promoted and suffering is to be avoided; but I can be unsure, either in particular cases or in general, whether one of these should enjoy priority over the other. Nihilism concerns justification, but it doesn't rest on generalized doubts about justifying normative claims. The person who doubts that *any* normative claim can be justified is different than the person who doubts that *weightings* of normative claims can be sufficiently justified. And that latter task is more difficult. There are all kinds of convincing reasons for according value to human life; but are there convincing reasons for granting it an inviolable status? There are all kinds of convincing reasons for caring about animal suffering; but are there convincing reasons for weighting it above competing concerns?

The nihilist can still think in evaluative terms. He can still prioritize certain ends over others. He can still refrain from satisfying various desires in order to pursue other ends. He can view himself as having reason to go to the gym even when he doesn't want to; he can take himself to have reason to donate to charity rather than spend the money on a nice meal. He can complain about fairness, worry about inequality, strive for justice. He just cannot see any sufficient justification for assigning relative weights to these sets of normative claims.

But consider a complication: might skepticism about *weightings* of normative claims spread to skepticism about the *normative claims themselves*? That is, if you start questioning your ability to justify relative weightings of normative claims, might you be led to question your ability to justify the normative claims themselves? If so, the type of nihilism that I am analyzing would be a precursor to a more radical form of nihilism, which would deny our ability to justify any normative claims at all.

I grant that this is possible. But it is not rationally mandated: from the fact that I don't know how to weight the value of environmental preservation against the value of happiness, it does not follow that I am committed to doubting the value of either of these things. On the contrary, I could be firmly committed to the idea that both of these valuations are justified while remaining uncertain about their respective weights. My inability to answer questions about how two values ought to be weighted needn't lead me to reject the values themselves, and my arguments for valuing these things needn't be undermined by my inability to argue for their relative weights.[12] More generally, it's certainly true that any localized form of

---

[12] This general point—that arguments for the value of X and the value Y are independent of arguments for the relative weights of X and Y—is widely accepted in the literature on incommensurable values. See, for example, Chang 2015.

skepticism could lead to a broader skepticism; but it needn't. Insofar as the nihilist endorses only the more limited form of skepticism—Normative Weighting Skepticism—she needn't endorse global skepticism about our ability to justify values.

With that in mind, let's return to our question: is the nihilist making a mistake? It's not obvious that she is. If the nihilist were insisting on absolute certainty; if the nihilist were willing to treat a justification as sufficient only if it were such that all procedurally rational agents would be compelled to accept it; if the nihilist demanded standards of proof for ethical claims that mirrored those in mathematics or logic; if any of this were the case, then questioning her standard would be precisely the right move to make. The question, though, is how weak we can allow justification to become before it ceases to deserve the name. Suppose we consider this point at the level of reflection upon competing philosophical theories. I study Kant and Mill and am torn between their theories. I see no *compelling* ground for deciding between them. I see no non-question-begging arguments that decisively favor one over the other. Am I then making some mistake in claiming that I lack sufficient justification for picking one over the other? It's not obvious. It's not absurd to think that no such justifications are available; one doesn't have to rely on an overly inflated conception of justification in order to reach this verdict. Or so, at any rate, I will assume.

5.7 The Motivational Impact of Nihilism on *Rational* Agents

So far, I've offered a definition of nihilism as well as some reflections on how we might be led to it. But does nihilism, so defined, matter? I suggested earlier that the standard form of nihilism is counterintuitive and potentially unlivable, whereas the existentialist version has limited significance. Will this form of nihilism be any different?

It will. I submit that the following claim is true:

(**Normative Dissipation**) Insofar as she is rational and lacks sacred values,[13] an agent who formerly regarded normative commitment N_1 as outweighing normative commitment N_2, but who now believes that she lacks sufficient justification for assigning greater weight to N_1, will experience motivational and behavioral changes. In particular, there will be a reduction in the extent to which her motives, concerns, and behavior reflect the idea that N_1 is to be prioritized over N_2.

---

[13] I include this caveat because one way of avoiding widespread normative dissipation is by having sacred values. I don't want to assume that rational agents must lack sacred values.

To see why we should accept Normative Dissipation, consider the debates about *motivational judgment internalism* (hereafter MJI). A weak form of MJI can be put as follows: if an agent sincerely judges that she has a reason to A, then insofar as she is rational she has at least some motivation to A. There are familiar debates about the scope of this principle, the way in which it should be formulated, and indeed whether it's true. But let's assume the weak version is true. Then we can ask: what happens when an agent used to believe that there's more reason to A than to B, but now believes that there's *not* more reason to A than to B? If we accept MJI, then insofar as she is rational, the original case is one in which she'd have some motivation to A instead of B, and the latter case is one in which she needn't. So, if we accept even this weak version of MJI, Normative Dissipation would be true.

So that's one reason to accept Normative Dissipation: it follows from a widely accepted claim about the connection between normative judgments and motivation. But there's also another reason. Consider what it would be to deny Normative Dissipation. In essence, Normative Dissipation simply says that for rational agents, thoughts about justification have an impact on motivation and behavior. To deny this is to treat thoughts about justification as epiphenomenal, seeing them as having *no* impact on a rational agent's motivation and behavior.[14] Someone who treats thoughts about justification as epiphenomenal for rational agents would have no obvious reason for caring about moral philosophy and reflection on normative commitments in the first place. After all, presumably one of the *points* of moral philosophy is that it could have some effect on the concerns and attachments of rational agents. Seeing that a value is justified will make the rational agent more likely to adopt it; seeing it as unjustified will make the rational agent less likely to accept it. Absent a commitment to a thought of this form, the traditional practice of moral philosophy might well seem pointless. So again, commitment to something like Normative Dissipation seems quite deeply rooted in our conception of moral philosophy.

Of course, a response is available: we can deny that practical reflection *in general* is inert while holding that in the special case of doubts about how to prioritize competing values, practical reflection should be inert. More specifically, we could hold that there is no problem with a case in which: I accept a set of normative claims N1; see that it's also reasonable to apply another set of normative claims, N2, to the case; see no justification for prioritizing N1 over N2; and yet continue to prioritize N1 over N2. As I mentioned above, some views of moral uncertainty endorse roughly this position.

---

[14] There are views that take this form. For example, Haidt's social intuitionist model of morality suggests that justification is always post-hoc and hence in an important sense epiphenomenal (Haidt 2012). Hume is sometimes read as endorsing a similar position.

I do think there are cases in which this makes sense. For example, consider a case in which I cannot articulate an adequate justification for prioritizing N1 over N2, but nonetheless think that someone else could. Then it would make sense to continue prioritizing N1 over N2. Or, rather differently: I might think that there is no fact of the matter about how N1 and N2 ought to be weighted against one another. It would be reasonable to prioritize N1 but also reasonable to prioritize N2. In a case like this, I could feel secure in continuing to prioritize N1, regardless of my inability to articulate what I regard as a good justification for doing so.

But those aren't the kinds of cases that we have been considering. We are focused on a particular type of case: I believe that prioritizing N1 over N2 requires a justification; I believe that I lack such a justification; and yet I continue to prioritize N1. To the extent that Normative Dissipation doesn't occur, I have commitments that don't track justificatory considerations in the ordinary way. These commitments are resistant to justificatory considerations. In the extreme case, they are Dialectically Invulnerable.

I want to mark just how peculiar it is. Consider an analogy with theoretical reason: in general, and to elide various complications, degree of credence should covary with degree of justification. Suppose we have a case in which Elvira, having checked various climate change models, believes that the average temperature will rise by 2 degrees in the next thirty years. But then she encounters additional models, some of which predict 1 degree, some 5 degrees, and so on. She finds these models reasonable and can't detect any good argument for accepting the 2-degree model over the 1-degree or 5-degree models. Yet she remains firmly committed to the belief that average temperatures will rise by exactly 2 degrees. This is very strange: it seems to me that a person in this situation *typically would* and *certainly should* reduce her credence in the 2-degree model. To the extent that she doesn't, she has insulated one of her beliefs from the effects of justificatory reasoning.

Just so with normative claims. People routinely dissociate normative claims from justificatory reflection, holding them despite lacking what they regard as sufficient justification. But this fact should strike us as surprising. In fact, it should strike us as *especially* surprising in the normative case. For normative commitments typically have costs. In prioritizing N1 over N2, I will typically forgo certain goods; encounter certain obstacles; make certain tradeoffs; be vulnerable to certain kinds of disappointments and loses; and so on. To the extent that I think there is no good reason for prioritizing N1 over N2, I will think that there is a sense in which there is no good reason for exposing myself to these costs. But then why persevere? Why not attenuate the commitment?

Let me summarize. If weightings of normative claims cannot be seen, by the rational agent, as sufficiently justified, what happens? Would everything go on as before? My answer: no, things wouldn't go on as before. Insofar as agents are rational, their commitment to normative weightings would dissipate.

If this is right, then nihilism, as I've defined it, is a form of anomie. Anomie is lawlessness. Here, it arises not form a lack of normative claims but from all too many normative claims. In the face of competing normative claims, the agent's commitments fade. Prioritizations are destabilized. Guidance is lost.

With this in mind, here's another way of putting nihilism. The point of normativity is that it concerns authority rather than power: the mere fact that I am disposed more strongly toward X than Y does not, from within practical reflection, settle the question of whether I should pursue X rather than Y. The problem with nihilism is that, when followed to its logical conclusion, the power/authority distinction is dissolved. Certain weighted commitments are experienced as more forceful than others, but not as more authoritative. And again, the result is a loss of direction, a loss of guidance. "Is there still any up or down?" Nietzsche asks. "Are we not straying as through an infinite nothing?" (Nietzsche 1974: Section 125).

5.8 The Motivational Impact of Nihilism on *Typical* Agents

But is this conclusion too quick? Normative Dissipation is a claim about what happens to rational agents who accept Normative Weighting Skepticism. But most of us fall short of the norms of rationality. If nihilism's practical effects show up only for those who both accept Normative Weighting Skepticism and are exemplary rational agents, we might find it somewhat less pressing.

In fact, there's a reason for thinking that nihilism is unimportant. Regardless of their thoughts about justification, everyone does in fact treat certain normative claims as outweighing others. I might not be able to justify prioritizing my own suffering above the suffering of animals, but that's not going to lead me to undergo intense suffering in order to save a bird. And so on. Even if the person can't discover any good reason for maintaining that one normative claim outweighs another, she will find that these skeptical doubts have no effect on her behavior; they will dissolve as soon as she engages in life. No one can get by without prioritizing certain norms, letting certain considerations outweigh others. So nihilism looks interesting as a theoretical claim but idle in practice.

I will argue that this is a mistake. Acceptance of nihilism actually would have an important effect. It would transform practical life.

First, though, a qualification. Individuals are idiosyncratic. Even if a particular individual could accept nihilism without exhibiting any practical effects, widespread acceptance of nihilism might still have important practical effects. After all, in any particular case, the fact that competing weightings of normative claims are perceived as equipollent might not matter. Preferences, attachments, and leaps of reasoning may sway the agent toward one side or the other. In the aggregate, though, the fact that competing weightings of normative claims are perceived as equipollent may prevent any normative claim from being genuinely overriding. The normative claims will be employed in an ad hoc fashion, with the agent sometimes assigning priority to one and sometimes the other. Recognition of the ad hoc nature of these weightings may make the commitments themselves dissolve. For the agent becomes indifferent to the conflict between them. Or, if not indifferent, at least detached from it; she can't see it as truly important.

To illustrate this, I will offer two deliberately clichéd examples. These are examples that involve reflection on foundational normative principles, although analogous cases could be constructed with more particular, derivative reasons or principles.

> (Sebastian) From his youth, Sebastian embraces a strongly materialistic view. He treats wealth as his highest value, overriding all other values. He conceptualizes a successful life in terms of the acquisition of wealth and property. He wholeheartedly devotes himself to his work, spending long hours and late nights working in an investment bank. Most of his waking life is spent at work, with all other interests subordinated to his career. He has enormous success, acquiring vast wealth, buying fine apartments in several cities, collecting cars, dining at extravagant restaurants.
>
> But then one day he reflects on his prioritization of wealth over all other values. He begins to wonder why he took that value to be so important. Other goals tempt him: he fantasizes about having a family, or devoting himself to travel, or becoming a monk. But he cannot find any good reason for adopting these goals; when pressed, he cannot justify them over his current pursuits. Nor can he find any adequate reason for continuing to prioritize wealth over these competing goals. As a result, he is troubled. Nothing seems to him worthy of wholehearted pursuit. His passion and commitment begin to die out. He drifts along, still pursuing the same materialistic ends, but without the same energy and engagement. He has achieved what he sought, but he sees no reason to value these attainments over others. He might as well have done something else, or nothing at all. To put it in our terminology: he cannot find a good justification for treating wealth as prioritized over other values. And, absent this justification, the commitment to the prioritization of that value begins to taper off. He still values wealth, but what once overrode all competing concerns is now something weaker, something whose motivational effects are attenuated, something that competes, often unsuccessfully, with other values, perhaps even with passing fancies and whims. So the man who never took a vacation, who worked tirelessly, now clocks out at 5pm, lingers on beaches, takes retreats, and yet is always drawn back again, halfheartedly.

Or consider a second example.

> (Madeline) Madeline grows up immersed in a religious culture. She's Catholic, let's say, and is raised by devoutly religious parents. Her social activities center

around her church. The religion provides a host of concrete norms and values with a strongly hierarchical structure. Certain norms are treated as inviolable; certain norms are treated as possessing a gravity that others lack. Mundane personal pursuits and comforts are subordinated to service to God. Devotion to God is treated as outweighing all competing normative claims.

But then she goes to college. She moves away to a distant city, making new friends and having new experiences. She is exposed to new normative weightings. In her new social group, equality and a respect for diversity are treated as sacred values; anything that conflicts with them is problematized. She sees some of the associated norms as conflicting with those of her religion. Homosexuality is wrong, according to her religious view, and yet the contrary position is adopted by her friends. Sex outside marriage is forbidden, she believes, and yet she finds herself surrounded by those who disagree.

So Madeline is directly confronted, in a very familiar way, by a challenge to her religious values. And let's suppose she reflects. She cannot find a decisive justification for her religious values. She sees that (an interpretation of) her religion forbids what the alternative values permit. And, again for perfectly familiar reasons, she is torn. She finds that she cannot give up her religious views. But she also cannot wholeheartedly condemn those who violate the norms that she sees as integral to that view.

So, while she still believes, she finds herself compromising her principles. Homosexuality is wrong, she tells herself, and yet her dear friend is homosexual; she can't bring herself to condemn him. Sex outside marriage is wrong, she sincerely believes, and yet the temptations are too great. So she compromises. And over time her religious principles feature less and less in her life. She recognizes that the religious values proscribe certain behaviors, such as sex outside of marriage. She recognizes that mundane material ends are outweighed by sacred ends. Nonetheless, the grip of these norms begins to fade. They do motivate her, to some extent; when she thinks about them she does feel guilt or unease. But not enough to change anything. And although at first these conflicts are great, these emotions strong, they wither. In time, she's just a casual adherent of Catholicism, who purports to accept the various religiously inspired principles, but doesn't let them play much role in her life, who lets them be overridden by any passing whim.[15]

---

[15] We can imagine an alternative response: perhaps Madeline will try to distinguish a *core, unwavering* religious belief from *subsidiary, negotiable* religious beliefs. Perhaps she will come to think that the spiritual core of her religion is something like *devotion to God*, and that prohibitions on various forms of sexuality are less important. If so, she might manage to preserve a lexically prioritized value by cleaving it off from subsidiary commitments. I take it that this is a fairly common occurrence; I defer it for now but return to it in Chapter 9.

I hope these examples seem familiar. They should seem like tropes, instantiated in many films, works of literature, and so on. Their ubiquity suggests something important. For these examples have an analogous structure:

- The person initially accepts some value (or set of values, or normative principles, etc.), believing (perhaps in an uncritical or unreflective fashion) that it should outweigh competing values.
- At some point, the person comes to believe that a justification for treating this value as outweighing others is unavailable. (In the first case, this is sparked by critical reflection alone; in the second, by new experiences that prompt critical reflection.)
- In light of this belief, the behavior associated with that value is modified. The person remains committed to the value, but her commitment is attenuated. Her behavior no longer reflects a commitment to the idea that the value is to be prioritized over competing values. Instead, the value is treated as fungible.

In short: once the person begins to question the justification for particular normative weightings, those weightings are destabilized. What was formerly treated as overriding is now treated as fungible. The original values (wealth in one case, religious commitments in the other) remain, but in an attenuated form.

Considering these examples, let's ask: if weightings of normative claims cannot be seen, by the person, as justified, what happens? Would everything go on as before?

I think these examples suggest that the answer is no. Ethical life wouldn't go on as before. Of course, people wouldn't stop weighting things. But their commitment to these weightings would dissipate; they'd come to play less central roles, in the aggregate. Although any particular individual might go on prioritizing particular normative claims, there would be a tendency for strong commitments to these normative weightings to dissolve.

That's what happens in these cases. The person initially treats certain norms as outweighing others, based on religious grounds or assimilation of materialistic cultural tendencies. Eventually, she abandons this weighting, coming to see it as lacking justification. This results in an attenuation of the behavior that was formerly governed by the sense that one normative commitment outweighs others. The person still holds the original value, and this value still exerts some influence; but what was once resolute and uncompromising is now wavering and fungible.

And we can imagine cultural analogues of these examples. Imagine a culture that accepts traditional Catholic values. It is strongly governed by these norms; most individuals in the community recognize them as valid and attempt to regulate their behavior by them. The norms are taken to be sourced in divine revelation, and their authority is incontrovertible. So everyone generally follows them. But then, over time, the religious beliefs grounding these norms fade. Belief in a divine entity is no longer taken as given, as incontrovertible. Doubt arises. And with it, conformity to the religious norms begins to drop off. Not completely, of course: people still follow them. But people talk about them less, and they come to play an altogether less pervasive role in the ethical life of the community. When asked, everyone can cite the relevant norms perfectly well. But they don't care as intensely about them. They may adopt these norms; they may regulate their behavior with them from time to time. But they aren't committed to them in any deep sense. They do not exert the authority that they once did. They are overridden when perceived as too demanding, too difficult, or too inconvenient to enforce. They are treated as fungible, whereas formerly they were incontrovertible.[16]

In fact, the problem may be even more pressing when conceived as a cultural rather than individual problem. For we can distinguish the way in which *I* hold certain values from the way in which a culture holds certain values. Any particular individual might treat a value as prioritized for idiosyncratic reasons involving personal preference, lack of imagination, laziness, stubbornness, and so on. For a culture to treat a value as prioritized, though, it might need to support the value with publicly available justifications. In a pluralistic culture, the unavailability of these justifications seems likely to erode the value's status.

Lacking justification and faced with competition from alternative values, the grip of these values tends to fade. Indeed, Adam Smith emphasized precisely this, arguing that religious zeal and fanatical devotion to sacred values would be tempered if society contained not just one or two, but many competing sources of sacred values:

> The interested and active zeal of religious teachers can be dangerous and troublesome only where there is either but one sect tolerated in the society, or where the whole of a large society is divided into two or three great sects...But that zeal must be altogether innocent where the society is divided into two or three hundred, or perhaps into as many thousand small sects, of which no one could be considerable enough to disturb the public tranquility.
> (Smith 1776/2000: V.1.197–9)

For, in what we'd today call a pluralistic society, the proponents of each ideal "would be obliged to learn...candour and moderation" so as to attract adherents; and, rather than preaching an "austere" set of ideals and gravely condemning violations, they would have to allow "a good deal of indulgence," and violations of norms would have to be "easily either excused or pardoned altogether" (Smith 1776/2000: V.1.197–9). Smith, hoping to attenuate the power of the clergy, held

---

[16] For perceptive discussions of a related phenomenon, see Taylor's discussions of secularization in Taylor 2007.

this out as an ideal. But it is a point made familiar by Nietzsche that, with the attenuation of religiously inspired ideals, the threat of nihilism emerges. For Smith's point is more powerful than he realizes: it is not just religiously inspired ideals that would lose their force when faced with a demand that they be justified over competing ideals. This is a potential problem for all normative weightings.

In light of these reflections, I submit that Normative Dissipation is a problem not just for exemplary rational agents, but also for typical, run-of-the-mill agents.

Of course, I don't mean that *every* agent who accepts Normative Weighting Skepticism will experience Normative Dissipation for *every* set of weighted norms. Certainly, there would counterexamples to the thesis if it were presented as an exceptionless generalization about human behavior. But that's true of all psychological generalizations. People are complicated. Exceptions arise. Even modest theses such as "people do what they desire" or "people avoid painful experiences" have multiple exceptions. In particular, we will find agents failing to manifest Normative Dissipation in cases that involve norms which are firmly rooted in powerful and largely fixed motivational tendencies. An agent who formerly regarded *self-preservation* as more important than *environmental preservation,* but who now finds himself unable to justify that claim, is probably still going to prioritize saving his life over recycling his bottles. Certain normative commitments are so tightly bound to powerful, recalcitrant motives (such as self-preservation) that they will almost certainly survive independently of any doubts about their justificatory status.

But these are exceptions. Many of our normative commitments are not like this. Commitments to justice, compassion, generosity, fairness, environmental preservation, and so forth might not be similarly immunized from critical reflection—especially when remaining committed to them necessitates surmounting challenges and making sacrifices. So, too, commitments that center on more distant or more abstract goals—counteracting climate change, reducing one's environmental impact, helping distant strangers, etc.—seem particularly likely to be good cases of Normative Dissipation for typical agents.[17]

5.9 Sacred Values Forestall Normative Weighting Skepticism

At the outset, I mentioned that Nietzsche associates nihilism with the loss of sacred values. We are now in a position to see why. In particular: sacred values

---

[17] Even if it's true in general that Normative Dissipation obtains, might we try to prevent this? Could it be rational to work on our behavior, inculcating a disposition to remain behaviorally committed to N_1's outweighing N_2 even when we think we lack a sufficient justification for treating it as doing so? Of course, one way of doing so would be by self-deception. We could falsify the evidence. We could cultivate ignorance. In short, we could *ignore, hide, or disguise* the fact that we lack justification for prioritizing N_1 over N_2. But could a rational agent clearheadedly and in full consciousness accept nihilism without succumbing to Normative Dissipation? I address this question in Chapter 9.

prevent Normative Dissipation, and thereby block a form of nihilism. Let me explain.

Normative Dissipation is a motivational problem that arises from a justificatory problem: because I see myself as lacking adequate justification for prioritizing one value over another, I experience a slackening of commitment to both values. But notice that this phenomenon cannot arise if one of the values is sacralized: the sacralized value will be seen as prioritized over the ordinary value, and the commitment to the sacred value won't be affected by justificatory reasoning (recall that sacred values are dialectically invulnerable). So, if you have sacred values, you can't be a (full-fledged) nihilist; if you don't, avoiding nihilism would require either avoiding critical reflection or finding convincing justifications for your normative weightings.[18] Nietzsche (on most readings) thinks we can't do the latter, so it's no surprise that he worries that the collapse of traditional sources of sacred values (principally religions) will usher in widespread nihilism.

That said, having sacred values won't rule out all forms of Normative Dissipation. An agent might have sacred values that apply only to a limited range of cases. Suppose the *only* sacred value that I accept is the dignity of human life. There will be many cases in which I deliberate about things that don't concern human life. For example, when I deliberate about whether it's permissible to eat animals, or whether to prioritize intellectual development over pleasure, or whether it's okay to drive an SUV, my sacred value won't apply in any obvious way. In these cases, I might face Normative Weighting Skepticism and hence Normative Dissipation.

We can also consider cases in which the agent experiences a conflict between two or more sacred values. Suppose, for example, that both *human life* and *territorial integrity* are treated as sacred values, yet a situation arises in which preserving territorial integrity requires sacrificing human life. Could Normative Dissipation arise?

It could not. Notice that this is true simply by definition. I have defined sacred values as Dialectically Invulnerable: one's degree of commitment to the value is not affected by justificatory reasoning. But Normative Dissipation is a claim about how justificatory reasoning affects one's degree of commitment to a value: it says, in effect, that when justificatory reasoning reveals the value to be problematic (in particular, when the reasoning reveals inadequate justification for prioritizing one value over another), the agent's behavior and motivation changes. Insofar as a value is Dialectically Invulnerable, this won't be true; so, insofar as a value is sacralized, Normative Dissipation won't occur.

That might seem like a cheat: it might seem like I am just defining sacred values in a way that enables them to escape the dilemma that I have articulated in

---

[18] I include the caveat "full-fledged" because, as I explain in the following paragraphs, restricted forms of normative weighting skepticism can still arise for those with sacred values.

this chapter. But recall that we have independent reasons for thinking that sacred values exhibit Dialectical Invulnerability: there are empirical psychological studies establishing that certain values have this feature. Part of the point of marking out a distinct class of values, the sacred, was to highlight this feature.

So anything that counts as a sacred value will be immunized from Normative Dissipation. And notice that this conforms to our experience of tragic conflicts (cases in which two sacred values conflict). In tragic conflicts, agents tend *not* to be motivationally disengaged from either of the conflicting values. On the contrary, agents tend to experience a moral remainder: regardless of which value they sacrifice, they feel that they have acted wrongly. This suggests that they remain committed to both values despite prioritizing one over the other. Moreover, in these cases agents often feel the need to engage in some form of moral cleansing: they attempt to atone for their violation of a sacred value. Again, this suggests that the motivational and behavioral components of the agents' valuing do not dissipate or slacken. For discussions of these points, see Chapter 2, Sections 2.1–2.2.

5.10 Conclusion

I have argued that although standard versions of nihilism may be problematic, there is a version of nihilism that presents more difficulties. The nihilist, as I've defined her, accepts Normative Weighting Skepticism. She thinks that in an important range of cases, it is reasonable to believe that we lack sufficient justification for treating one normative commitment as outweighing another. Given that reaching an all-things-considered judgment about what one ought to do in a given case typically requires assigning relative weights to competing normative claims, the nihilist finds herself unable to determine which actions she ought to perform. I've argued that this position does not require the agent to have any generalized doubts about the project of justifying normative claims. The nihilist is happy to see various normative claims as justified; what she denies is that we can find sufficient justification for assigning relative weights to normative claims. While this version of nihilism is not immune to challenges and does depend on certain presuppositions about responses to moral uncertainty, I've argued that it is a reasonable position. Moreover, I've suggested that nihilism, so understood, is no idle concern: if accepted, rational agents would experience Normative Dissipation; and this would tend to alter their behavior. Finally, I have suggested that we can avoid full-fledged nihilism by holding sacred values.

6
The Enlightenment Account of Fanaticism

So far, I have been focusing on the positive aspects of sacred values: I have shown how they sustain certain valuable forms of ethical life and how they stave off a type of nihilism. But sacred values aren't unambiguously positive. Consider some of the examples of sacred values that I mentioned in the introduction: sacred values pertaining to territorial integrity, gun rights, nationalism, authoritarianism, and certain religions. It's obvious that certain sacred values promote division, opposition, and sometimes outright violence.

There are two ways of viewing this. One view is that sacred values are objectionable merely in virtue of their formal features. In other words, *any* value that prohibits tradeoffs, prohibits comparisons, and is dialectically invulnerable will be objectionable. I hope my arguments in the previous chapters have shown that this is false. Instead, we should endorse a more nuanced view. Some sacred values are objectionable merely in virtue of their content, rather than their status as sacred; others are objectionable because of the combination of particular contents with the sacralizing attitudes. But this leaves room for unobjectionable and even praiseworthy sacred values. The mere fact that a value is sacralized is not in itself a reason for treating it as objectionable.

Nonetheless, there is something to the idea that sacred values promote violence and opposition. In Chapters 6-8, I examine the way in which sacred values can promote certain forms of pathology at both the individual and group levels. In particular, sacred values can give rise to *fanaticism*.

* * *

The term "fanatic" has lately come to enjoy a central place in discussions of political orientation, religion, and, especially, terrorism. We are told that proponents of certain political views are fanatics; that fanaticism inspires terrorism and religious extremism; that fanaticism drives us to violence; that fanaticism is becoming increasingly widespread. But what, if anything, is fanaticism? Does the term pick out a single condition? Or does it merely serve as a term of abuse, picking out any class of passionate behavior that the speaker views as misguided?

Philosophy of Devotion: The Longing for Invulnerable Ideals. Paul Katsafanas, Oxford University Press.
© Paul Katsafanas 2022. DOI: 10.1093/oso/9780192867674.003.0006

Today, philosophical analyses of fanaticism are rare.[1] But it was not always so: in the early modern period, the "fanatic" or the "enthusiast," as he was alternately called, was one of the central targets of ethical theory. Philosophers including Locke, Hume, Shaftesbury, Wolff, and Kant endeavored to provide an account of fanaticism. While the details varied, there was agreement on three central points: fanaticism was analyzed as (1) unwavering commitment to an ideal, together with (2) unwillingness to subject the ideal (or its premises) to rational critique and (3) the presumption of a non-rational sanction for the ideal. Thus, the prototypical fanatic is the person who "raves with reason" (Kant 1999: 5:275), insisting on a personal sanction for some ideal or goal to which he is committed, while refusing to submit this ideal or goal to rational critique. Call this the Enlightenment account of fanaticism.

This chapter has two goals. First, I argue that the Enlightenment account of fanaticism is inadequate. The Enlightenment account does define a particular type of rational failing, which I call being a *true believer*. But you can be a true believer without being a fanatic. Which brings me to my second goal: while their account fails, Enlightenment thinkers were right to attempt an analysis of fanaticism. For, I argue, there is a particular type of *vice* or *practical defect* that merits the label fanaticism. And it's a peculiar kind of vice: it blends a purely rational failure with a distinctively moral failing. In characterizing this state, I will try to bring into view an underappreciated mode of ethical critique: we can show that certain ethical views, or certain ways of understanding ethical distinctions, are defective not because they are false or incoherent, but because they promote distinctive forms of individual or social pathology. (This is a mode of philosophical critique that certain nineteenth century thinkers, including Kierkegaard and Nietzsche, discuss and rely upon; but it has been largely forgotten. When remembered, it is usually dismissed as a mode of *ad hominem*.)

The plan of the chapter is as follows. Section 6.1 introduces central cases of fanaticism and considers the possibility that the term "fanatic" fails to pick out any unified class. Section 6.2 explicates the Enlightenment account of fanaticism. Section 6.3 argues that this account does not succeed: it characterizes a rational defect that I call being a *true believer,* but the true believer is not necessarily a fanatic. This will put us in position, in the next chapter, to offer a different and more successful account of fanaticism.

6.1 Central Cases of Fanaticism

First, let's address a concern about the very attempt to analyze fanaticism. Might fanaticism be nothing more than a term of abuse? After all, one person's fanatic is

---

[1] There are a few exceptions, including Colas 1997, Toscano 2010, Crosson 2003, Passmore 2003, and Cassam 2022. And there are many explorations of the early modern accounts; see, for example, Klein and La Vopa 1998, La Vopa 1997 and Zuckert 2010. I will discuss some of these works below.

another person's rational actor. History indicates that this is a danger. The early modern period witnessed various branches of Christianity each accusing the other of fanaticism.[2] More recently, the Abolitionists declared the proponents of slavery to be fanatical, and were, in turn, labeled fanatical by their opponents.[3] Kant tells us that Taoists are fanatics; Nietzsche says that Kant himself is a fanatic.[4] Today, the label is often applied to proponents of religious fundamentalism and, most notably, to members of terrorist groups. But not exclusively: witness Newt Gingrich's claim that "secular fanaticism" is responsible for attempts to ban displays of crosses on public property, or the Discovery Institute's missives against "animal rights fanaticism."[5]

It's tempting to conclude that the charge of fanaticism is based on nothing more than denunciation of commitments that the speaker regards as unreasonable. And the term surely does function in that way in ordinary discourse.[6] But it would be a mistake to take this as decisive. Terms such as "psychopath," "nihilist," "skeptic," and "egoist" also have loose uses in ordinary discourse, but can be rendered precise enough to pick out philosophically interesting kinds. Just so, I will argue, with fanaticism.

To see this, let's focus on some paradigm cases. Although the term is widely used, the prototypical western image of the fanatic is the violent religious extremist, who takes himself to have divine sanction for terrible acts of cruelty and oppression. The term acquires these connotations in the 1500s, when Martin Luther employs it with alarming frequency to denounce his opponents: he never tires of warning of the dangers of the frenzied swarms of peasants and field preachers, raving about illusory religious revelations and upending the social order: these *swarms* of fanatics, compared to beasts and herds driven mad, must be stopped at all costs (see La Vopa 1997).[7] Analogously, in the early modern period we find Locke, Shaftesbury, and others presenting the fanatic as the

---

[2] For example, Melanchthon writes, "The Anabaptists scorn both priests and their ordination and imagine it necessary to wait for new revelations and illuminations from God, which they seek to obtain by means of bodily macerations such as monks and other enthusiasts have invented. Their fanatic ravings should be abominated" (quoted from Colas 1997: 12).

[3] In 1836, Calhoun addressed the US Senate, claiming that abolitionists wage "a war of religious and political fanaticism...the object is to humble and debase us [i.e., white men]" (Cralle 1864: 483–4). In 1816, Wilberforce had responded to this trope of identifying abolitionists with fanatics as follows: "If to be feeling alive to the sufferings of my fellow-creatures is to be a fanatic, I am one of the most incurable fanatics ever permitted to be at large."

[4] Kant 2001: 8:335–6 and Nietzsche 1997: Preface §3.

[5] See, for example, http://politicalticker.blogs.cnn.com/2011/04/27/gingrich-blasts-secular-fanaticism-at-prayer-breakfast/comment-page-1/; http://www.discovery.org/a/25261; and http://www.evolutionnews.org/2016/09/the_human_cost103118.html.

[6] Consider just how broadly the term is applied: we might speak of the football fan who riots after his team's win as a fanatic, or we might speak of the fanatical tendencies present in the Trekkie who goes to each convention, or the groupie who appears at each performance of the band. Here, too, we have little more than denunciation of commitment that outsiders judge to be unreasonable.

[7] Before Luther, the term wasn't strongly associated with violence. In antiquity, for example, the term simply picked out those who were inspired to passionate or frenzied behavior by temple rituals.

religious individual who diverges from the mainstream view and condones violence. Today, the idealized member of ISIS provides a clear case: imagine a jihadi who embraces a set of values that are extremely demanding, requiring devotion and great personal sacrifice. He views his activities as profoundly meaningful. He views his values as excluding competing ways of life. His values make possible a distinctive community. And, of course, his ideals demand violence.[8] Violent white nationalism has the same structure, with individuals making extreme personal sacrifices and engaging in horrific violence in pursuit of (what they take to be) divinely sanctioned ideals that confer meaning on their lives (see Stern 2003 for interviews with some of these individuals).

But I think it will help to consider an actual case, described at some length. Although the DSM-5 doesn't treat fanaticism as a psychological condition, it used to be recognized as a mental disorder. In 1880, the *Boston Medical and Surgical Journal* (which later became the *New England Journal of Medicine*) published case histories of fanaticism. Examining one such case in detail will be useful.

Charles Freeman worked as a farmer and mail carrier in a small Massachusetts village. He lived with his wife and two daughters. In February 1878, at the age of thirty-three, he was struck by a sermon while attending church: "he heard the Old Testament preached" and reflected that "no one lived up to the religion which he professed to believe" (Folsom 1880: 265). He resolved to "lead a new life of devotion to the Word and Spirit of God" (Folsom 1880: 265). Shortly thereafter, he began experiencing personal "communications" from God, which constituted "direct relations with God" (Folsom 1880: 266). He described these communiques thus: "In these communications from the Lord there was no act of the will, but they came beyond his power to bring them or prevent their coming. They were always accompanied with a peculiar, indescribable sensation" (Folsom 1880: 265). These communications placed demands upon Freeman. For example, in one communication, "the Lord required him to give up [sexual] relations with his wife."

A few months later, on April 29, his wife read him a paper discussing Abraham's sacrifice of Isaac, and asked him if he could perform such a great sacrifice. Within a day, Freeman concluded that the Lord required him to sacrifice someone, though he was not sure whether this was his wife or one of his children. On April 30, a "tramp" asked Freeman for food; Freeman provided him with a generous meal, and, in gratitude, the tramp gave Freeman an old knife. That night, around 1am, Freeman woke and believed himself to have a vision: "the Lord meant to test his faith by asking him, as did Abraham, to kill his beloved child" (Folsom 1880: 266). His wife tried to dissuade him, but he collected the knife. He assured his wife that "all God wanted was a test of his faith... He would not require the deed to be done." He went to his child's room, where she was sound

---

[8] My concern isn't whether this is accurate; all that matters, for my purposes, is that this is the way that those who use the term "fanatic" envision its target. For this type of reading of ISIS, see Wood 2015.

asleep. "He then raised [his knife] to the highest, kept it up a long time to give God plenty of time, brought it down and struck the bed. He then raised it again, and, on bringing it down pierced the walls of the heart, when the child died almost instantly" (Folsom 1880: 266).

Freeman was untroubled by the murder of his daughter. Almost immediately after the murder, he experienced a new revelation that the child would be resurrected by the morning. After convincing his wife of this, they went to sleep. In the morning, when the child remained dead, "he had another revelation that she would [rise] on the third day" (Folsom 1880: 267). He invited twenty Adventists over to his house, explaining his revelations and showing them the corpse of the child. "He finally convinced them of her resurrection on the third day" (Folsom 1880: 267). The following day, having learned of the murder, the constable arrested Freeman and his wife. The pair still believed that his act was justified and that the child would be alive the next day: "He told his family physician that he should kill the other child if the Lord required it, and his wife sat quietly by darning stockings... sure that whatever happened the resurrection on the third day would fully justify the deed." The passage of the third day, with the child remaining dead, had no effect on Freeman's certainty: "When the child did not rise on the third day he was not troubled in the least, as he said the word day was used in the scriptural sense, and he did not know its length" (Folsom 1880: 267).

The author of the case history tells us that the fanaticism of "Mr. F. and his wife cannot be a matter of dispute among competent persons" (Folsom 1880: 271). I will take this as an uncontroversial case: if anything is fanaticism, this is.

These cases display several intriguing features:

Unwavering commitment to an ideal: the fanatic is willing to make extreme sacrifices, including even his own life, in order to promote or preserve his ideal. The costs of this course of action do not sway him. So, whereas most individuals make tradeoffs, abandoning their commitments when the costs of holding to them prove too high, the fanatic treats his ideal as warranting any sacrifice. Relatedly, the fanatic is willing to persevere in his ideal even when the prospects for achieving or promoting his ideal seem, at best, highly dubious. Instrumental calculations of the likelihood of attaining that ideal do not feature prominently in his reasoning.

Unwavering certainty about the ideal: the fanatic's confidence in his ideal does not track what others would describe as its rational warrant. Most of us would experience some doubts about the veracity of these experiences; most of us would take their outlandishness and peculiarity to undermine them. But not the fanatic. Although he sees that others do not accept the ideal, he treats them as making a profound mistake. Rational critiques of the ideal hold no force for him.

Localization of this certitude: the fanatic is unconditionally committed to the truth of some set of claims, and won't let contrary evidence sway him. But what's astonishing about the fanatic is the degree to which the rational defect is localized. Freeman is calm, collected, with a veneer of rationality. He doesn't rave. He sincerely believes that he is correct, that his actions are justified. Contrary evidence is explained away, often quite skillfully. For example, it's true that Biblical terms such as "day" are often interpreted as having ambiguous or uncertain meanings. He's not being irrational in insisting on this point; it's actually quite clever. And this is typical of the fanatic: he embraces goals that we view as unsupported or misguided, but he's entirely sensible in his pursuit of them. The prototypical proponents of ISIS, too, fit that mold: although we see their goals and their methods as abhorrent, they reason quite well about the implications of those goals, the strategies for implementing them, and so on. Thus, ISIS's online magazine *Dabiq* contains FAQs about permissible behavior, reasoning about whether it's permissible to rape children (yes, so long as the child is old enough for it to be physically possible; otherwise, you must be content with forcing the child to perform other sexual acts) and enslave women (yes for Jews and Christians; no for apostates.)[9] The answers, grotesque as they are, are not arbitrary: they are reasoned conclusions from accepted premises. They aspire to norms of consistency and coherence. So what's odd is that the fanatic's rational defect is quite local: the fanatics themselves don't display a generalized inability to assess evidence, to draw rational conclusions, and so on. Rather, they display fixity in just one area or even on just one point.

Intolerance and violence: what stands out about fanaticism is its intolerance, its violence. The central cases of fanaticism involve attempts to impose some ideal or value on others who do not share it. The child doesn't consent to her murder; the person enslaved by ISIS doesn't consent to enslavement; even the looser uses of fanaticism, such as Gingrich's tirades against "secular fanaticism", focus on the perceived attempt to impose values on one who doesn't share them. So the fanatic manifests a particular form of intolerance: he attempts to impose his values on those who do not share them, and is often willing to undertake violent means in order to do so.

Religious provenance of the ideals: the ideals accepted by fanatics often have a religious provenance. Both of my examples fit that mold. It's commonly assumed that fanatics are religiously inspired. Locke tells us that the fanatic has unrestrained "fancies" of personal revelation; Kant tells us that the fanatic "believes itself to feel an immediate and extraordinary communion with a higher nature";

---

[9] See the pamphlet entitled "Questions and Answers on Taking Captives and Slaves." A translation and excerpt is available in Roth 2015. "Question 13: Is it permissible to have intercourse with a female slave who has not reached puberty? It is permissible to have intercourse with the female slave who hasn't reached puberty if she is fit for intercourse; however if she is not fit for intercourse, then it is enough to enjoy her without intercourse." "Question 3: Can all unbelieving women be taken captive? There is no dispute among the scholars that it is permissible to capture unbelieving women [who are characterized by] original unbelief [*kufrasli*], such as the *kitabiyat* [Jews and Christians] and polytheists. However, [the scholars] are disputed over [the issue of] capturing apostate women. The consensus leans towards forbidding it, though some people of knowledge think it permissible. We [ISIS] lean towards accepting the consensus..."

A.P. Martinich defines a fanatic as "a person who purports to place all...value in things of some transcendent realm [and attaches]...no or only derivative value...to this world" (Martinich 2000: 419). Nietzsche extends this: for him, it is not necessarily a religious belief that motivates fanaticism, but it will at least involve an aspiration to something beyond this world, as in Kant. (Below, I will suggest that fanaticism needn't be religiously inspired.)

Group orientation: the fanatic is part of a group and thinks of his identity as constituted by his commitment to this group. Freeman, for example, is an Adventist and sees this as a central feature of his identity. Isolated fanatics are very rare, and even when we find an apparently isolated fanatic the individual often identifies with some broader group of like-minded individuals.[10] Moreover, the fanatic typically needs another group to react against. For the fanatic takes his personal revelations to legitimate the elimination or overturning of widely accepted norms. He sees those who don't accept his ideals not as people embracing valid alternatives, but as foes to be contended with, dealt with, or simply eliminated.

The prototypical fanatic, then, is the individual who is unconditionally committed to the truth of some claim, unwilling to let his degree of certainty in the claim track rational assessment of its warrant, intolerant, willing to resort to violence, typically religious, and oriented toward groups. But this is an odd cluster of features. They seem unrelated: people can manifest some of them without manifesting others. I can be supremely confident in some ideal (equality, environmental preservation, justice, etc.); this confidence can outstrip my rational warrant for the ideal; and yet I can be perfectly tolerant and peaceful. Or, I can be exceptionally intolerant, forcibly and even violently imposing my ideals on others, without displaying any deep commitment to these ideals and while thinking that these ideals are questionable. And so on.

So we might wonder: is there anything philosophically interesting about fanaticism? Or is it just a cluster of unrelated features, together constituting a type of dogmatism and intolerance that we regard as objectionable?

6.2 The Enlightenment Account of Fanaticism

Several Enlightenment thinkers offer a philosophical diagnosis of fanaticism. These thinkers don't see fanaticism as a haphazard series of disconnected states.

---

[10] As I explain below, the fanatic need not be in physical or even temporal proximity to the individuals with whom he identifies. For example, the Unabomber (Ted Kaczynski) was physically isolated but identified with certain Christian anarchists such as Jacques Ellul. Or, for a more recent example, consider Anders Behring Breivik, who spent nine years planning his 2011 Norwegian terrorist attacks (which killed 77 people). Although he acted alone and was socially isolated, he identified with several right wing extremist groups; see his 1500-page manifesto entitled "2083: A European Declaration of Independence."

Instead, they treat it as arising from a defect of rationality. In this section I will introduce the defect; in the next section I will argue that the Enlightenment account is inadequate.

Sparked by Enlightenment optimism and pervasive religious conflicts, philosophers including Locke, Hume, Shaftesbury, and Kant offered philosophical analyses of fanaticism.[11] Many of these thinkers treat fanaticism as a product of irrational commitments fostered by religious dogma. The excessive enthusiasm cultivated and promoted by religion could, they argue, be reduced by the development of more rational approaches to meeting human needs.

To see this, consider some characteristic accounts of fanaticism. Locke emphasizes the way in which the fanatic is impervious to rational argumentation:

> Reason is lost upon [fanatics], they are above it: they see the light infused into their understandings, and cannot be mistaken; it is clear and visible there, like the light of bright sunshine; shows itself, and needs no other proof but its own evidence: they feel the hand of God moving them within, and the impulses of the Spirit, and cannot be mistaken in what they feel. (Locke 1975: chapter 19)

For Locke, the fanatic is the person who presumes to have religiously sanctioned, unerring insight about some point. He cannot be reasoned with; rational argumentation won't dislodge his presumed insight.

Hume makes the same point:

> The inspired person comes to regard himself as a distinguished favorite of the Divinity; and when this frenzy once takes place, which is the summit of enthusiasm, every whimsy is consecrated: Human reason, and even morality are rejected as fallacious guides: And the fanatic madman delivers himself over, blindly, and without reserve, to the supposed illapses of the spirit, and to inspiration from above. Hope, pride, presumption, a warm imagination, together with ignorance, are, therefore, the true sources of ENTHUSIASM.
> (Hume 1985: "Of Superstition and Enthusiasm")

Again, the fanatic is the person who presumes to have divinely inspired insight, which goes beyond the domain of rational thought. Hume notes that this presumption leads to unreserved devotion to the ideal.

And, of course, unreserved devotion sanctioned by ideals that are taken to be unassailable can be quite dangerous. Here's Shaftesbury:

---

[11] The term "enthusiast" is initially more common than "fanatic," but I will take these as equivalent.

Fury flies from face to face, and the disease [enthusiasm] is no sooner seen than caught. They who in a better situation of mind have beheld a multitude under the power of passion, have owned that they saw in the countenance of men something more ghastly and terrible than at other times expressed on the most passionate occasions. Such force has society in ill as well as in good passions, and so much stronger any affection is for being social and communicative.
(Shaftesbury 1999: 10)

There's palpable fear of the fanatic here. The fanatic's refusal to entertain doubts about his belief makes him unwilling to compromise, unwilling to tolerate alternative views. So the fanatic is not only irrational and immune to argument: he is also dangerous.

One more example, from Kant. Kant complicates this standard account by introducing a distinction between *mere enthusiasm* and *fanaticism*.[12] He writes,

Fanaticism [*Schwärmerei*] must always be distinguished from *enthusiasm* [*Enthusiasmus*]. The former believes itself to feel an immediate and extraordinary communion with a higher nature, the latter signifies the state of the mind which is inflamed beyond the appropriate degree by some principle, whether it be by the maxim of patriotic virtue, or of friendship, or of religion, without involving the illusion of a supernatural community.   (Kant 2007: 2:251n)

For Kant, enthusiasm is simply heightened, excessive attachment: the enthusiast is "inflamed beyond the appropriate degree." The football fan who celebrates his team's win by cheering with friends is not an enthusiast; the fan who riots, destroying property in an orgy of feeling, is an enthusiast.

Fanaticism is different: the fanatic takes himself to have some access to a "higher nature," such as a divine revelation. As Kant puts it elsewhere, the fanatic "is properly a deranged person with presumed immediate inspiration and a great familiarity with the powers of the heavens. Human nature knows no more dangerous illusion" (Kant 2007: 2:267). So the fanatic, for Kant, is enthusiastic, but takes this enthusiasm to be certified by some insight that is beyond the realm of rational inquiry. Once you calm down the riotous football enthusiast, once the passion dissipates and he heads home, he won't try to certify his behavior by appeal to divinity; if he's an ordinary enthusiast, he will admit that he was carried away, that his behavior was inappropriate, and so on. Not so with the fanatic: the fanatic will insist that his behavior is correct or justified. So, while enthusiasm is principally an affective or emotional matter—it consists simply in having and acting on passions to an inappropriate degree—fanaticism is, additionally, a defect

---

[12] Zuckert 2010 offers a helpful reconstruction of Kant's views on this topic.

of *reason*. The fanatic is the enthusiast who presumes an authoritative justification for his "inflamed" passions and actions.

As these passages indicate, there is substantial agreement between Locke, Hume, Shaftesbury, and Kant on the nature of fanaticism.[13] All four of these philosophers take the fanatic to be characterized by the following traits:

E1. Unwavering commitment to an ideal.
E2. Unwillingness to subject the ideal (or its premises) to rational critique.
E3. The presumption of a non-rational sanction for the ideal (or its premises).

The first claim picks out a certain type of behavior: the individual is wholehearted with respect to his ideal. One form of this is Kantian enthusiasm: inflamed passions consume the individual. Enthusiasm needn't devolve into fanaticism, but it can. Suppose the second feature is present: the individual refuses to engage in serious critique of the ideal. The individual may, of course, offer elaborate arguments for his ideal, may reason about his ideal's implications, and so forth. But at some point, there will be something about which the fanatic refuses to entertain doubts. And claim (E3) explains why: the fanatic takes his ideal to have some kind of non-rational sanction, some support beyond the domain of shared rational inquiry. When these features are present, we have fanaticism.

Conditions (E2) and (E3) require some clarification. In particular, consider condition (E3)'s appeal to the presence of a non-rational sanction for the ideal. What, precisely, is the distinction between rational and non-rational sanctions?

Several of the quotations above mention refusing to entertain doubts and abstaining from rational critique (condition E2); accordingly, we might conclude that the Enlightenment accounts treat a justification as non-rational if the person is unwilling to entertain doubts about it. However, this would be too hasty. Strictly speaking, the Enlightenment account is not committed to the claim that *unwillingness to doubt* is always problematic. After all, it might be perfectly rational to refuse to doubt that triangles have three sides or that emeralds are green. What distinguishes the fanatic is not simply the refusal to entertain doubts (condition E2) but the *ground* for this refusal (condition E3). The Enlightenment thinkers emphasize that the fanatic refuses to entertain doubts *for a particular reason:* he takes himself to be in possession of distinctive type of ground for his belief; specifically, a ground that the Enlightenment thinkers judge to be non-rational.

So condition (E3)'s distinction between rational and non-rational sanctions plays a crucial role. The philosophers I've mentioned tend to illustrate this distinction with examples involving direct experiences of divinity. In the

---

[13] Although Locke, Hume, and Shaftesbury use the term "enthusiast" more often than "fanatic," I will take them to be referring to fanaticism.

quotations above, Locke speaks of feeling the "hand of God moving within"; Hume focuses on giving oneself over "to inspiration from above"; and Kant cites "an immediate and extraordinary communion with a higher nature." Thus, the Enlightenment account treats claims about direct experiences of divinity as paradigmatic examples of non-rational sanctions. Notice that this upends traditional claims about the authority of religious revelation. Take the Biblical tale of Saul on the road to Damascus: Saul certainly took himself to have an immediate experience of an extraordinary communion with a higher nature.[14] The Enlightenment account thus seems to classify him as a fanatic. Some philosophers—notably Hume—would presumably welcome this result. Others do not directly address the Biblical examples and focus, instead, on cases that their audiences are likely to regard as less controversial: thus, following the above passage on "extraordinary communion with a higher nature," Kant cites Mohammed and John of Leyden (a sixteenth-century Anabaptist who led a rebellion in Münster).

Of course, the claim that these sorts of religious experiences constitute non-rational sanctions for belief is controversial (to put it mildly). It is also dispensable.[15] We could accept the Enlightenment account of fanaticism while rejecting the claim that *all* grounding in religious experience is non-rational. And this brings us back to the original question: how, exactly, does the Enlightenment account draw this distinction between rational and non-rational justifications for ideals? We need more than just examples; we need a good account of the distinction.

And, in fact, we're given it: each of the Enlightenment thinkers I've mentioned (Locke, Hume, Shaftesbury, and Kant) does provide such an account. Familiarly, they defend comprehensive and systematic epistemic theories which aspire to provide us with a way of distinguishing legitimate and illegitimate grounds for belief. Thus, for example, Kant doesn't attempt to explain this rational/non-rational distinction merely in the case of the fanatic; instead, he offers a systematic epistemological and metaphysical theory that, if successful, would enable us to distinguish legitimate and illegitimate grounds for belief in general. This theory can then be applied to the particular case of the fanatic and his beliefs, explaining why, for example, Freeman's appeals to divine revelation would count as non-rational.[16]

---

[14] Acts 3–6: "As he neared Damascus on his journey, suddenly a light from heaven flashed around him. He fell to the ground and heard a voice say to him, "Saul, Saul, why do you persecute me?" "Who are you, Lord?" Saul asked. "I am Jesus, whom you are persecuting," he replied. "Now get up and go into the city, and you will be told what you must do."

[15] As G.K. Chesterton put it: "The secularist and the sceptic have denounced Christianity first and foremost, because of its encouragement of fanaticism; because religious excitement led men to burn their neighbors and to dance naked down the street. How queer it all sounds now. Religion can be swept out of the matter altogether, and still there are philosophical and ethical theories which can produce fanaticism enough to fill the world. Fanaticism has nothing at all to do with religion..." (Chesterton 1991: 37).

[16] To simplify a bit, Kant claims that the fanatic's ground for his belief counts as non-rational because the fanatic presumes to have experience of something which is, in fact, beyond the bounds of possible experience. See Zuckert 2010 for discussion.

As this discussion indicates, while the general idea that there is a distinction between rational and non-rational justifications for beliefs is a truism, any *particular* way of drawing this distinction will require substantial argumentation. Kant, Hume, Locke, and other Enlightenment thinkers do provide that argumentation: they each defend systematic theories. Their accounts of condition (E3) are thus embedded in much larger philosophical projects. An examination of those projects is beyond the scope of this book. Nonetheless, we can step back from the details of these projects and focus on a more restricted point. We can grant, for the sake of argument, that there is a distinction between rational and non-rational justifications for beliefs, as expressed in condition (E3). We can then ask whether this distinction, together with (E1) and (E2), enables us to account for fanaticism.

Thus, while there will be some obvious cases of meeting condition (E3) (Freeman, perhaps), there will also be some controversial cases (Saul on the road to Damascus). Fortunately, our goal in this chapter is not to adjudicate particular cases, but to investigate and analyze the conditions for fanaticism as such. I rely on the distinction embedded in condition (E3) in what follows; if it turns out that there is no way of drawing that distinction, then the account of fanaticism will not succeed.

6.3 Problems with the Enlightenment Account of Fanaticism

The Enlightenment account treats fanaticism as enthusiasm for some ideal that is taken to be warranted in a non-rational manner. At a certain point, the fanatic is cut off from rational argumentation and unwilling to entertain doubts. He seeks to secure a certainty that is, in fact, inaccessible. His certitude blinds him to potentially legitimate competing ideals, and therefore makes him dangerous. Or so, at any rate, the Enlightenment thinkers argue.[17]

The Enlightenment account does capture certain traits of the fanatic. The religious extremist, for example, manifests (E1)–(E3). But is this account sufficient?

There's one glaring difficulty with the account: a crucial feature of the fanatic is *intolerance*, which is often manifest in violent behavior. The Enlightenment thinkers agree on this; Shaftesbury, Locke, and others emphasize the fanatic's intolerance. But the rational defects that these thinkers focus upon—features (E1)–(E3)—have no direct connection to intolerance.

---

[17] Hegel offers a rather different account, which links fanaticism to excessive abstraction: fanaticism is "enthusiasm for something abstract—for an abstract thought which sustains a negative position toward the established order of things. It is the essence of fanaticism to bear only a desolating destructive relation to the concrete..." (Hegel 1900: 358).

To see this, it suffices to note that there are individuals who exhibit features (E1)–(E3) to very high degrees, yet do not seem properly describable as fanatics. Imagine a committed but tolerant Christian, such as Pope Francis. There's good evidence that Pope Francis exhibits extremely high degrees of features (E1)–(E3). First, his commitment to Catholic doctrine has been lifelong and unwavering (feature E1). Second, though he is open to debate about the applications and implications of Christian ideals, he insists that the core ideals are not subject to rational scrutiny (feature E2): as he puts it, the Apostles' "revealed truths of faith were theologically formulated and transmitted as our nonnegotiable inheritance ... There are things that are debatable, but – I repeat – this inheritance [i.e., the "revealed truths of faith"] is not negotiable. The content of religious faith is capable of being deepened through human thought, but when that deepening is at odds with the inheritance, it is heresy" (Bergoglio and Skorka 2010: 26). Third, these ideals are not subject to standard forms of rational scrutiny precisely because they have a distinctively religious sanction: as he puts it in the quotation above, they are "truths of faith."

So Pope Francis appears to meet conditions (E1)–(E3).[18] (Of course, the specifics don't matter: if you don't think Francis meets these conditions, imagine a hypothetical individual who does.) But does he seem like a good case of fanaticism? Francis isn't dangerous, or at least isn't dangerous in the way that we associate with fanaticism. Shaftesbury's description—the "ghastly and terrible" countenance, the violence—seems out of place here. On the contrary, he is peaceful, condemns violence, preaches religious toleration, and so on. I think most of us will hesitate to label Francis a fanatic.

If an account of fanaticism entails that a paradigmatically peaceful and tolerant individual qualifies as a fanatic, then the account misfires. And it misfires on grounds that the Enlightenment thinkers accept: they associate fanaticism with violent intolerance.[19]

If that example isn't convincing, consider another one. Surprisingly, Kant claims that Taoists and Buddhists are the ultimate fanatics. He tells us that the meditative quest for a release from self is the most extreme form of fanaticism

---

[18] The evidence here is not beyond dispute. I've read the Francis quotation, above, as indicating that he refuses to entertain doubts about certain "non-negotiable" religious commitments. But we could instead read him as claiming that certain teachings are fixed commitments of the Catholic faith: although one can reason critically about them, privately doubt them, and so forth, one must remain committed to them in order to be a Catholic. If we do read Francis that way, then he wouldn't manifest feature (E2). Nonetheless, this doesn't affect the larger point: we can imagine a slight variant of Francis who does manifest feature (E2). Presumably there are many individuals who manifest unwavering commitment to an ideal, refuse to submit the ideal to rational scrutiny, assume a non-rational sanction for the ideal, and yet remain peaceful and tolerant.

[19] Of course, we could respond to this problem by limiting the aspirations of the account. For example, if we take the Enlightenment account to be identifying something that leads to a moral failure or an epistemic vice rather than specifically to violent intolerance, then it might succeed.

(Kant 2001: 8:335–6).[20] We can see why he says that. Consider an idealized Buddhist sage who is utterly committed to his ideal of, as Kant puts it, annihilation of the self. Several branches of Buddhism take progress toward this ideal to require a kind of insight that goes beyond ordinary rational thought. In other words, the ideal is taken to have a non-rational sanction.[21]

The prototypical Buddhist sage, of the sort Kant is envisioning, manifests conditions (1)–(3) to an extremely high degree. So Kant is right that, if we accept the received account, the Buddhist sage is the paradigmatic fanatic. But again, this result seems quite peculiar. The Buddhist sage does presume a sanction for his ideal that is not accessible by standard rational inquiry. And he does display an admirable degree of commitment. But is he a fanatic? Again, that seems to me to miss something essential.

So far, we have two cases that, I think, won't strike us as fanaticism, but which qualify as paradigmatic fanaticism on the Enlightenment account. This gives us good reason to question the account. But there are two additional problems.

First, notice that conditions (E1)–(E3) are degreed; people can manifest these traits to greater or lesser extents. My examples of Pope Francis and Buddhist sages, above, involve people who score exceptionally highly on these traits. They thus indicate that manifesting high degrees of (E1)–(E3) is not correlated with fanaticism. Indeed, I suspect that many paradigmatic fanatics are less strongly committed to (E1) than are Francis or the Buddhists. Freeman is a prototypical fanatic, yet the particular commitments that he embraces seem to vary based on what he's read or experienced in the past few days. Insofar as we want to count certain members of ISIS as fanatics, we know, from interviews, that many of them display remarkably little knowledge of the ideals to which they are purportedly committed. Indeed, an interesting feature of fanatics is that the *content* of their commitment often seems less important than the *manner* of their commitment. Eric Hoffer says of fanatics from opposed camps: "They hate each other with the

---

[20] Specifically, Kant derides the "monstrous system of Lao-kiun [Laozi, the founder of Taoism] concerning the highest good, that it consists in *nothing*, i.e. in the consciousness of *feeling* oneself swallowed up in the abyss of the Godhead by flowing together with it, and hence by the annihilation of one's personality; in order to have a presentiment of this state Chinese philosophers, sitting in dark rooms with their eyes closed, exert themselves to think and sense their own nothingness" (Kant 2001: 8:335–6).

[21] Traditionally, Buddhists claim that attainment of nirvana requires "Right Insight" into the nature of reality; this is the first step on the Noble Eightfold Path to Buddhism's goal. Different Buddhist schools interpret Right Insight in divergent ways, but several schools take it to require something beyond ordinary rationality. For example, consider Garfield's discussion of Nāgārjuna: "to see things as Buddha sees them...one must see things independently of the categories that determine an ontology of entities and a dichotomy of existence and nonexistence. That this is inconceivable to us...only indicates the fact that we are trapped in conventional reality through the force of the delusion of reification.... Emptiness is the final nature of all things...This fact entails, for Mahāyāna philosophers, the possibility of any sentient being to be fundamentally transformed—to attain enlightenment" (Garfield 1995: 282). As Garfield's explication indicates, while the claims about Right Insight are rationally articulable, the full understanding and appreciation of them is taken to require something beyond discursive rationality. In this sense, the justification of the ideal is non-rational.

hatred of brothers. They are as far apart and as close together as Saul and Paul" (Hoffer 2010: 85). His suggestion is that what appeals to the fanatic, what motivates unconditional commitment, is not the particular content of the ideal, but the way in which the ideal demands unflinching devotion. I will return to this point.

A second problem is that the Enlightenment criteria are instantiated very widely. Many ordinary individuals exhibit (E1)–(E3) to some degree. (E2) and (E3) in particular may be pervasive: many adherents of religions manifest them, and yet it's odd to attenuate the notion of fanaticism to such an extent that these people would qualify as fanatics.

In light of these problems, there are reasons for doubting that (E1)–(E3) properly characterize the fanatic. Now, (E1)–(E3) do characterize a particular type of rational failing. Just to have a label for this, let's call it being a *true believer*. The true believer, so defined, is strongly committed to some ideal, unwilling to critique the ideal, and takes the ideal to be justified in some non-rational manner (whether by divine revelation, some non-rational ability to limn the structure of reality, etc.). This is a unified phenomenon, exhibited in many religious individuals to a high degree, but also by many nonreligious individuals. It has, as far as I can tell, only a contingent connection to the intolerant behavior that we associate with fanaticism.[22]

It is important to note that this is not just a linguistic dispute about the connotations of "fanatic" in the early twenty-first century. What matters is not whether the word "fanatic" seems applicable to the Buddhist. What matters is whether there really is a unified trait shared by the Buddhist and the violent extremist. That's possible. It's possible that conditions (E1)–(E3) sometimes result in peaceful tolerance, and sometimes in violent behavior; it's possible that when the latter occurs, we label the individual fanatical. So fanaticism would just be (E1)–(E3) plus violence. But this wouldn't be especially interesting as a philosophical phenomenon.

What would be interesting, philosophically speaking, is if there were some way in which the rational defect characterized by (E1)–(E3), when coupled with an additional feature, did generate fanaticism. Of course, any number of things could cause a true believer to become a fanatic. A propensity toward aggression, the acceptance of values whose content directly mandates oppression, a craving for excitement, or a bump on the head might spark violence. But these would be contingent external factors, of no philosophical interest. What I want to do is explore whether there's an internal logic to the true believer-to-fanatic transition. In the next chapter, I will suggest that there is.

---

[22] I describe true believers as exhibiting a rational *failing* or *defect*. This is tendentious. The Enlightenment thinkers, with their commitment to the idea that we should embrace only those commitments that survive critical reflection, do regard being a true believer as a defect of rationality. But subtler views are available. I pass over this complication here, as nothing in my argument turns on it.

7
Fanaticism as Individual Pathology

In the previous chapter, I argued that the Enlightenment account of fanaticism is unsuccessful: it characterizes an epistemic failing that is at best contingently connected to fanaticism. In this chapter, I want to offer a different account of fanaticism. Rather than tying fanaticism to a purely epistemic defect, I will argue that fanaticism is best understood as a form of pathology resulting from a cluster of mutually reinforcing tendencies. In particular, the following sections argue that the fanatic is distinguished by four features: the adoption of one or more sacred values; the need to treat these values as unconditional in order to preserve a particular form of psychic unity; the sense that the status of these values is threatened by lack of widespread acceptance; and the identification with a group, where the group is defined by shared commitment to the sacred value. If my account succeeds, it not only reveals the nature of fanaticism but also uncovers a distinctive form of ethical critique: we can criticize the fanatic not for the content of his view, but for the form of pathology that he exhibits. As I mentioned in the last chapter, this is an underappreciated mode of philosophical critique: we can show that some value or some way of conceptualizing ethics is defective because it promotes a form of individual or social pathology.

7.1 Sacred Values and the Enlightenment Account

As I explained in the last chapter, the Enlightenment account claims that fanatics manifest the following three features:

E1. Unwavering commitment to an ideal.
E2. Unwillingness to subject the ideal (or its premises) to rational critique.
E3. The presumption of a non-rational sanction for the ideal (or its premises).

While these aren't characteristic of fanaticism, they do characterize an epistemic failing that I call being a *true believer*. In this chapter, I want to ask whether there's a pathway from being a true believer to being a fanatic.

The reader will have noticed that being a true believer is *very* close to having sacred values. Recall our account of sacred values:

(**Sacred Values**) Let V1 be a value or normative commitment. Then V1 counts as sacred iff it displays the following three features:

1. **Inviolable**: if V2 is an ordinary value, then it is prohibited to sacrifice V1 for V2, regardless of the quantities of V1 and V2.

2. **Incontestable**: It is prohibited to *contemplate* trading or sacrificing V1 for most or all other values.

3. **Dialectically Invulnerable**: The agent insulates her commitment to V1 from the effects of justificatory reasoning. That is, while the agent may think about V1's justification, consider objections to V1, consider alternatives to V1, engage in thought experiments with respect to V1, and so on, the agent does not stake her commitment to V1 on the outcome of this justificatory reasoning. There is no dialectical move that would disrupt the agent's commitment to V1.

Inviolability can be understood as a form of (E1); incontestability and dialectical invulnerability can be manifest in (E2) and (E3). The chief difference between the true believer and my account of having sacred values is simply that the true believer thinks (albeit incorrectly) that he has a decisive justification for his commitments: he has direct access to divinity or metaphysical insight or some such. In a sense, we could say that the true believer exhibits Dialectical Invulnerability, for we could argue that the fanatic doesn't engage in *genuine* critique of his ideal; genuinely critiquing the ideal would require modifying it in light of ordinary rational and evidential standards, and the true believer doesn't do that. But this would rely on a controversial and disputable premise about what counts as genuine critique. Moreover, it would risk conflating the person who has sacred values and insulates them from critique with the person who has sacred values and also takes them to have (e.g.) a divine sanction.

In order to keep these cases apart, we can simply say that the true believer, as characterized by the Enlightenment account, is the person who has sacred values *and* believes he has some sort of non-rational sanction for them. In other words, we can condense (E1)–(E3) as follows: the true believer has and acts on sacred values, which he takes to be non-rationally justified.

In the following sections, I will investigate the connection between being a true believer and being a fanatic. Strictly speaking, I don't think the belief that these values are non-rationally justified is necessary for the fanatic. I will explain why below, but even before getting into the details we can imagine a paradigmatic fanatic who just doesn't give much thought to the justificatory status of his values. Members of ISIS are often treated as paradigmatic fanatics, but interviews tend to reveal that most of these individuals know very little about and give little thought to the ideals to which they are purportedly committed (see Stern 2003, Stern and Berger 2015, Berger 2018). Insofar as they have any justifications at all, these justifications tend to be quite amateurish and superficial, and indeed often display inconsistencies. Even if these individuals happen to believe that their values are divinely revealed, this justificatory belief is not the factor that distinguishes them from non-fanatics.

So let's set aside the point about non-rational justifications and focus, instead, on the fact that the fanatic has sacred values. Let's make this the first condition for fanaticism:

(F1)   Sacred values: the individual adopts one or more sacred values.

For the reasons I discussed in the previous chapter, having sacred values doesn't by itself entail intolerance. However, in the following sections I will suggest that a particular way of understanding and relating to sacred values does promote fanaticism.

7.2 Recent Psychological Research on Individual Fanaticism

I will begin by reviewing some empirical work on fanaticism. There's quite a bit of work on this topic, as well as on related notions such as extremism and radicalization. Reviewing some key findings will be useful in orienting our discussion.

7.2.1 Accounts Focusing on Cognitive Features

One body of empirical literature focuses on epistemic traits which, while not unique to extremists, have a far higher rate of occurrence among extremists than within the general population. Chief among these are *rigid thinking* and *intolerance of uncertainty*.

Let's start with rigid thinking. Recent work in neuropsychology defines *cognitive rigidity* as "the inability to adapt to novel or changing environments and a difficulty to switch between modes of thinking" (Zmigrod 2020: 35). To measure this capacity, some studies quantify people's capacity to inhibit habitual or impulsive responses while performing a task; others examine the capacity to switch rapidly between different tasks or different paths to a goal (Goschke 2014; Merien 2010; Koch, Grade, Schuch, and Philipp 2010; Miyake et al. 2000). The general idea is that rigid thinkers are those who tend to persevere in one way of thinking or behaving, especially in situations where this way of thinking or behaving is less effective than alternative modes (cf. Kashdan and Rottenburg 2010).

The view that cognitive rigidity might promote intolerance and extreme prejudice arose in the 1950s. In early works such as *The Authoritarian Personality* (Adorno et al. 1950), psychologists and philosophers argued for links between these notions, sometimes drawing on empirical studies, sometimes on psychoanalytic theory, sometimes on abstract philosophical reflections. A few decades' worth of studies have established connections between cognitive rigidity and the acceptance of extreme social and political views. According to what's now known as the *rigidity-of-the-extreme* view, political and social extremism is associated with rigid thinking. For example, a recent survey article concluded that "the evidence suggests that cognitive rigidity is linked to ideological extremism, partisanship, and dogmatism across political and non-political ideologies" (Zmigrod 2020: 34).

So cognitive rigidity is clearly associated with extremism, at least in the sense that extremists are likely to display cognitive rigidity. And that's not the only cognitive feature associated with extremism. Consider *intolerance of uncertainty*. Kruglanski and other psychologists have developed scales for measuring the extent to which individuals desire *cognitive closure*, which is understood as the elimination of uncertainty, confusion, and ambiguity (Kruglanski and Fishman 2009; Webster and Kruglanski 1994). People who are highly intolerant of uncertainty are unwilling to embrace ambiguity or to remain in a position of uncertainty; they seek quick answers that present simple solutions to complex problems. As one would expect, individuals vary greatly in their tolerance for uncertainty. Those with extreme political views tend to score quite highly on the cognitive closure scale, indicating a potential connection between the need for cognitive closure and extremism.

While this data is interesting, we should be aware of its limitations. Most of the studies look for correlations rather than causation: they examine groups of extremists and non-extremists, and try to determine whether the groups differ in their cognitive features. This leaves it open whether rigid thinking (and/or intolerance of uncertainty) causes extremism; whether extremist views cause rigid thinking; or whether there is a feedback loop between the two, with people who have slightly more rigid thinking being attracted to extreme views, which then increase the rigidity, which then increase the extremity of their views, and so on.

Aside from that, if we're interested in fanaticism rather than extremism these views will be of limited use. There is a very significant step between having extreme social and political views and being a fanatic. The former is much more widespread than the latter. So, suppose we had the strongest possible version of these cognitive views: suppose studies decisively established that rigid thinking and intolerance of uncertainty were the most significant causal factors in producing extreme political views. (To be clear, nothing like this has been established.) Even if this were so, we would still need to explain what leads from political extremism to fanaticism.

7.2.2 Accounts Focusing on Motivational Factors

So far, I've discussed empirical work on *cognitive* features, or facts about the way in which information is selected, processed, and evaluated. But another strand of research focuses on *motivational* factors, trying to uncover distinctive desires, goals, and ideals that might be linked to extremism.

Again, there is a massive literature on this topic, and I won't offer anything resembling a comprehensive overview. But I will mention a few of the most influential accounts. Let's start with *Significance Quest Theory*. Arie Kruglanski has argued that suicide bombers and other violent extremists are motivated by a "quest for personal significance": roughly, these individuals undertake extremist actions because they want to be viewed as significant or as mattering by other members of their communities. Other accounts broaden their scope, mentioning features such as a quest for some determinate personal identity, or the need to overcome diminished sense of self-worth (Bhui and Dinos 2012; Kruglanski et. al. 2009). These, too, are often classified as quests for significance.

However, as Bloom (2009) and Jensen et al. (2018) have pointed out, these accounts face a very simple problem: most people have a desire for personal significance and very few carry out terrorist attacks. There is, as far as I am aware, no compelling evidence that terrorists in particular or extremists in general display a greater need for personal significance than do ordinary individuals. So, while the quest for significance is obviously one factor that could motivate an individual to join an extremist group, it's very far from sufficient.

Some studies try to address this concern by introducing multiple psychological constructs that, while individually widespread, tend to occur together in violent extremists. For example, in one recent study (Jensen et al. 2018), psychologists examined 56 representative cases of extremism in the United States over the 1960–2013 period. Of these 56 cases, 31 were violent and 25 nonviolent. The authors' goal was to determine whether the dominant empirical psychological theories of violent extremism would apply to these cases. The authors reviewed dozens of these theories, sorting them into ten main camps. Their findings were striking. Eighty-five percent of the cases of violent extremism shared the following three features:

- Psychological vulnerability: the person exhibited cognitive or emotional characteristics that revealed his sense of self to be threatened; in particular, the person exhibited "uncertainty over issues of identity of community membership" (Jensen et al. 2018: 7).
- Community vulnerability: the person identified with a group and took this group to have "collective feelings of intense trouble, difficulty, or danger" (Jensen et al. 2018: 7). The group was seen as in some way threatened and at risk of becoming unstable.
- Psychological rewards: the agent experienced violent activity as psychological rewarding, either because it gave the individual a sense of significance, bolstered his sense of group identity, or seemed instrumentally rational.

Agents who exhibited only *one* of these traits were no more likely to engage in violent extremist behaviors than those who lacked the trait. But agents who had all three traits were *far* more likely to engage in violent extremist behavior. Of course, these aren't sufficient conditions: we can imagine cases in which a person exhibits all three conditions but nonetheless remains peaceful and tolerant. Nonetheless, 85% of cases of violent extremism had all three conditions, suggesting that these conditions jointly dispose the agent toward violence.

While these studies are intriguing, we can wonder how illuminating they are. Do people become extremists because they antecedently feel psychologically vulnerable, think their group is threatened, and see some pathway to reward? Or does the fact that a person is an extremist explain why they are drawn toward views that present their groups as threatened and violence as a path to rewards? It's hard to sort out the direction of causality.

In fact, it's unsurprising that we lack clear answers to these questions. People are complex. We wouldn't expect to have a clear, generalizable causal account of what draws people to being architects or playing football or being selfish or appreciating Renaissance art or enjoying travel or being political moderates or drinking coffee. Why think we can generate an account that explains why people become extremists?

In light of these problems, I suggest that a different approach is more promising. We can outline a particular kind of pathology, fanaticism, which is much more specific and distinctive than extremism. We shouldn't expect a unique causal pathway leading to this state: just as any number of things could lead to someone's becoming egotistical or enjoying Renaissance art or appreciating football, so too any number of things could lead to someone's becoming a fanatic. But, once the pathology is in place, we will see that it strongly disposes individuals to the behavioral and psychological traits that we associate with fanaticism.

7.3 Fragility of the Self

It seems clear that fanaticism has something to do with the way in which we relate to our commitments, goals, and values. So let's begin by considering different ways of doing so. Kant sometimes associates fanaticism with an attempt to escape from the demands of autonomy: he tells us that the fanatic is "kept ever distant from the good based on self-activity" (Kant 2001: 6:83). The fanatic seeks a form of passivity: he wants to be directed from without.

Of course, that's not distinctive of the fanatic; many people escape self-direction and look for external guidance. But we escape self-direction for different reasons. There's a difference between someone who is *unwilling* to self-direct and someone who is *unable* to do so. The latter—a *need* for external regulation—is one of the features that Nietzsche associates with fanaticism. He claims that for certain individuals, lack of fanaticism would "lead to crumbling and disintegration" (Nietzsche 1989: §30). For "fanaticism is the only 'strength of the will' that even the weak and insecure can be brought to attain, being a sort of hypnotism of the whole system of the senses and the intellect for the benefit of an excessive nourishment (hypertrophy) of a single point of view and feeling that henceforth becomes dominant..." (Nietzsche 1974: §347).[1]

While the language is imprecise, I think Nietzsche is pointing to an important phenomenon. There is a family of views about self-constitution and personal identity which take the self to be constituted by its commitment to either principles, ideals, values, or narratives. There is a vast literature on this topic, and the differences between these views have been explored in depth. I wish to focus only on the common ground: there is a sense of the term "self" which picks out a particular type of orientation toward a principle, ideal, value, or narrative. Absent that commitment, the self evaporates. Thus, Frankfurtian theories hold that the self is constituted by the person's identifying with elements of her mental economy (Frankfurt 1988). Kantian views take the agent to be constituted by her identification with principles of choice (Korsgaard 1996). Narrative identity theories hold that what makes an event or psychological characteristic properly attributable to a person is its incorporation into a narrative of the person's life, as told by that person (MacIntyre 1984; Schechtman 1996). And so on. If some view of this form is correct—and the details don't matter—then, in order to preserve a unified self, the agent needs to commit herself to some ideal, principle, value, or narrative.

We could also describe this phenomenon in a rather different way: rather than focusing on agential unity, we could examine a person's sense of her own *identity*. People understand themselves under different descriptions: when asked who you are, you might cite your activities, your job, your skills and abilities, various social roles that you occupy, groups that you align yourself with, goals that you have, ways in which you characteristically behave, traits that you take yourself to have, and so on. And perhaps more abstractly: you might cite your *values,* which (at least in ideal cases) would inform and perhaps underwrite your commitment to the aforementioned things. I occupy a particular social role because I take it to have some value; I align myself with groups that share my sense of what's worth doing; and so on.

If we abstract from the individual's participation in particular roles, groups, activities, and so on, we can speak of the agent's identity in terms of the values that her various commitments express. And then we can ask: why does the agent have the values that she does? Take someone who identifies herself in terms of her quest for social justice. That's what she regards as most important; that's what she

---

[1] For a helpful analysis of this point, see Reginster 2003.

appeals to when she wonders why she participates in various activities, why she has a certain job, why she lives as she does. Some people can preserve a sense of themselves independently of their commitment to *particular* values. I value philosophy, but can envision myself living a different life that doesn't involve that valuation or that commitment. Other things are worthwhile and one isn't making a mistake by privileging them. But others are too firmly wedded to their values to envision their being optional: some people need to treat their values as unconditional in order to preserve their sense of self.

So suppose Nietzsche is right—suppose some of us can achieve unity of selfhood or a sense of personal identity only by becoming fanatics. The "strong" individuals, in Nietzsche's language, can bind themselves to an ideal that they see as rationally optional. Part of my identity is constituted by my commitment to my profession and my wife; if I had been a doctor instead of a philosophy professor, or if I had married a different partner, I would be a very different person. I can admit to myself that nothing mandated my commitment to these ends. I could have chosen a different profession; I could have met and married a different partner, or none at all. The recognition of the contingency of these commitments doesn't disrupt them.

But Nietzsche's suggestion is that, for some of us, the recognition of contingency would disrupt our identities. Aware of this at some level, we block recognition of the contingency of our commitments. Although we see that our commitments can't be rationally justified as non-contingent, we take ourselves to have some source of special authority that legitimates and binds us to them. Uncertainty and doubt are thereby eliminated, and self-integrity preserved.

So let's add a second condition:

(F2) Fragility of the self: the agent needs to treat a value as sacred in order to preserve her identity.

What Nietzsche is suggesting, in other words, is that some individuals exhibit an inability to preserve their identity absent a commitment to a value that they treat as inviolable, incontestable, and dialectically invulnerable. The *content* of this commitment is less important than the fact that it is treated as sacred.

For a particularly vivid example of this phenomenon, consider the recent case of Devon Arthurs. In May 2017, police arrested Arthurs for murdering his two roommates. Arthurs confessed and explained his crime as follows: he and his roommates were active neo-Nazis (they participated in online neo-Nazi groups, their apartment was full of neo-Nazi documents, they had a framed photo of Timothy McVeigh, and so on). However, Arthurs had very recently decided to convert to Islam. Given that neo-Nazis encourage violence against Muslims, Arthurs decided that he should retaliate by killing his neo-Nazi roommates. Here we have an astonishingly clear case of the structure mattering more than content:

one authoritarian ideology (neo-Nazism) is substituted for another (a violent interpretation of Islam). This is just one example but we can imagine many others.

One qualification: notice that Nietzsche seems to be assuming that any value to which we bind ourselves will be rationally optional; thus, he takes *all* cases of treating values as non-optional to result from factors such as confusion, ignorance, or motivated reasoning, including the type of motivated reasoning picked out by (F2). It's important to note that we need not follow him on this point in order to accept claim (F2) as a condition for fanaticism. Suppose there is a rationally obligatory sacred value. Still, we can ask whether a particular agent's commitment to this value is driven primarily by epistemic factors or, instead, by motivations that hinge on the preservation of psychic unity. In the former case, condition (F2) would not obtain; in the latter case, it would. This distinction may be clearer in a straightforwardly factual case: suppose a husband believes that his wife is unfaithful. We can ask whether the husband's belief is primarily driven by epistemic factors (evidence of infidelity, etc.) or by other factors (jealousy, possessiveness, etc.). Determining this in any particular case will be difficult, but the distinction can nonetheless be drawn and is important (contrast Othello with a dispassionate investigator of potential infidelity). Just so with sacred values.

7.4 Fragility of the Value

Condition (F2) focuses on fragility of the self. But we can also look at this from the other side. It's not just the *self* that is fragile, but the value as well.

Suppose you took yourself to need external legitimation for some value, found this legitimation unavailable through standard rational argumentation, and accordingly lapsed into being a true believer about the value. Suppose, in other words, that you manifested features (F1)–(F2). Still, this wouldn't by itself constitute fanaticism. To return to Kant's example, a Buddhist could do this. So could Pope Francis. But again, they don't seem to qualify as fanatics. Knowing that they exhibit fragility of the self would make us think that they were unfortunate, that they displayed some defect of autonomy; but it wouldn't, just by itself, render them fanatics.

But what if you also thought the value itself were fragile? That is, what if you thought that the value's status could be imperiled by the way in which *other people* relate to this value?

Some individuals do treat values in this way. Compare the rhetoric surrounding protecting the integrity of marriage, with some groups arguing that allowing same-sex marriage threatens or undermines the institution of marriage itself.[2] Or, to take a relatively trivial example (trivial because not yet dangerous), consider

---

[2] For an overview of court cases on this matter, see Busch 2011. I return to this example below.

the idea of a "war on Christmas", wherein ostensibly non-religious corporations are taken to be attacking, demeaning, or threatening Christianity by acknowledging the possibility of non-Christian holidays.[3] In these cases, we have groups that take the status of their own values to be threatened by the fact that other groups do not share them.

Let's put the point this way:

(F3) Fragility of the value: the value's status is taken to be threatened when it is not widely accepted.

To understand (F3), we need to distinguish it from closely related claims. First, some values can only be *realized* when they are widely accepted. Suppose, for example, that Genevieve values environmental preservation. She can do her part to realize this value, but she's one among many; in order for environmental preservation actually to occur, the value needs to be held not just by Genevieve, but by a sufficiently large percentage of the population. So, in valuing environmental preservation, she might also aspire to have others accept this value. This seems sensible and entirely unproblematic; it bears no interesting connection to fanaticism.

Condition (F3) is not meant to be a claim about the *realization* of values. It is a claim about the *status* of values. To illustrate the distinction, consider the debates concerning same-sex marriage. Suppose Arthur thinks that heterosexual marriage has sacred value; he opposes same-sex marriage, which he sees as in violation of this value. Let's stipulate that in opposing same-sex marriage, Arthur isn't worried about the realization of his value; he doesn't think that allowing same-sex marriage will cause fewer heterosexual marriages to occur. Rather, he worries that allowing same-sex marriage will render heterosexual marriage less significant, less sacred. So, the lack of broad acceptance of Arthur's value seems to him to imperil not the realization but the status of his value. He thus meets condition (F3).

I take it that this stance is familiar. A common form of argument against same-sex marriage hinges on the claim that allowing same-sex marriage undermines the value of heterosexual marriage.[4] How should we understand this claim? Suppose heterosexual marriage is held to be sacred, to have a value that other forms of committed relationship lack. By allowing other forms of committed relationship to carry the title "marriage," heterosexual marriage is no longer publicly marked off as something with a distinctive form of value. It is no longer publicly

---

[3] For an introduction to this topic, see Stack 2016.
[4] For a typical statement, consider the Archbishop of Canterbury, Justin Welby, in 2013: allowing same-sex marriage "weakens" marriage, for "The concept of marriage as a normative place for procreation is lost; the idea as marriage as covenant is diminished; the family in its normal sense, predating the state, and as our base community of society, as we have already heard, is weakened" (quoted from http://www.telegraph.co.uk/news/politics/10096579/Gay-marriage-weakens-society-says-Archbishop-of-Canterbury.html). In a 2003 Pew Poll, 73% of Americans who opposed same-sex marriage said that allowing it would "undermine" heterosexual marriage and/or heterosexual families.

acknowledged as possessing a different status than same-sex committed relationships. And this seems, to some opponents of same-sex marriage, to render heterosexual marriage less significant, less valuable, or less sacred.

Notice that not everyone shares this concern about whether their sacred values are widely held. Some individuals and communities hold distinctive sets of values and practices, and yet evince no concern whatsoever about whether the broader society acknowledges these values and practices. The Amish are, perhaps, an example of a community that traditionally maintains certain sacred values without staking their own acceptance of these values on the stance of the broader non-Amish community. To some extent, the New York Hasidic community is analogous: although there have been well-publicized exceptions, in general this community seems to maintain its sacred values without concern for whether non-Jewish individuals in the surrounding communities also accept them. Non-interference is regarded as sufficient.

As these examples illustrate, some individuals and groups see the status of their own values as threatened by the absence of widespread acceptance, whereas others don't. I think that it is precisely those individuals and communities that accept the former claim that are most strongly associated with fanaticism. Take violent religious extremism, neo-Nazism, and so forth; a distinguishing feature of many of these communities is the attempt to enforce compliance with and acceptance of a particular set of values. The fanatic typically wants his values to be accepted by everyone; he is not content to acknowledge alternative sets of values as acceptable for other individuals. Thus, whereas the non-fanatic might be strongly committed to his values without attempting to enforce compliance with these values on all, and without seeing these others as needing to hold these values in order for the values to preserve their legitimacy for him, the fanatic tends to have the opposite reaction.

For these reasons, I think feature (F3), when coupled with (F1)–(F2), brings us quite close to an analysis of fanaticism. (I will shortly suggest that one additional feature is needed.) In other words, part of what's criterial for fanaticism is the need to treat some value as inviolable, incontestable, and invulnerable; when we couple this with the sense that these values are fragile, that failing to accept them imperils their status, we come quite close to fanaticism.[5]

7.5 Group Orientation

Are features (F1)–(F3) sufficient? Is the fanatic a true believer about sacred values who exhibits psychic fragility and also sees his values as fragile? I think this takes us almost all the way to fanaticism. But there's one final feature.

---

[5] Durkheim claims that one of the characteristic features of the sacred is that it must be continually protected from incursions by the profane (1915/1955: 33–44).

I mentioned in the introduction that the individuals we typically think of as fanatics are members of groups, rather than isolated individuals. There's no such thing as an isolated fanatic, and there's no such thing as a fanatic who bears ordinary relations to other individuals. As Gabriel Marcel writes,

> The fanatic cannot be an isolated being... he exists among others and... between these others and himself there is formed... a unity of identity or harmonic range. This unity... is felt as a link which exalts, and the fanaticism of one man is always kept alight by contact with the fanaticism of another. (Marcel 2008: 102)

The fanatic's group is constituted by shared commitment to a sacred value, as well as the sense that membership in the group is necessary for preserving this value. To be clear: the fanatic may *in fact* be physically isolated, adrift in a society in which he feels unwelcome or alienated. But he sees himself as defined by membership in some group. The group can be merely notional; physical or even temporal proximity isn't necessary. The fanatic can identify with some group that lives across the world (think of the cases of teenagers in affluent liberal democracies identifying with or even attempting to join ISIS). The fanatic can identify with a group all of whose members are dead (think of the individual who identifies with a lost movement or a past age).

More precisely:

(F4) Group identity: the fanatic identifies herself with a group, where this group is defined by shared commitment to a sacred value.

Let's link these features together. The agent's sense of self is vouchsafed by his commitment to a sacred value, where the value is taken as definitive of a group. The value is seen as compromised by dissent. Thus, the group's identity, which hinges on its adherence to the value, is seen as compromised by dissent. So, too, the agent's psychic integrity. These relations of dependence make group orientation essential.[6]

And this is where the behavioral element becomes prominent. The relations of value-dependence make opposition to other groups essential. The fanatic sees outsiders as opposed to his group. These outsiders threaten not only his value, and not only his group, but his very identity.

This oppositional tendency can be present to different degrees. In the minimal case, the individual simply notes that outsiders exist and are potentially

---

[6] Passmore focuses on a similar feature. He claims that fanatics treat some set of beliefs as authoritative, and that what "fanatics have in common is the notion that those who do not share their beliefs are in some way morally inferior to them" (2003: 219). Crosson agrees: analyzing Marcel's account of fanaticism, he claims that fanaticism is a group-phenomenon in which outsiders are seen third-personally, as objects to be contended with rather than agents to be reasoned with (Crosson 2003).

threatening. In the extreme case, the fanatic sees these outsiders as to be dealt with rather than reasoned with. After all, the fanatic accepts some ideal which is not itself subject to rational justification. Rational argumentation won't sway the other side. They are to be contended with, suppressed, or simply eliminated. The fanatic thereby denies them their status as potential subjects of rational engagement, i.e., persons. It is a short step from there—the denial of personhood—to the characteristic life of the fanatic: the rage, the propensity toward violence.[7]

Consider Foucault:

> The polemicist . . . proceeds encased in privileges that he possesses in advance and will never agree to question. On principle, he possesses rights authorising him to wage war and making that struggle a just undertaking; the person he confronts is not a partner in the search for truth, but an adversary, an enemy who is wrong, who is harmful and whose very existence constitutes a threat. For him, then, the game does not consist of recognising this person as a subject having the right to speak, but of abolishing him as an interlocutor, from any possible dialogue; and his final objective will be, not to come as close as possible to a difficult truth, but to bring about the triumph of the just cause he has been manifestly upholding from the beginning. The polemicist relies on a legitimacy that his adversary is by definition denied.   (Foucault 1984: 382)

Foucault is discussing "polemicists" rather than fanatics, but his points carry over. Fanaticism is a constellation of traits that make this disposition to deny humanity to outsiders quite likely; the psychic dependence on an unquestionable ideal, when coupled with the sense that the ideal is threatened by non-acceptance by outsiders, promotes thinking of those outsiders not merely as fellow persons with different values, but as enemies. And this disposes the fanatic to violence.

There's empirical psychological research that makes a related point. Some psychologists use the term *identity fusion* to refer to cases in which a person's identity is becomes bound up with the identity of a group: the personal identity and the group identity become "fused" or melded together. As Scott Atran puts it, "Identity fusion occurs when personal and group identities collapse into a unique identity" (Atran 2016: 193; cf. Swann et al. 2012). So, for example, the nascent white supremacist might join Stormfront; and might increasingly find his own sense of personal identity becoming inextricable from his sense of what Stormfront is. Or, in a more neutral context: the person who joins a football team might increasingly find his personal activities, values, commitments, even his sense of humor and his ways of relating to the world becoming increasingly

---

[7] Of course, this violence isn't exclusively directed at the out-group. It's common for groups of fanatics to participate in ritualized violence directed at their own members. But this violence may have a different explanation: it can serve as a way of ensuring total compliance with the group's ideals.

aligned with and inextricable from his sense of what the team does. This is obviously a matter of degree, and the notion is somewhat imprecise, but we needn't delve into the details here. The relevant point, for our purposes, is that some psychologists have argued that we can generate an account of extremism by linking this notion of identity fusion to sacred values:

> People will become willing to protect morally important or sacred values through costly sacrifice and extreme actions, even being willing to kill and die, particularly when such values are embedded in or fused with group identity, becoming intrinsic to "Who I am" and "Who We are." (Atran and Ginges 2015)

Psychologists call this the *Devoted Actor Hypothesis:* in essence, they claim that fusing one's identity with a group while having sacred values predicts extreme behavior.

My own claim (F4) expresses a similar point, so we can ask how the Devoted Actor Hypothesis relates to my account of fanaticism. Fanatics are devoted actors. But not all devoted actors are fanatics (being a devoted actor only requires meeting F1 and some analogue of F4). So I am suggesting that fanatics should be understood as people who are driven to being devoted actors out of a kind of fragility or weakness: they manifest not only (F1) and (F4) but also (F2) and (F3).

Notice that the constellation of traits (F1)–(F4) generates a *propensity* or *disposition* toward violent intolerance; it does not *necessitate* violent intolerance. Given the vagaries of human psychology and the complexity of situational factors bearing on individuals' behavior, it would be foolhardy to claim that (F1)–(F4) guarantee violent intolerance. And this point generalizes: I doubt that there is *any* trait, commitment, or view which would, independently of other psychological and situational factors, necessitate violent behavior. Consider a more familiar example. Racist beliefs tend to promote morally problematic behavior (people with overtly racist beliefs are more likely to discriminate, to treat members of other races unfairly, to favor policies that disadvantage members of other races, and so forth). Nonetheless, there may be particular cases in which racist beliefs are accompanied by morally acceptable behavior (perhaps the racist individual has no opportunity to act on his beliefs, or faces social pressure against doing so, or—as in the case of Huck Finn—finds his racist beliefs overruled by other passions or commitments). This does not reduce the interest in analyzing the way in which racist beliefs generate a propensity to morally problematic behavior. Just so with (F1)–(F4) and violent intolerance.

So (F1)–(F4) generate a disposition to violent intolerance. This disposition can be blocked, and some of the ways in which it can be blocked are important. In particular, there may be cases in which the *content* of a value puts it in tension with some of the conditions for fanaticism. Put differently, there may be certain values that are unlikely to generate fanaticism. By way of illustration, suppose we have a group whose members treat freedom from coercion as a sacred value. Could members of this group be fanatical with respect to that value? I think the answer is no, or at least not wholeheartedly. To the extent that the person wholeheartedly accepts the value of freedom from coercion, he will not attempt to coerce others into accepting this value (though, of course, he might *wish* or *hope* that others will come to these values on their own). He will see that some others do not accept this value; but he will see this as something that they themselves must put right. Thus, he will be unlikely to exhibit conditions (F3)–(F4). Or, if he does exhibit these conditions, he will experience some tension or fragmentation of his commitments. We can generalize this point: certain values will be in tension with fanaticism.

7.6 Refinements

7.6.1 The Connection between (F3) and Intolerance

Condition (F3) focuses on whether a value's status is taken to be threatened when the value is not widely accepted. Notice that there is an interesting connection between (F3) and *tolerance*. Typically, the concept of tolerance is applied to cases in which a set of evaluative beliefs or practices is viewed as objectionable, yet is in some way accepted. There are different accounts of what exactly tolerance requires. Minimal conceptions of tolerance treat it as requiring only non-interference with dissenting views; more robust conceptions claim that tolerance involves respect or even esteem for these dissenting views (cf. Scanlon 1996, Forst 2002, Raz 1988).

I think tolerance itself is widely treated as a sacred value, especially in liberal democratic cultures.[8] But notice that if you treat tolerance itself as a sacred value, then you will experience persistent tragic conflicts between tolerance and other sacralized values. So, to use one of my earlier examples: a person like Pope Francis could be fully committed *both* to the idea that human life has sacred value from the very moment of conception *and* to the idea that we must tolerate dissenting views, such as political views that allow abortion and hence involve denying that human life is sacred from the moment of conception. Insofar as he treats both of these values as sacred, he would experience tragic conflicts. For, insofar as he is committed to tolerance, he will see himself as barred from interfering with those who accept abortion. He might try to reason with them; he might try to convince them of his view; but he will not impose his views on them by force, as this would violate his sacred value of tolerance. So he would experience a tragic conflict: his

---

[8] Which is not to say that it is *universally* treated as such. Many strands of recent political discourse are directly opposed to tolerance.

sacred valuation of tolerance prohibits him from certain forms of interference with those who endorse abortion rights, whereas his sacred valuation of human life (as he understands it) requires him to interfere. These values can be neither reconciled nor abandoned.

As this example indicates, a person who treats tolerance as a sacred value and who also has other sacred values will be prone to experiencing tragic conflicts. So (F3), which states that values are seen as threatened when not widely accepted, is not simply an illusion or a mistake: it is picking up on a real feature of ethical life, one that an emphasis on toleration defuses only imperfectly and at great cost.

Does this suggest that fanaticism necessarily involves a form of intolerance? I think we should resist that conclusion. Fanatics tend to be intolerant, but not all intolerant individuals are fanatics. Nor are all fanatics intolerant: if the fanatic is surrounded by like-minded individuals, intolerance needn't arise (except perhaps in counterfactual cases). Nonetheless, it may be that fanaticism only arises as a distinct phenomenon when tolerance is sacralized or at least treated as highly valuable. In other words: we see fanaticism as a pathology in part because we treat tolerance as a sacred value.

The fanatic does get something right: the fanatic is correct in thinking that there is a genuine tension between treating a value as unconditionally overriding (Inviolable) and tolerating the fact that others don't adopt this value. This is why (F3) can arise and is always tempting. But (F3) is not *directly* entailed by the Inviolability of a value.

To see this, consider a distinction. Some sacred values are taken to apply universally: to treat human life as sacred is, at least in the usual cases, to treat *all* human life as sacred and *all* violations of this value as problematic. Other sacred values are taken to apply to some more restricted group: the Amish take their commitments to apply to other Amish, but not to members of the surrounding non-Amish communities. The values that are taken to apply universally will generate the tension; the ones that are taken to apply only to restricted groups needn't.

But that's not all. Some sacred values require institutionalization in order to be effective; others don't. Contrast a person who treats *racial equality* as having sacred value with a person who treats *love* as having sacred value. Valuing racial equality requires certain institutional mechanisms, whereas valuing love requires only personal and perhaps idiosyncratic commitments. So again, the tensions are more likely to arise in the former kind of case than in the latter.

With this in mind, what differentiates the fanatic (who is characterized in part by (F3)) from the agent who maintains a sacred value in a non-fanatical form? If we think about Pope Francis again, we can see a crucial difference: while non-acceptance of the sacred value of human life is seen as a mistake, and while efforts at conversion might be undertaken, he does not see this value's sacred status as imperiled by dissent. Seeing a value as widely violated or widely disrespected is compatible with seeing the value as sacred. In the case of the fanatic, by contrast, suppression of dissent is needed in order to buttress the agent's commitment to the sacredness of the relevant value. For the agent feels that the value's status as sacred is threatened by dissent; he and his value are fragile.

7.6.2 Cassam on Fanaticism and Extremism

In a work that appeared as I was finishing this book, Quassim Cassam critiques my account of fanaticism (originally published as Katsafanas 2019) and provides his own alternative. Cassam offers two arguments.

First, Cassam claims that there are counterexamples to my account of fanaticism. He focuses on Reinhard Heydrich, who was a leading figure in Nazi Germany; he led the Reich Security Main Office and had chaired the 1942 conference at Wannsee, where he outlined the "Final Solution to the Jewish Question." Cassam notes that other Nazis, including even Himmler, viewed Heydrich as "the perfect Nazi" (Cassam 2022: 115). Cassam claims that given the depth of Heydrich's commitment to Nazi ideals, "Heydrich was the fanatic's fanatic, a true fanatic in every sense" (116). But, according to Cassam, Heydrich lacks a sacred value and doesn't seem to be psychologically fragile (123–5). If this is right, Heydrich fails to meet my conditions F1 and F2. Nonetheless, Cassam claims, Heydrich is a fanatic—and not only that, he's a *paradigmatic* fanatic. If this is right, then my account is not only subject to a counterexample but, worse yet, it fails to account for a paradigm case of fanaticism.

However, Cassam's claims are questionable. First, it seems clear that Heydrich does in fact have sacred values: the Nazi ideals seem like obvious candidates. And indeed, Cassam quotes a biography of Heydrich which notes his "mindless and total assimilation of Nazi ideology," his "lack of recognition of any possible alternative to the Nazi world-view... Nazi ideology appeared to be for Heydrich something utterly impersonal, an unquestioned set of ideas and attitudes that it was his ambition to put into effect with cold, passionate efficiency" (Evans 2008: 276, quoted by Cassam 2022: 116). Not only that: Cassam later goes on to say that fanatics must have some "pre-eminent good" for which they will sacrifice themselves and others (125–6) and which they are unwilling to doubt (131–2). That certainly sounds like a sacred value: it sounds like these pre-eminent, unquestioned ideals involve Inviolability, Incontestability, and Dialectical Invulnerability. So I suspect that Cassam and I are actually in agreement that Heydrich in particular, and fanatics in general, meet condition F1. We use different terminology—Cassam speaks of indubitable pre-eminent goods, I speak of sacred values—but the core idea seems very close indeed.

The deeper disagreement is over F2. As Cassam puts it, "There is no evidence that Heydrich needed to treat Nazi values as sacred in order to preserve the unity of his self...Heydrich was a unified self before he became a Nazi" (124). I completely agree with Cassam that this is a plausible interpretation of Heydrich. There is no indication (at least in the material Cassam has provided) that Heydrich is psychologically fragile. Cassam concludes, from this, that my account of fanaticism is wrong. I would conclude, instead, that Heydrich is not a fanatic.

This might seem like a terminological dispute, but I think it points to a deeper disagreement concerning the *work* that we want the concept of fanaticism to do. Notice that Cassam and I agree on many details of this case. We agree that Heydrich is an extremist; that he is a person with a morally reprehensible ideal; that he is dogmatic about that ideal; that he is self-sacrificing in pursuit of that ideal; that he takes abhorrent means to the realization of his reprehensible ideal; and so on. We disagree only on whether he is a fanatic. In my view, we want the term *fanatic* to do some distinctive work. If the term is just picking out people who have extreme and misguided views, who take extreme methods to the realization of their goals, and so on, it's not really doing any distinctive work. We can see this when we turn to Cassam's positive account. Here's Cassam's account of fanaticism:

> Fanatics have *unwarranted* contempt for other people's ideals and interests, are willing to trample on those ideals and interests in pursuit of their own *perverted* ideals, and impose their ideals on others, by force if necessary. Fanatics are unwilling to think critically about their ideals because they regard them as indubitable. However, they are willing to sacrifice themselves and others in pursuit of their ideals. (Cassam 2022: 133, emphasis added)

This account might appear quite close to mine, insofar as Cassam and I agree that fanaticism involves some form of insulation from justificatory reflection, treating an ideal as overriding, and so on. The key difference emerges in the terms that I have italicized in the quotation above. Cassam thinks that a purely *formal* account of fanaticism cannot be successful. A formal account, like my own, analyzes fanaticism in a way that does not make reference to the *contents* of the fanatic's ideals; a substantive account, like Cassam's, makes essential references to the contents. Thus, Cassam writes:

> It was not just his irrational commitment to his ideals that made Heydrich a fanatic but also the fact that these were morally *perverted* ideals.
> (Cassam 2022: 122)

Note the implication: a psychological duplicate of Heydrich who differed from him only in that his ideals were morally respectable would not count as a fanatic.

I have no monopoly on the notion of fanaticism; if someone wishes to define the term in a way that makes essential reference to morally perverted ideals, that is their prerogative. But I think an account of Cassam's form loses much of the point of singling out fanaticism. Notice that if we interpret fanaticism in the way that Cassam suggests, then the core problem with the fanatic is simply that he has morally objectionable attitudes or ideals. And that brings me to my chief disagreement with Cassam: it's one thing to have morally objectionable ideals and attitudes; it's another to be a fanatic. It seems to me to make perfect sense to say: not only does that person have morally perverted ideals and unwarranted contempt for others, but in addition to that he's a fanatic. This additional charge picks out something about the way in which the agent relates to his ideals, rather than merely rejecting the ideals' content. And that is what my account captures: the fanatic is distinguished in part by his fragility.

This brings us back a point I mentioned previously (see Chapter 3). Sometimes, sacred values are problematic solely because of their contents: the content would be objectionable if treated as an ordinary value and is equally objectionable when sacralized. Sometimes, sacred values *magnify* the problem: a content that would be objectionable when valued in the ordinary way becomes still more objectionable when sacralized. And sometimes, sacred values *create* problems: a content that would be *un*objectionable when valued in the ordinary way becomes objectionable when sacralized.[9] Cassam's account elides these complications. In focusing only on *perverted ideals,* it ignores the way in which the perversion can lie in the sacralization of an ideal, rather than in the content of the ideal. And, more generally, it ignores the way in which commitments to ideals can be problematic not solely in virtue of the content of these ideals, but in virtue of the way that the agent relates to these ideals. That is what my account of fanaticism attempts to identify.

That said, as I have discussed above, certain contents are more likely to promote fanaticism, and certain contents are likely to impede it. Any content that focuses on toleration will impede it; any that focuses on intolerance will promote it. So Cassam is certainly right that there is *some* connection between the contents of ideals and the question of fanaticism. But I hope the remarks above show why we should not adopt a purely content-based account of fanaticism.

7.7 Conclusion

I've attempted to provide an account of the fanatic. The Enlightenment accounts of fanaticism focus on three features:

E1. Unwavering commitment to an ideal.
E2. Unwillingness to subject the ideal (or its premises) to rational critique.
E3. The presumption of a non-rational sanction for the ideal (or its premises).

---

[9] The reverse is also the case. In Chapter 3, I presented cases in which it seems objectionable to value some content merely in the ordinary way, and praiseworthy to sacralize it.

I've argued that (E1)–(E3) do not offer an adequate characterization of fanaticism. They do characterize a state that I've called being a *true believer*. These are purely rational moves that can go wrong; they consist in displaying inappropriate certitude about some ideal, which is preserved by refusing to subject the ideal to rational critique and taking it to have a non-rational provenance.

But this alone doesn't constitute fanaticism—the peaceful Buddhists and the tolerant Christians are fully committed on these fronts, and may even exceed the fanatic in the degree to which they meet each of these conditions, but are not properly characterized as fanatics. For they lack the propensity to violent intolerance that is characteristic of fanatics. In short: (E1)–(E3) have no direct bearing on whether the individual is disposed to violent intolerance.

I've argued that the true believer can develop in a certain way, and when he does fanaticism emerges. There are four mutually reinforcing properties that can jointly lead such an individual to fanaticism:

F1. Sacred values: the agent adopts one or more sacred values.

F2. Fragility of the self: the agent needs to treat a value as sacred in order to preserve her identity.

F3. Fragility of the value: the value's status is taken to be threatened when it is not widely accepted.

F4. Group identity: the fanatic identifies herself with a group, where this group is defined by shared commitment to a sacred value.

Each of these lends support to the other. An agent whose self is robustly unified independently of commitment to an unquestioned ideal won't be liable to treat the ideal as threatened by criticism, nor will he see those who share his ideal as a unified front against an enemy who, by rejecting or questioning the ideal, puts the ideal at risk.

I began by asking whether "fanaticism" picks out anything objective or is a mere term of abuse. The above account does pick out a constellation of mutually reinforcing traits. Conditions (E1)–(E3) are common, perhaps pervasive. But (F2)–(F4) are not. None of these connections are necessary; an agent could exhibit a few of these traits without exhibiting all of them, or could exhibit some to a high degree and others to a minimal degree. There will be borderline cases. But (F2)–(F4) do tend to be reinforce one another; and when all present to high degrees, we tend to have paradigmatic cases of fanaticism.

In this chapter, I have merely tried to get the phenomenon of fanaticism into view. Thus, my account does leave several unanswered questions. Is there a way of blocking the progression from (E1)–(E3) to (F1)–(F4)? In other words, is there a way of blocking the progression from true believer to fanatic? Nietzschean accounts tell us to be stronger, to be more self-reliant—in effect, to get rid of condition (F2). But is that realistic? Is it desirable? Toleration-based accounts might focus on (F3): let the ideal be questioned. Do not reject those who oppose it. But can it then serve its function of promoting psychic integrity? I can't answer these questions here. But my hope is that the account of fanaticism at least puts us in a position to investigate them. I return to a version of them in Chapter 9, asking whether we can be devoted to an ideal without being fanatical.

I conclude by noting that what is philosophically fascinating about fanaticism is that a purely rational failure—being a true believer—can, when coupled with an additional practical defect concerning one's psychic integrity and a particular view of the fragility of value, produce a moral defect. A tacit philosophical view concerning the status and fragility of value can promote a dangerous pathology.

8
Group Fanaticism and Narratives of Ressentiment

The two previous chapters analyzed individual fanaticism. In this chapter, I ask how individual fanaticism relates to *group fanaticism*. In ordinary discourse, we speak both of individual fanatics and of fanatical groups. Just as in the individual case, the labeling of a group as fanatical can be mere rhetoric; perusing newspapers, you can find everyone from vegans to environmentalists to the Republican party to supporters of Bernie Sanders labeled as fanatical groups. Much of this is just invective, of no philosophical interest; it consists in nothing more than insulting and condemning groups with whom one disagrees. But, just as in the individual case, I think there is a philosophically interesting phenomenon that we can uncover. There are some groups that actually merit the label. Or so I will argue.

I begin, in Section 8.1, by reviewing two accounts of individual fanaticism. I ask how these accounts could be extended to groups. Section 8.2 considers a very simple but ultimately mistaken view of group fanaticism, according to which a group qualifies as fanatical if a sufficient number of its members are fanatics. The failure of this account indicates that features of the group, rather than merely features of the individual members, must be linked to fanaticism. Section 8.3 clarifies this point by distinguishing between the features of fanatical groups and those of other types of problematic groups, such as extremist and cultish groups. This puts us in a position, in Section 8.4, to argue for the *generative view* of group fanaticism. On this view, a group qualifies as fanatical only if it has features that promote individual fanaticism. This raises the question of *how* groups might promote individual fanaticism. While I don't think there is any one unique way of doing so, I do think that there is a very common feature of fanatical groups: they encourage an emotion that philosophers sometimes call "ressentiment." Section 8.5 examines this point, explaining what ressentiment is, how it can be fostered, and how it can lead to fanaticism.

8.1 Two Accounts of Individual Fanaticism

In the previous chapters, I distinguished two views of fanaticism. The *Enlightenment account* treats fanaticism as a purely epistemic failing. In particular, it maintains that a fanatic is distinguished by:

(E1)   Unwavering commitment to an ideal.

(E2)   Unwillingness to subject the ideal (or its premises) to rational critique.

(E3)   The presumption of a non-rational sanction for the ideal (or its premises).

But there's a problem with this account. The Enlightenment thinkers believe that fanatics tend to be violently intolerant. I argued that the Enlightenment account of fanaticism fails to explain *why* fanatics would have a tendency toward violent intolerance. For (E1)–(E3) are only accidentally connected to violent intolerance. Rather than uncovering genuine fanaticism, features (E1)–(E3) are better associated with an epistemic failing that I call being a *true believer*.

Thus, I introduced an alternative account:

(F1)   Sacred values: the agent adopts one or more sacred values.

(F2)   Fragility of the self: the agent needs to treat a value as sacred in order to preserve his identity.

(F3)   Fragility of the value: the value's status is taken to be threatened when it is not widely accepted.

(F4)   Group identity: the fanatic identifies himself with a group, where this group is defined by shared commitment to a sacred value.

I suggested that this account is superior insofar as (F1)–(F4) do dispose individuals to violent intolerance. This doesn't mean that every individual who exhibits (F1)–(F4) will be violent and intolerant; particularities of the individual's psychology and circumstances may block these tendencies. But, I argued, (F1)–(F4) do generate a disposition toward violence and intolerance.

With this account at hand, I can now state my question more precisely. Suppose we accept this psychological account of individual fanaticism. How do we account for fanatical *groups?* Can we just apply some analogue of (F1)–(F4) to groups, or do we need a different account?

8.2 The Simple Account of Group Fanaticism

Let's start with the most obvious possibility.

<u>The simple account:</u>   a group is fanatical iff all or most of its members are fanatical.

The problem with the simple account is that it makes the connection between group and individual fanaticism *accidental.* Suppose a group of fanatical neo-Nazis happens to form a knitting club. And suppose the knitting club focuses exclusively on knitting: during the hours they spend there, the neo-Nazis talk about nothing but knitting. The knitting group's members are entirely fanatical. But the knitting group itself is not fanatical in any interesting sense. We can see this by contrasting the neo-Nazi knitting club with a group that actually does encourage violence, such as the violent white supremacist group Atomwaffen. Consider the words of one Atomwaffen member, announcing the formation of this group and calling for new members:

> We are very fanatical, ideological band of comrades who do both activism and militant training. Hand to hand, arms training, and various other forms of training. As for activism, we spread awareness in the real world through unconventional means. (keyboard warriorism is nothing to do with what we are.). Joining us means serious dedication not only to the Atomwaffen Division and its members but to the goal of ultimate uncompromising victory. With this means only those willing to get out on the streets, in the woods, or where ever we maybe in the world and work together in the physical realm. As started earlier, no keyboard warriorism, (we do however do a lot of hacking, you won't hear about this though) if you don't want to meet up and get things done don't bother.
>
> (October 12, 2015 post by Clint Russell on the "Iron March" website)[1]

Atomwaffen explicitly presents itself as encouraging its members to participate in violent activities in the real world, seeking "ultimate uncompromising victory" over nonwhites.

As a comparison of the knitting club and Atomwaffen makes clear, there is an important difference between genuinely fanatical groups and groups all of whose members are fanatics. If the complex nature of fanaticism makes this point hard to see, we can illustrate it with a simpler example. There's a difference between violent groups and violent individuals. Suppose, for example, that we have a hiking club. And suppose that for a decade or so all of the members of this group, which is organized merely around hiking, happen to be violent, prone to outbursts of anger, gripped by strong angry passions. Yet the group itself is just focused on hiking: all of the group's statements, ideals, and commitments concern only the enjoyment of the outdoors. I think we'd say, in such a case, that the group itself isn't violent, but the members are.

But now consider a twist: suppose that group begins endorsing or encouraging violence. Perhaps its leaders praise those who fight. Perhaps its goals and ideals come to be tinged with things encouraging violence. Suppose it is no longer an accident that it is composed largely of violent individuals: suppose it seeks out those individuals, encourages its members to display violence, and so forth. Then

---

[1] https://web.archive.org/web/20170615224829/http://ironmarch.org/index.php?/topic/5647-atomwaffen-division-central-topic/

it seems much clearer that we'd want to label it a violent group, rather than just a group whose members happen to be violent.

Why is this? The answer is clear enough: in our modified case, the group itself has features that encourage violence. The connection between group membership and violence is no longer purely accidental.

We can capture the difference in terms of collective intentionality. I won't defend any particular view of collective intentionality, but in rejecting the Simple View I will rely on the idea that there's a difference between collective intentions and aggregates of individual intentions. It's widely accepted that there's a difference between these two scenarios: (1) you intend to visit New York and I intend to visit New York; (2) we intend to visit New York. Sums of individual intentions aren't identical to collective intentions. A group may comprise individuals all of whom, individually, have the intention to participate in violent activities; but that doesn't mean that the group has a collective intention to participate in violent activities. And that's just what's on display in the above cases: the hypothetical knitting club members have a collective intention to knit, and individual intentions to participate in violent activities; but they lack the collective intention to participate in violent activities. Atomwaffen's members, by contrast, do have a collective intention to engage in violent activities.

That's the problem with the Simple Account. On the Simple Account, the group's features bear no connection to the individual fanaticism of its members. But presumably the *point* of labeling a group fanatical is to identify features of the group that bear some interesting connection to fanaticism. As I will discuss below, certain *types* of groups, or certain *features* of groups, either attract or are conducive to fanatics. An account that merely labeled groups fanatical when a sufficient number of their members were fanatical would ignore this fact. It wouldn't explain which features of the group were responsible for the fanaticism.

8.3 Distinctions between Types of Problematic Groups

It's conceptually possible for there to be non-fanatical groups all or most of whose members are fanatics. So we need a different account of fanatical groups. How might we generate that account? Well, another straightforward possibility presents itself. I've just pointed out that we can distinguish violent groups in terms of their collective intentions. So why not employ a similar account to fanatical groups? Perhaps we can find something that fanatical groups collectively intend.

Already, though, I think we can see a problem with this proposal. Violent groups collectively intend to engage in violence but fanatical groups don't collectively intend to engage in fanaticism. Fanaticism, as I've been analyzing it, needn't involve any particular intention. Consider individual fanaticism: if my account is correct, fanaticism pertains to the manner in which one selects, relates to, and engages with various values rather than to the contents of these values. So, if we wanted to find a collective intention for fanatical groups, it's not clear what the content of the intention would be.

It is, however, true that fanatics tend to behave in certain ways: they tend to engage in violent intolerance. Might we then define fanatical groups in terms of their tendency to promote violent intolerance? For example, perhaps we could define fanatical groups in terms of collective intentions to engage in violent actions against other groups or individuals.

I think there are several problems with this kind of approach. First, the account is too broad. It captures too many groups that we would ordinarily classify as non-fanatical. For example: during World War II, the Allied governments promoted violence against the Axis powers. But it would be odd to conclude that the UK was fanatical in responding violently to the Nazi attacks. Or: Nelson Mandela co-founded the armed branch of the African National Congress, Umkhonto we Sizwe (Spear of the Nation). At his behest, group members began attacking government installations and contemplated a campaign of guerilla warfare. This group certainly promoted violence, but it's not obvious that it should be characterized as a fanatical group. Many see its actions as rational. Examples can be multiplied.

We might also try to define fanatical groups in terms of the contents of their views; but this seems hopeless. There's too much diversity in the groups. There's very little ideological overlap in the views of ISIS and Atomwaffen, for example.[2]

We might try to avoid this problem by stepping back from the particularities of the group's ideology and focusing on more general claims that tend to be accepted by fanatical groups. For example, in a recent book J.M. Berger defines extremism as follows: "the belief that an in-group's success or survival can never be separated from the need for hostile action against an out-group" (Berger 2018: 44). This does seem to be a common thread in many fanatical groups: ISIS and Atomwaffen have different in- and out-groups, different methods, and different goals, but they do agree that the in-group is threatened by an out-group, which must be attacked.

Again, though, I worry that this account is too broad. Under this definition, most of the United States and Soviet administrations during the Cold War would have qualified as extremist groups. The Allied governments during WWII would have been just as extremist as the Axis powers; both meet the definition equally well. After all, as the WWII case demonstrates, it's sometimes *true* that in-group's success or survival can't be separated from the need from hostile action against an

---

[2] Of course, we could try to characterize the content in other ways. For example, perhaps fanatical groups share the idea that outsiders are nothing more than threats. Or perhaps fanatical groups share the idea that outsiders are not deserving of respect. I won't try to offer a full rebuttal of these proposals here. I think they suffer from the same flaw as content-based accounts of individual fanaticism: a group can view outsiders as threats, deny that they are deserving of respect, and so on, without being fanatical. Fanaticism picks out an *additional* problem with groups, a problem that is not reducible solely to the contents of the group's ideal.

out-group. And, depending on how we define "hostile action," the notion could cover even more cases: groups fighting climate change will have success only if they overcome out-groups who deny climate change; groups fighting for universal health care in the US will be successful only if they overcome out-groups who fight against those plans; groups fighting for mandatory vaccinations will be successful only if they overcome anti-vaxxers; and so on.[3]

This brings us to another problem with the proposal: it risks conflating a number of different types of groups. Consider a few types of groups that are potentially problematic:

- Violent groups: groups that encourage violence.
- Intolerant groups: groups that attempt to overrule, suppress, or eliminate opposed views.
- Extremist groups: groups that endorse values that are considered extreme or who advocate extreme measures toward more widely accepted values.
- Cultish groups: groups whose members venerate a leader, treating the leader as having unquestionable authority to direct the lives of his followers.

Fanatical groups are often violent. They are often intolerant. They are often extreme. They are often cultish. But I don't think that any of these features are sufficient for a group to qualify as fanatical. A group can be violent, intolerant, extreme, or cultish without thereby being fanatical.

Of course, it might be possible to define *types* of violence, intolerance, extremism, or cultishness that correlate more closely with fanaticism. And certainly if a group has *all* of these features, it is likely to be fanatical. Still, I think we should keep these notions apart. I've already given some examples of the way in which the promotion of violence comes apart from fanaticism, so let's consider the other cases.

Let's start with intolerance. While fanatical groups tend to be intolerant, intolerance alone isn't sufficient for fanaticism. After all, there are groups that are intolerant of hate speech, or anti-vaccination movements, or climate change denial, that don't seem to be fanatical.

Extremism is sometimes associated with fanaticism, but these don't have to align. The first thing to notice is that groups are labeled extreme in relation to some baseline of what's considered normal or acceptable (see Cassam 2022). But the standards for normalcy and acceptability shift over time. By the standards of the US South in the 1960s, the Freedom Riders were an extremist group.

---

[3] More generally, we might consider whether a fanatical group could be defined roughly as follows: the members of the group have a shared intention to protect a sacred value that is perceived as threatened by outsiders. Again, I think this is too broad, as the examples above indicate. It might be a necessary condition, but it is not yet a sufficient condition.

Analogously, the National Woman's Party, which picketed in front of the White House during World War I in order to promote female suffrage, was widely seen as extreme group. But I doubt that most of us would today see these groups as fanatical. Aside from that, it's possible for a group to be fanatical while aiming to realize values that are politically and socially moderate. Violent environmental groups are a good example: recent surveys show that the majority of respondents endorse coordinated responses to climate change; but few would approve of the tactics of the Earth Liberation Front when it firebombs housing. Or: many people are opposed to nuclear power, but few would endorse Chaïm Nissim's 1982 rocket attack on the French Superphénix nuclear power plant. The goals are moderate but the methods aren't.

Fanatical groups are often cultish—Aum Shinriko, which carried out the Tokyo subway sarin attack in 1995, is a good example. But fanatical groups needn't be cultish. Insofar as we take white nationalist and jihadist groups as examples, it's a familiar fact that many of them are organized as independent cells without a central authority figure. The various affiliates of Al Qaeda are exemplary in this regard. And, looking at this from the other direction, not all cultish groups are fanatical. For example, if we define cultishness as I've done above—treating a leader as having unquestionable authority to direct the lives of his followers—then some organized religions with central authority figures will qualify (so long as the authority is not dispersed or checked by others within the religion).

In light of these considerations, I think it makes sense to distinguish fanatical groups from violent, intolerant, extreme, and cultish groups. Of course, these considerations aren't decisive. Someone who wanted to identify group fanaticism with cultishness, extremism, intolerance, or violence could refine the view, adding qualifications or complications. That might work. But I will pursue a different strategy.

I suggest that it's helpful to think of fanatical groups in the following way: fanatical groups are groups that *encourage fanaticism amongst their members.* I will call this the *generative view* of group fanaticism.

<u>Generative View of Group Fanaticism</u>: a group qualifies as fanatical iff it promotes individual fanaticism.

Why might we want to accept the generative view?

Presumably, the point of labeling a group as fanatical is to pick out some distinctive problem with the group. Many groups encourage violence, intolerance, and so forth. But some groups are problematic for a different reason: they encourage the emergence of fanaticism. Insofar as fanaticism is a distinctive pathology, and insofar as we can identify the way in which certain groups promote this pathology, we would have reason to single out these groups with a special term.[4]

---

[4] Note that condition F4, above, already linked individual fanaticism to a certain form of group identification. Thus, a particular form of collective belonging is part of the definition of individual

Turning to historical work on fanaticism, it's notable that many writers are concerned to study fanatical groups precisely because they see these groups as producing ever more fanatics. A number of writers treat fanaticism as *contagious*. Fanaticism spreads on contact, like a disease. This claim is endorsed by several early modern philosophers, including at least Shaftesbury and Voltaire. Consider again a quotation from Shaftesbury:

> Fury flies from face to face, and the disease [fanaticism] is *no sooner seen than caught*. They who in a better situation of mind have beheld a multitude under the power of passion, have owned that they saw in the countenance of men something more ghastly and terrible than at other times expressed on the most passionate occasions. Such force has society in ill as well as in good passions, and so much stronger any affection is for being social and communicative.
>
> (Shaftesbury 1999: 10; emphasis added)

Fanaticism spreads: it is "no sooner seen than caught." And Voltaire agrees, claiming that fanaticism is a "spiritual pestilence," "a malady of the mind, which is taken in the same way as smallpox" (Voltaire's *Philosophical Dictionary*, "Fanaticism" entry). Martin Luther warns of the same thing: his term for fanatics, *Schwärmer*, was intended in part to draw attention to the way in which the "insane peasants in their raging" *swarm*, like flies or locusts, across the countryside. For, he warns us, they "betake themselves to violence, and rob and rage and act like mad dogs." These peasants are "like a great fire, which attacks and lays waste a whole land... Therefore let everyone who can, smite, slay and stab, secretly or openly, remembering that nothing can be more poisonous, hurtful or devilish" than these fanatics (Luther, "Against the Murderous, Thieving Hordes of Peasants", 1525).

Disease; pestilence; swarms; great fires. These claims are metaphorical and are certainly imprecise. But I think they contain a truth. Fanaticism tends to flare up at certain times and in certain conditions; it can be dormant for a long while, then spread quickly. In some cases, mere exposure to fanatical groups seems to draw ordinary individuals into fanaticism. For example, a recent review article sifted through over 5000 empirical studies of radicalization and concluded that there is "tentative evidence that exposure to radical violent online material is associated with extremist online and offline attitudes" (Hassan et al. 2018: 1). If correct, this is striking: *mere exposure* to a radical position is associated with affective changes.

---

fanaticism; and, I will be arguing, a particular form of relation to individuals is part of the definition of group fanaticism. So individual fanaticism and group fanaticism are often intertwined. That said, it is possible for individuals to be fanatical in relation to groups that are not themselves fanatical. An individual could manifest features F1–F4, and thereby qualify as a fanatic; in virtue of F4, he would be related to some group that defines itself in terms of a sacred value; but the group itself could be non-fanatical (assuming it has no tendency to encourage the emerge of individual fanatics).

Some of the recent empirical work on radicalization also operates on this assumption. People are said to *radicalize* when they move from ordinary lives to extremism, fanaticism, or terrorism. In a review of this literature, Quassim Cassam writes,

> The model of radicalization to which many Western governments are committed is what might be called a 'contagion' model. This represents radicalization as an ideological disease or virus to which some individuals are vulnerable, and they catch the disease by contact with infectious agents, in the form of radicalizers with extremist ideologies.... This leads to the suggestion that vulnerable people can be prevented from catching the extremist virus by being prevented from coming into contact with radicalizers... (Cassam 2018: 195)

In general: many of these studies try to show that there are certain groups that exert a corrupting influence on prospective members. And many of these studies accept the contagion model, the idea that fanaticism spreads by mere contact.

But this is probably too simplistic. Cassam critiques the contagion model, quite rightly noting that the dominant accounts of radicalization are unable to make any predictive claims. After all, *many* people have contact with extremist ideas (I do, for example; and, in virtue of reading this book, you have a bit of contact with them as well); but very few people are turned into extremists by this mere contact. At most, as Hassan et al. 2018 demonstrate, prolonged contact with extremist viewpoints may tend to lead to extremist attitudes; but most people with extremist attitudes don't perform actions that we'd characterize as extreme. There's a world of difference between sympathizing with ISIS and joining ISIS. There's a world of difference between having racist attitudes and joining Atomwaffen.

I think Cassam is right that the contagion model can't serve in a predictive capacity. The effects are just too weak; there's too much distance between having extremist affects and being a fanatic; and there are too many confounding factors, including the relationship between the fanatical ideology's claims and the individual person's values, commitments, circumstances, relationships, capacity for openminded critical thought, and so on. Nonetheless, I also think there's something right about the idea that fanatical groups generate new fanatics. So let's look more carefully at how this might work. How might a fanatical group generate new fanatics?

I think there are two main pathways. Sometimes, the spread of fanaticism is individually managed: some fanatical groups actively try to recruit new members on an individual basis. At other times, fanaticism seems to spread without this kind of overt contact and management of individuals. Let's look at cases of each.

We will start with a case of intentional cultivation of an individual, an attempt to shift a person toward fanaticism. Consider an interviewee who went by the pseudonym Alex.[5] Alex lived in a rural area of Washington State. At the age of twenty-three, she'd dropped out of college and was supporting herself by babysitting and by teaching Sunday school at her church. She was isolated, living with her elderly grandparents and having little contact with anyone else. But she spent hours and hours online. These online activities were initially innocuous; she mainly streamed movies. But on August 19, 2014, she—like so many others—was horrified by the news that ISIS had beheaded the American journalist James Foley. ISIS had uploaded a video to YouTube entitled "A Message to America." The video starts with Obama announcing airstrikes against ISIS; it then cuts to Foley, kneeling in a desert next to a masked ISIS member; Foley, dressed in an orange jumpsuit intended to invoke those worn by US prisoners in Guantanamo Bay, reads a message condemning American activities, reproaching his family members by name, expressing a wish not to have been an American; Foley is then beheaded with a knife; after the execution, the terrorist shows another journalist prisoner and warns that he will be next (and, two weeks later, he is).

Before seeing this video, Alex knew nothing at all about Foley or ISIS. But she became absorbed by the images of the beheading. She searched for more information; she logged on to Twitter, looking for explanations from sympathizers. As she put it, "I was looking for people who agreed with what they were doing, so that I could understand why they were doing it." And she had no trouble: "It was actually really easy to find them."

She began chatting with people who identified themselves as members of ISIS. She was struck by their apparent kindness: "Once they saw that I was sincere in my curiosity, they were very kind. They asked questions about my family, about where I was from, about what I wanted to do in life." This was new for her: she was an object of attention; people wanted to know about her. Over the next six months, she spent thousands of hours talking to several dozen accounts, several of which were operated by people who identified themselves as ISIS members. People behind these accounts sent her money, gifts of chocolate, copies of the Qur'an, hijabs, prayer rugs, gift certificates to an Islamic book store; they advised her on becoming a Muslim; on religious rituals; on breaking off contact with non-Muslims (i.e., with everyone in her town). She converted to Islam; after doing so, she posted on Twitter: "I actually have brothers and sisters. I am crying." One of her online contacts attempted to arrange a marriage for her to a forty-five-year-old man in Syria. He offered to purchase her tickets to Austria and arrange travel from there. Before that could take place, Alex's grandmother intervened, contacting the FBI.

In the space of six months, Alex went from knowing absolutely nothing about ISIS, Islam, Syria, or any related matters to readying herself for a trip to Syria to marry an ISIS member to whom she'd never spoken. The appeal was obvious,

---

[5] The details of this case are drawn from Callimachi 2015.

deliberate: the ISIS recruitment manuals specifically enjoin recruiters to target lonely, isolated individuals, offering them a sense of community and purpose. In particular: see the fifty-page handbook by Abu ʿAmr al-Qaʿidi, *A Course in the Art of Recruitment*.[6] It provides a five-stage process for cultivating recruits, together with metrics for measuring success, flow charts to guide the process, and so on. To simplify a bit, the five stages are: (1) selecting a target and making their acquaintance, with advice on which types of people are most susceptible (youth in remote areas are mentioned as easy to recruit); (2) building a personal relationship with the target, largely by discussing personal matters and becoming friends while avoiding controversial topics; (3) awakening generalized religious sentiments in the target, in particular by isolating the recruit from his family and society, by emphasizing punishment and reward (the book claims that successful recruitment "normally happens to those who fear the torment of the afterlife and who come to know that jihad is the salvation from eternal damnation; the result is that jihad is desired and craved"), and encouraging the target to view videos of "paradigms" such as Osama bin Laden and Ayman al-Zawahiri; (4) instilling jihadist concepts in the recruit, with a particular focus on adherence to the Qur'an, the religious duty of jihad, and the idea that democracy is unacceptable; (5) the formation of a cell that will carry out violent jihad. Alex had made it to stage (3) and was on the cusp of (4).

Alex is an example of deliberate, intentional recruitment. She is carefully managed.[7] But other cases involve a more self-driven process. There's a large literature on what's sometimes called *self*-radicalization. Alex is radicalized by a group of people who seek to recruit her. But others aren't actively recruited, or at least aren't actively recruited until late in the game. They somehow shift from more or less ordinary lives to fanaticism, and they do this on their own.

How does this happen? The stories of radicalization are as multifarious as the stories of any other attachment: people are drawn into relationships with fanatical groups at times through loneliness, at times through rage; at times through despair, at times through certitude. Nonetheless, there are massive research projects underway on this topic. Most of these projects focus on how individuals become terrorists or members of terrorist groups. Terrorism and fanaticism aren't equivalent: you can be a fanatic without being a terrorist, and vice versa. But, insofar as fanaticism involves a disposition toward violent intolerance, it could be a factor in explaining individual's commitment to terrorism. So some of these points will be transferable.

---

[6] One translation is available here: https://archive.org/stream/ACourseInTheArtOfRecruiting-RevisedJuly2010/A_Course_in_the_Art_of_Recruiting_-_Revised_July2010_djvu.txt

[7] ISIS explicitly encouraged this. Its members were in regular contact with those who considered joining, offering advice on even the most trivial matters. One example: when a potential recruit asked what he should bring to Syria, Abu Turab, a twenty-five-year-old American who had joined ISIS, wrote "Cargo pants (combat trousers), 511 brand is good. I have Old Navy, lol, but water-resistant stuff is the best" (quoted in Stern and Berger 2015: 84–5).

The first potential explanation of radicalization treats it as analogous to any other form of human activity: some individuals turn to terrorism or join fanatical groups because, in light of their beliefs and evaluative commitments, doing so is instrumentally rational. For example, given certain beliefs a person might conclude that terrorist activity is the best way of achieving a putatively valuable political goal. Al Qaeda, at least in its early days, justified its actions in that way: it produced at least two versions of a seven phase, twenty-year plan, which began with provoking the US to attack Muslim countries, inciting local resistance and opposition to the US, broadening the conflict into new territories, and so on. Several phases of this plan have come to pass exactly as predicted, and Bin Laden correctly noted that "All we have to do is to send two mujahideen to the furthest point east to raise a piece of cloth on which is written al Qaeda in order to make the generals race there."[8] So we shouldn't discount a very straightforward explanation for radicalization: certain beliefs and evaluative commitments will make radicalized behavior appear eminently rational.

The question, though, is how we get to those beliefs and values. And this is where the real work begins. There is little agreement in the work on radicalization; theories abound.[9] Let me give a few examples. Proponents of *Significance Quest Theory* (which I discussed in the last chapter) argue that people—especially people in precarious social or economic circumstances—seek goals or quests that provide them with a sense of meaning (Kruglanski et al. 2014). People are attracted to fanatical groups insofar as these groups offer a significant goal toward which one can strive. Another strand of research focuses on *peer groups*. To simplify, this research project relies on the idea that fanatical groups provide a welcoming community for otherwise isolated individuals (see, for example, Klausen 2015). Finally, some researchers advocate *Identity Theory*, which states that "experiencing identity conflict or confusion—whether because of a struggle to adapt to a new culture, one's stage of life (e.g., adolescence), or other challenges—is often viewed as potentially leaving individuals more open to adopting new ideas and behaviors, including those associated with terrorism" (Smith 2018). One could go on, but these are three of the major theories. In short: interviews and studies reveal that radicalized individuals are often driven by three factors: a desire for something that gives life importance or provides a goal toward which one can strive; a longing for a sense of acceptance or community; and the attempt to forge a new sense of identity.[10]

---

[8] "Full Transcript of Bin Ladin's Speech," Al Jazeera, November 1, 2014. See also Crenshaw 1990.

[9] McCauley and Moskalenko 2017 is a helpful recent overview.

[10] There are disputes about whether one of these factors is more powerful than the other. For example, Sageman claims that "social bonds play a more important role in the emergence of the global Salafi jihad than ideology" (Sageman 2004: 178). But even he admits that evaluative changes or changes in ideals are also central: "With the gradual intensity of interaction within the group and the progressive distance from former ties, they [members of the group] changed their values. From secular people they became more religious. From material rewards, they began to value spiritual rewards,

Suppose something like that is right. It's certainly true that paradigmatically fanatical groups tend to offer narratives that would be attractive to those seeking goals, community, and identity. But one thing that's left out of these explanations is the simple fact that *lots of groups* do this. To be sure, ISIS provides goals, community, and identity; but so does a knitting club. Stormfront provides goals, community, and identity; but so does Oprah's book club. So, while I certainly don't want to dispute the idea that some people join radical groups because they seek goals, community, or identity, this explanation isn't particularly illuminating. These are reasons for joining groups in general, rather than fanatical or extremist groups in particular.[11]

Let's take stock. I've noted that those who study fanatical, extremist, or radical groups often claim that these groups exert an attractive force on potential recruits, pulling them into the group, perhaps even spreading like disease to those sufficiently exposed to the group. I do think there's something right about this. Fanatical groups are groups that generate individual fanatics. That's the common theme both in the Enlightenment account and in modern work on radicalization. And that's why fanaticism is distinct from the other group pathologies that I mentioned above: you can be intolerant, extreme, or even cultish without suffering these particular forms of damage. But there's a problem: aside from the actively managed cases of individual recruitment, we lack an explanation of how fanatical groups would generate new fanatics. The accounts with which we've been provided are just general explanations of why individuals join groups. They don't single out any distinctive features of fanatical groups. So, we have a question: is there anything distinctive about the way in which fanatical groups generate fanatics? I will suggest that there is.

8.4 Group Fanaticism as the Tendency to Encourage Individual Fanaticism

I've given some reasons for accepting the following account:

<u>Generative View of Group Fanaticism:</u> a group qualifies as fanatical iff it promotes individual fanaticism.

---

including eventually otherworldly rewards. From the pursuit of short term opportunities, they turned to a long term vision of the world." (Sageman 2008: 86–7). See also work by Jessica Stern, Deeyah Khan, Eli Saslow, Graeme Wood, and Jerrold Post.

[11] Of course, proponents of these views do have responses. For example, proponents of Identity Theory can agree that knitting clubs also provide the agent with a sense of identity, but argue that they do so *to a much lesser degree* than fanatical groups. After all, fanatical groups tend to provide extremely clear criteria for belonging to the group; they encompass many or all aspects of the person's life, rather than providing merely an isolated diversion; and so on. In short: while the knitting club and the fanatical group don't differ in the functions that they perform, they do differ in the *degree* to which they perform these functions. While I lack the space to do full justice to this point, I think my objection retains its force: if it is to be more than a mere accident that fanatical groups clearly demarcate their members, are all-encompassing, and so on, we need some further explanation of why this is so. Below, I will postulate a mechanism that explains why fanatical groups have these kinds of features.

Of course, this account is to some extent stipulative. I am not claiming that we *must* understand group fanaticism in this way. Rather, I am claiming that it's illuminating to do so. It helps us to see a distinct problem with certain types of groups. Some groups are problematic because they are violent; others, because they are intolerant; others, because they are extreme; others, because they are cultish. But in addition to all of that, some groups are problematic for another reason: because they encourage individual fanaticism. This isn't equivalent to or reducible to any of the other problems. It thus merits its own label.

But we need to explain this account in more depth. We've struggled to identify a distinctive mechanism by which fanatical groups would generate new fanatics; the existing literature on the topic doesn't seem particularly helpful, insofar as it specifies mechanisms that are not unique to fanatical groups. I will try to specify a unique mechanism.

The first thing to notice is that the account of group fanaticism relies on an account of individual fanaticism. I've defended the psychological account of individual fanaticism, which analyzes individual fanaticism in terms of features (F1)–(F4), above. For the remainder of this chapter, I will simply assume that this account is correct. Thus, the Generative View says that a group qualifies as fanatical iff it promotes features (F1)–(F4) in its members.

It's relatively easy to see how feature (F1), the acceptance of sacred values, could be promoted. All that we would need is for the group to promulgate the idea that some particular value is inviolable, incontestable, and dialectically invulnerable. Many groups do this. Certain groups even make acceptance of sacred values a condition of group membership: for example, as I pointed out in Chapter 2, Catholicism defines *de fide truths* as claims the rejection of which constitutes heresy. In other words, acceptance of these claims is a necessary condition for being a Catholic. There is a list of these claims; they include: "the soul, for the immediate vision of God, requires the light of glory"; "there is only one God"; "God is infinitely just"; "the world was created for the glorification of God." Some of these express sacred values.

Or, even more directly: consider Catholic statements about the sacred value of human life. Here are a few: "Human life is sacred and inviolable at every moment of existence" (John Paul II 1995: 61); "The absolute inviolability of innocent human life is a moral truth", so that "the direct and voluntary killing of an innocent human being is always gravely immoral" (John Paul II 1995: 57). These are clear and explicit statements of sacred values.

So condition (F1) is straightforward. But conditions (F2)–(F4) are more complex. No doubt (F2)–(F4) can be encouraged in a number of ways. But I will focus on just one method, which I take to be quite common among fanatical groups, and which does distinguish them from more innocuous groups: the fostering of *ressentiment*. To be clear, I am not trying to specify the *single correct* account of how groups promote fanaticism. Rather, I am trying to elucidate one common but underexamined process.

8.5 Fanatical Narratives Encourage (F2)–(F4)

In this section, I will argue that a common and perhaps universal feature of fanatical groups is their tendency to foster an affective condition that Nietzsche describes as "*ressentiment*". When a person accepts a ressentiment-fostering narrative, features (F2)–(F4) are likely to emerge. Thus, by promoting ressentiment-fostering narratives, groups can promote the emergence of fanatical individuals. To see this, though, we'll need to do several things. Section 8.5.1 explains what ressentiment is. Section 8.5.2 explores the way in which certain narratives can promote the emergence of ressentiment. Section 8.5.3 argues that ressentiment and certain kinds of narrative can generate a feedback loop, with each strengthening the other. Section 8.5.4 shows how these features jointly promote conditions (F2)–(F4), and thereby encourage individual fanaticism.

8.5.1 What Is Ressentiment?

To start, we need to say what ressentiment is. Ressentiment is just the French word for resentment. But it acquired a special technical sense in Nietzsche's *Genealogy of Morality*. There, Nietzsche uses "ressentiment" rather than the ordinary German word for resentment, *Groll* (or related words such as *Abneigungen*, or speaking of someone who is *nachtragend* or *übelnehmerisch*). He uses this French word to pick out a state that differs from ordinary resentment. While I won't be endorsing every aspect of Nietzsche's account, I will follow him and other philosophers in distinguishing ressentiment from ordinary resentment.

First, let's define ordinary resentment as *indignation resulting from the belief that one was wronged*. Although nothing that I say will depend on accepting exactly this definition of resentment, I do think this corresponds to the standard usage.

Notice that resentment needn't involve individual wrongs; it can also be responsive to perceived collective wrongs. I can resent someone for shoving me on the subway; or I can resent someone, or some group, for wronging a group or collective with which I identify (Stockdale 2013). A black US citizen who has never himself been subject to mistreatment by the police could nonetheless experience resentment when considering the way in which black people are wronged by the police; a Palestinian living in the US, with no direct connection to people in Palestine, could nonetheless experience resentment when reading of Israeli interactions with Palestinians; a white nationalist, who has never himself experienced any economic hardships or episodes of oppression, could nonetheless experience resentment when contemplating the perceived oppression or diminution of his group. This type of collective resentment, though subject to less philosophical attention than the individual cases, is extremely common.[12]

So resentment can be individual or collective. In either case, it's crucial that resentment requires the agent to perceive herself or her group as wronged. It thus has fairly complex presuppositions and will be dependent upon certain beliefs about the world. Minimally, the agent will have to be capable of identifying a wrongdoer, an act of wronging, and so on. And the resentment will be responsive to these beliefs: if the agent ceases to believe that Bill has wronged her, she should cease to feel resentment; if she believes that Bill has corrected or atoned for the wrong, she should again cease to feel resentment.

Ressentiment shares some of these features. It, too, involves indignation resulting from the belief that one (or, more commonly, one's group) was wronged. But it's more complex. Briefly: ressentiment is a form of resentment coupled with a self-reinforcing, self-perpetuating narrative. I will explain. Although I won't be doing exegetical work, I do think that Friedrich Nietzsche and Max Scheler have identified core features of ressentiment. So let's look at their account.

First, Scheler claims that ressentiment has a particular etiology: it originates from a desire for revenge. But what is revenge? As Scheler understands it, a desire for revenge emerges when (i) the agent perceives himself (or his group) as in some way slighted, injured, or wronged by (ii) some person or group and (iii) seeks some response to this wrong, but (iv) is unable to respond *immediately* to this wrong in a way that he regards as satisfactory, so that (v) gratification is delayed. For example: someone insults me, but I am unable to respond immediately; instead, I fantasize about ways of getting back at him. By contrast, if someone insults me and I immediately respond, it would be at least a little odd to speak of my desiring revenge; the desire for revenge arises only when immediate compensation is unavailable. If we understand revenge in this way, then all cases of desiring revenge will involve a perceived inability to respond immediately to some wrong; and this constitutes an awareness of one's own impotence. In experiencing the desire for revenge, one *wants* to respond, but can't yet do so; so gratification is delayed.

Scheler is here emphasizing the way in which ressentiment is linked to a feeling of impotence. Originally, the feeling of impotence need not have any particular source; the agent could feel impotent because of perceived personal failings, inadequacies, the objective difficulty of attaining what he seeks, and so forth. However, ressentiment leads the agent to see this impotence as attributable to some person or group that is wronging the agent. The feeling of impotence can relate to any number of things: a goal that I see myself as blocked by others from achieving; a social status that I see others as denying me; or, in more complex

---

[12] There is a large literature in political theory that addresses these cases. See, for example, Brown 1995.

cases, a particular self-conception, a particular sense of my own identity, that I see others as threatening or preventing me from attaining.

Let's dwell on that last case for a moment. Ressentiment can arise when an agent wants to attain or preserve some self-conception, but sees others as illegitimately threatening this. One is wronged because one is prevented from attaining or maintaining one's self-conception. In many cases, the person of ressentiment wants to attain a sense of identity that presents him as superior to or at least equal to the person or group that he resents. And this desire is not fulfilled.

This desire for acknowledgement is always present in ressentiment, though it doesn't have to be fully explicit. Unrequited love, unacknowledged talent, unreciprocated admiration, and so forth can give rise to ressentiment even if the person never conceptualizes himself as spurned, unacknowledged, or in any way lacking.[13] And this is what distinguishes ressentiment from mere desire for revenge, which needn't be linked to this desire for acknowledgment. I might seek a secret revenge on someone, sabotaging his romantic prospects without caring whether he ever learns what I've done; or I might damage someone's property without concern for whether he discovers that *I* was the one who damaged it; and so on. But ressentiment is more demanding: it wants not only revenge but also acknowledgement of superiority or at least equality. So in ressentiment the desire for acknowledgment persists; in revenge it needn't.

Third, ressentiment is a dynamic, ramifying psychological process. The desire for revenge can be stable and discrete: I can feel wronged in some specific way and seek some specific compensation. This desire can be satisfied once vengeance is taken. But, all else being equal, ressentiment grows. It is not extinguished by vengeance. It seeks objects, but doesn't dissipate even if these objects are attained. Consider an example: someone embarrasses me by drawing attention to my disheveled appearance; a few days later, I call attention to the food stuck in his teeth; and then I feel restored. The issue is dropped. By contrast, in a case of ressentiment I might feel humiliated by a colleague; and I might continuously seek, over the years, to get back at him in a variety of ways, grimacing as he talks, pointing out his faults to other colleagues, making fun of him behind his back, keeping an eye out for opportunities to point out his faults. So whereas revenge can be directed at a specific, limited act or circumstance, ressentiment recurs. Scheler writes that ressentiment involves "the repeated experiencing and reliving of a particular emotional response reaction against someone else" (Scheler 1994: 2).

---

[13] For a nuanced, insightful discussion of the way in which some cases of resentment involve unreciprocated emotions, see Carlsson 2018. For accounts that treat a need for mutual acknowledgment as playing a fundamental role in social relations and the development of the self, see for example Honneth 1992 and Fraser and Honneth 2003.

Why is this? Why does ressentiment grow? Different answers are available. We might think that ressentiment, like some other emotional processes, has a typical trajectory. Some emotions extinguish quickly, whereas others take the form of long arcs in which they grow and then subside (compare surprise and grief). But there's also a deeper explanation: insofar as ressentiment arises from the attempt to maintain a self-conception, and insofar as this self-conception is seen as threatened by another, the person of ressentiment can find himself in a situation where his very identity is dependent upon the rejection of some out-group. Maintaining one's self-conception requires maintaining one's antagonistic, negating stance toward the one who purportedly threatens it. So the person of ressentiment will be motivated to seek out new occasions for rejection and negation.

This is an important difference between ressentiment and resentment. Some philosophers think that resentment aims at reconciliation; it motivates the agent to seek a form of redress, which eliminates or mitigates the original wrong. Maybe that's true of resentment but it's not true of ressentiment. Eliminating ressentiment would eliminate the agent's identity, or at least a core component of it. Thus, rather than aiming at extinction, ressentiment aims at expansion, growth, perpetuation.

This brings us to the fourth key feature: ressentiment leads to fantasies, imaginative compensation, and the construction of vindicatory narratives. Scheler describes this by saying that ressentiment is a "falsification of the worldview [*Weltanschauung*]" (Scheler 1994: 47); and Nietzsche famously chronicles the process by which ressentiment can lead to a shift in a group's evaluative commitments. Ressentiment tends to draw the person into a new perspective on the world. It doesn't leave things as they are. "Regardless of what he observes, the world has a peculiar structure of emotional stress," so that the person of ressentiment "concentrates increasingly" on the negative: "he has an urge to scold, to depreciate, to belittle whatever he can" (Scheler 1994). The characteristics of the resented person or group are belittled, demeaned, mocked, disparaged.

Scheler offers a helpful characterization these ressentiment-inspired fantasies. He writes that in ressentiment, the person "seeks a feeling of superiority or equality, and he attains his purpose by an illusory *devaluation* of the other man's qualities or by a specific 'blindness' to these qualities. But secondly—and here lies the main achievement of *ressentiment*—he falsifies the *values themselves* which could bestow excellence on any possible objects of comparison" (1994: 34). The person of ressentiment first ignores A's qualities, but second begins to regard those qualities as disvaluable. So, suppose Bill feels threatened by intellectual attainments: never much educated himself and holding on to a vague suspicion that intellectuals would look down on him, Bill disparages intellectuals as effete, as charlatans, as self-important buffoons. He is aware of these judgments. But he is not aware that these judgments and attitudes are manifestations of ressentiment.

So the surface attitudes have connections and presuppositions of which Bill is unaware.

The same structure emerges in Nietzsche's original discussions of ressentiment. Briefly, Nietzsche imagines that in antiquity a vengeful underclass of slaves and priests chafes under the dominance of a noble class. The nobles view the slaves and priests as of lesser worth: according to the noble values, the exemplary individual is the heroic warrior, the Achilles or the Agamemnon, and the slaves and priests are not that. The slaves and priests come to resent the disdain and indifference that the nobles bear them. This, in Nietzsche's story, motivates the devaluation of the noble. The priest, in particular, recognizes that the noble regards the priest as less worthy; recognizes, too, that this judgment is justified by the dominant evaluative system; cannot bear this negative judgment on the part of one whom he esteems; and is thus driven to "revalue values," promulgating a new system of values that champions subservience, humility, and so forth while labeling the heroic warrior evil. The revaluation both degrades the nobles, making them no longer objects of esteem, and makes their contempt for the priest unwarranted and unjustifiable. In essence, the priest develops and comes to accept a narrative according to which the noble is evil and the priest is exemplary; and, under this interpretation, the priest both finds some outlet for his vengeful impulses (e.g. by imagining that the evil noble will be punished in the afterlife) and reduces the negative impact of the noble's disdain (for disdain from one whom you esteem hurts much more than disdain from one you despise).[14]

We don't have to accept the details of Nietzsche's story in order to see its power. In essence, he is describing a characteristic feature of ressentiment: it arises from impotent vengefulness and gives rise to fantasies that involve recharacterizing the world. It is also tied to a desire for acknowledgment of one's status, either as superior or equal or at least as not inferior; and it rankles all the more when this status as inferior is legitimated by the values that one accepts.

Scheler sometimes suggests that ressentiment is just an expression or consequence of a "psychological law" which he states as follows: "we have a tendency to overcome any strong tension between desire and impotence by depreciating or denying the positive value of the desired object" (1994: 45-6). I don't know if that's a psychological law but it's certainly a common occurrence. Everyone will experience episodes of ressentiment from time to time; we've all had a day or an hour when we lapse into these experiences. But, for some, these episodes become pervasive. Nietzsche speaks of the *person of ressentiment* to pick out those in whom this tendency is firmly entrenched. So I now want to ask: is there an explanation for why people of ressentiment arise?

---

[14] See *The Genealogy of Morality,* First Essay. Nietzsche associates these priestly values with Judaism and early Christianity; his examples of individuals propounding those values include Tertullian and Aquinas (see *Genealogy* Part I, Sections 7 and 15).

8.5.2 Fanatical Narratives

I think there is. The structure of the explanation is present in Nietzsche's story about the ancient world: the person experiencing ressentiment gropes for some way of reconceptualizing his felt impotence and attaining a feeling of superiority over the resented group; certain *stories,* especially stories that vindicate the person of ressentiment and demean his opponent, become attractive; once these stories are accepted, they legitimate the ressentiment while offering the agent a way of experiencing himself as superior or at least as unjustly oppressed; and, once that happens, a feedback loop emerges, with the narrative enabling the ressentiment to grow and spread, while the growing ressentiment then more firmly entrenches and supports the narrative.

That's the quick version. But let's take it more slowly.

Like resentment, ressentiment is bound up with certain ways of interpreting the world. Ordinary resentment requires that the agent perceive herself as wronged. Ressentiment requires that but also more: not only am I wronged, but by fixating on this wrong and demeaning the person or group who perpetrates the wrong, I bolster my sense of my own identity.[15]

Throughout the last few chapters, I've mentioned the narratives, worldviews, or perspectives offered by various fanatical groups. There is a common core: many fanatical groups view themselves as oppressed or threatened by an out-group; and they see violent or coercive responses to this out-group as the only way of rectifying the threat. That general structure is present in ISIS, in Al Qaeda, in Stormfront and the various branches of white nationalism.[16] Call these *fanatical narratives*. These fanatical narratives have several intriguing features.

First, the fanatical narrative is *goal-providing*: it provides group members with something toward which to strive. Second, the fanatical narrative is *exculpatory*: it treats the faults, failings, and negative features of the in-group as forced upon

---

[15] I have been arguing that in ressentiment, the person's self-conception incorporates as an essential element the idea of being rejected or damaged by the other. It is important that this sense of being aggrieved is fostered and maintained, rather than contingently present. Consider two people, Pia and Ted, who have been wronged in a significant way, such that they regard the wrong as part of their identities (we might, for example, consider victims of oppression). Suppose time passes and the wrong is addressed adequately; some form of amends, which the agents take to be adequate, occurs. Suppose Pia ceases to regard *being wronged* as a significant constituent of her identity, whereas Ted immediately seeks to identify some new sense or new way in which he is being wronged. Whereas both people initially regarded *being wronged* as a constituent of their identities, Pia is willing to alter this conception when conditions change. Ted, on the other hand, is not; he seems more interested in maintaining his condition of *being aggrieved* rather than in correcting any particular aggrieving condition; the particular wrongs are adventitious, whereas the state of being aggrieved seems desired. It is the latter condition that I am associating with ressentiment.

[16] Indeed, this structure is so widespread in extremist groups that some authors identify extremism with its acceptance. For example, as I mentioned in Section 8.3, J.M. Berger tells us that extremism is "the belief that an in-group's success or survival can never be separated from the need for hostile action against an out-group" (Berger 2018: 44).

them by the out-group. Third, the fanatical narrative is *fixated on a rejected group*: it offers a rather simple account of the source of negative features in one's life. Fourth, the fanatical narrative tends to be *all-encompassing*. While the agent may initially focus on some particular wrong, the scope of the wrong tends to grow. In the extreme case, the agent sees most of his (or his group's) shortcomings and failures as explained by the wrong that is being perpetrated against him by others. Fifth, the fanatical narrative tends to present individuals as *impotent on their own but powerful as a collective*: while the putative wrongs are beyond the individual's power to rectify, collective action can correct them. Sixth, and relatedly, the agent is thus offered *deferred compensation*: the agent tends to envision a future in which the perceived wrongdoers are punished, eliminated, or rendered subordinate. These six features aren't universal in fanatical groups, but they are extremely common.[17]

I will give a few examples of narratives with these features. First, consider Al Qaeda's best known propaganda film, *The State of the Ummah*, which was released in 2001. The film is divided into three parts. The first part describes a series of problems facing Muslims around the world: it lists atrocities committed against Muslims in Afghanistan, the Philippines, Somalia, Chechnya, Bosnia, and other countries. It claims that hundreds of thousands of Muslims have been killed, maimed, and raped, providing graphic detail. The second part, entitled "Causes", then defines al Qaeda's enemies: the "near enemy" is a series of allegedly corrupt Arab regimes (including Saudi Arabia and Egypt), whereas the "far enemy" includes the United States and the Jewish people. The film connects these groups by presenting the near enemy as propped up and supported by the far enemy. The third part, "Solution," is introduced by Osama bin Laden. He claims: "Thus if we know the disease, this is the remedy. Hijrah [emigration] and Jihad...So it is incumbent on the Muslims...to migrate for the sake of Allah, and find a place where they can raise the banner of jihad, and revitalize the Ummah to safeguard their religion and life. Otherwise they will lose everything."

Second, consider an excerpt from a June 2009 speech by Yahia Al Libi, an Al Qaeda commander (who was killed in 2012):

> This path, and I mean the path of jihad, despite the calamities, sufferings, difficulties, and all forms of ordeals and distress, is the path which pleases the Almighty God and achieves his obedience. It is the evidence of truly loving God and the distinguisher between the people of honesty and faith from the people of deception and trickery. The path of Jihad is the way to purge the ranks of

---

[17] Of course, someone who doesn't experience ressentiment could embrace narratives with these features. The person could then be driven to individual fanaticism, without himself experiencing ressentiment. I am not arguing that ressentiment is a necessary feature of fanatics or of fanatical groups. Rather, I am arguing that ressentiment has been underappreciated; it deserves attention and analysis because it is at once quite common and overlooked.

Muslims and the mean to uphold the banner of monotheism, and exterminate the infidelity and desecration.

So the jihad for the sake of God is the refuge of the weak, the shelter of the oppressed, the peace of mind of the faithful and the hermits, the place of safety for the frightened and petrified, and the way to lift the humiliation from the suppressed and restrained. The corruption will not be eliminated from this world except with jihad and fighting.

Today, jihad in Algeria is your hope; God's willing, in order that you should be salvaged from the Hell of the unjust regimes whose prisons have become full of your youths, sons and even your women. In addition, they have made their armies, police forces and intelligence agencies hold sway over you, and have opened the doors to them to practice tortures against you. . . . Unify your efforts in cooperation with them [Al Qaeda members in Algeria], provide them with your capabilities, and unify your ranks under their banner, command and emirate . . . Be aware of the fact that their victory is your victory, their empowerment leads to your empowerment, and their salvation leads to your salvation.[18]

In both of these cases, we have all of the features that I mentioned above: the narrative provides a purpose; it treats current problems as traceable to the activities of an outgroup, on which it focuses; the narrative is all-encompassing, treating a vast array of social, political, economic, and religious problems as having a singular cause; it treats these wrongs as capable of being rectified through unified action, thus offering a form of deferred compensation.

The same features arise in many white nationalist narratives. The white nationalist Richard Spencer believes that the "white race" should be unified in "white ethnostates" in the US and Europe. In these proposed states, citizenship would be limited to white people. Spencer bases this claim on the idea that America's white population is oppressed and endangered due to immigration and multiculturalism. The American Identity Movement (formerly called Identity Evropa), which is open only to "those of European, non-Semitic heritage", advocates the same goal: their slogan is "You will not replace us"; they warn of "white genocide" and they present themselves as opposing "those who would defame our history and our rich cultural heritage." The leader of the American Identity Movement, Nathan Damigo, has repeatedly compared the plight of modern white people to that of Native Americans.[19] In a 2016 speech, he said:

---

[18] Accessible through the Global Terrorism Research Project at https://scholarship.tricolib.brynmawr.edu/bitstream/handle/10066/4707/AYL20090622.pdf?sequence=4

[19] For an overview, see https://www.splcenter.org/fighting-hate/extremist-files/individual/nathan-benjamin-damigo

Even though horrible things did happen to the indigenous people... there was land set aside where they could be who they were and express themselves how they wanted to, and they could have a form of government that reflected them. And I think that is something that we want. (Branson-Potts 2016)

In other words: Damigo thinks that white Americans are being persecuted in a way that's comparable to the nineteenth-century persecution of Native Americans; and he thinks that, as a result, white Americans should be given or should form a separate nation.

Again, the fanatical narrative provides a purpose; it treats contemporary failings or difficulties as traceable to a root cause; it focuses on an out-group (nonwhites); the narrative is all-encompassing, again treating a vast array of social, political, and economic problems as having a singular cause; and it treats these wrongs as capable of being rectified through unified action, thus offering a form of deferred compensation.

8.5.3 Feedback Loops between Fanatical Narratives and Ressentiment

What's interesting about the structure of these fanatical narratives is that they seem tailor-made for stoking ressentiment. Recall that ressentiment issues from felt impotence, coupled with a sense that one's impotence is due to a wrong perpetrated by some other person or group; this feeling grows; and it motivates reconceptualization of one's experiences. A person with incipient ressentiment—or even just a person who feels slighted or impotent—could latch on to these fanatical narratives, finding in them strong support for his emotional state; but, at the same time, in working himself into one of these narratives, the ressentiment would find new outlets, new targets, becoming ever more encompassing.

Nietzsche and Scheler are interested in ressentiment in part because they see how it can arise from simpler and more innocuous states. We're all susceptible to desires for revenge, desires to correct wrongs, feelings of impotence when we can't, and so on. We're all attracted to stories that present us as capable of overcoming faults, of getting back at those who have wronged us. Narratives of the sort that I've examined in the previous section can feed on these states, generating a feedback loop between ressentiment and the perspectives that it induces. For the narrative can make ressentiment seem appropriate; once ressentiment begins to emerge, it then cements the agent's attraction to that narrative. And, to the extent that the narrative presents not just some but many or all failings as traceable to a singular cause; to the extent that it treats this cause as a group; to the extent that it presents a path toward the correction of this wrong; to the extent that it does all of this, the narrative encourages ressentiment to spread. Fanatical narratives are narratives of ressentiment.[20]

8.5.4 Ressentiment Encourages (F2)–(F4)

We're now in a position to pull some threads together. Recall that I've said that a group qualifies as fanatical iff it promotes individual fanaticism. I then pointed out that some of the groups that are paradigmatically fanatical provide perspectives or narratives that generate ressentiment. I will now argue that ressentiment encourages individual fanaticism.

Here's the short version: in defining the individual in terms of group membership, and in defining the group as wronged by some out-group, the ressentiment narrative fosters features (F2)–(F4). How so? The ressentiment narratives tend to become all encompassing, treating the central failings of one's life as traceable to some singular root cause. One's identity is seen as fundamentally damaged or wounded by some other. The injury, damage, or wound is not just some past causal factor which is eventually overcome; it provides a central, continuous focal point. So ressentiment *fixates* on some object. The object fixated upon is defined as evil, threatening, and so on. So one's identity becomes bound up with opposition to that object; one defines oneself in opposition to it. Insofar as one's identity is dependent on a characterization of X as Y, revaluing X, interpreting it differently, will be costly. To the extent that one's perspective on the world is in this way all-encompassing and fixated, breaking out of it requires not just local adjustments but abandoning classifications, distinctions, and beliefs that create larger upheavals in the perspective.

Let's look at this in more depth. We'll start with feature (F2): fragility of the self. To the extent that certain components of one's identity are sacralized (by being treated as nonfungible and dialectically invulnerable), the agent will be psychologically fragile.[21] This kind of fragility can arise in any number of ways: certain

---

[20] Or, to be more precise, we could say that fanatical narratives are *one kind of* narrative of ressentiment: whereas all fanatical narratives are narratives of ressentiment, not all narratives of ressentiment are fanatical narratives. For fanatical narratives present a goal or a path to recovery, whereas narratives of ressentiment needn't do so. Part of what makes the fanatical narrative attractive is that it (at least implicitly) offers a putatively reasonable response to ressentiment. That said, a person who doesn't experience ressentiment could still embrace fanatical narratives. In general, a person can accept a narrative that promotes and characteristically accompanies a particular affective condition without experiencing that affective condition. For example, I can accept a narrative of loss, or grief, or bereavement, without experiencing a sense of loss, or grief, or bereavement. Just so, a person could accept a fanatical narrative without experiencing ressentiment. I am not arguing that ressentiment is a *necessary* feature of fanatics or of fanatical groups, only that it is a *typical* or *characteristic* feature.

[21] Notice that (F2) is designed to pick out individuals whose identity is dependent upon their treating certain values as sacred. This differs from individuals who do, but needn't, treat certain values as sacred. For more on this distinction, see the discussion in the previous chapter.

people might be more predisposed to it than others; one's culture will impact it; one's relationships to others will affect it. But it can also be encouraged.

Suppose an agent accepts a narrative with features that make it seem indispensable. These could include (i) treating other, competing narratives as untenable; (ii) encouraging close-mindedness or cognitive inflexibility; (iii) encouraging the agent to define himself wholly in terms of commitment to the narrative, so that departures from it become more costly and less imaginable; (iv) presenting those who reject the narrative as vicious or even as enemies; (v) making the narrative all-purpose, covering many aspects of the agent's life. Insofar as these features are in place, departures from the narrative will become increasing costly and imagined alternatives to it more difficult. By contrast, the person who accepts a range of relatively localized narratives; or who sees each of his commitments as important yet dispensable or modifiable; or who sees the possibility of standing back from and altering each of his commitments; or who sees situations as complex and ambiguous; that person will be less likely to exhibit psychic fragility.

Ressentiment narratives have features (i)–(v). Given this, they will encourage psychological fragility.

Let's now turn to feature (F3): fragility of the value. As I noted in the previous chapter, some groups treat values as fragile and some don't. Take the Amish or the Hasidic: when we consider their basic principles, they typically don't care whether non-Amish or non-Hasidic people share their values. What matters is that everyone in the community accepts the values. The Amish are a particularly clear case, given that it is encouraged for individuals to go out into the world and explore other ways of life before committing fully to the Amish values. If you're going to be Amish, you need to accept the value; but it doesn't matter whether non-Amish people respect the values.

But contrast this with extremist groups. If we consider jihadist and white nationalist groups, we can see that these groups typically *do* claim that it matters whether the value is widely accepted. The group's values are presented as endangered by dissent. I've already given several examples of this, ranging from ISIS to white nationalism.

By presenting the value as endangered by dissent, you encourage feature (F3) in group members. I think this is a common feature of the groups that we're inclined to label extremist or fanatical: they present their core values or beliefs as under threat. Indeed, if you can get individuals to regard *mere disagreement* about a value as a *threat,* then you've moved most of the way to fanaticism. Ressentiment narratives, which trace disagreement about a value to a perceived systematic wrongdoing, are particularly effective ways of doing this.

So let's turn to feature (F4): group identification. The group identity condition (F4) states that the fanatic identifies himself with a group, where this group is defined by shared commitment to a sacred value. Again, it's easy to see how a group can encourage this. All we need is a group that identifies itself in terms of acceptance of a sacred value. If the group encourages its members to define themselves in terms of group membership, and if the group is centered on a sacred value, we will have this feature.

Some groups do this and some don't. For example, consider a hiking club that treats environmental appreciation as a sacred value. It may be that the group doesn't particularly encourage its members to define their identities in terms of environmental appreciation. Suppose it's just a casual group, with members who enjoy getting together now and then but have diverse interests. We can contrast this with a group that does try to foster a particular sense of identity. The clearest cases of encouraging one to define one's identity in terms of a group will be cases in which the group advocates an us/them dichotomy, where being one of the "us" requires endorsing some sacred value. Again, ressentiment narratives do this. They strongly encourage the individual to classify the world into two groups: the damaged/wronged and the wrongdoers.

So an individual gripped by a fanatical narrative will tend to exhibit features (F1)–(F4). Thus, by promoting fanatical narratives, groups can encourage fanaticism.[22]

I haven't claimed that ressentiment is unique. It's clearly not the only way that a group can induce its adherents to manifest features (F1)–(F4). But it is a powerful and widespread mechanism.

Given the above features, ressentiment tends to grow and spread. Incipient ressentiment, sometimes merely in the form of felt impotence, disposes the person to accept ressentiment-narratives; these narratives give the agent further opportunities for expressing ressentiment; they also focus the negative emotions on some person or group; which gives ressentiment more opportunities for expression; and so on. The process ramifies.

8.6 Conclusion

I have argued that we should reject the Simple View of group fanaticism. Instead, we should accept the Generative View of Group Fanaticism, according to which a group qualifies as fanatical iff it promotes individual fanaticism.

---

[22] I have been focusing on fanatical narratives, which have two important features: they present their members as oppressed or threatened by an out-group and they present violent or coercive responses to this out-group as the only way of rectifying this threat. But fanatical narratives are not the only types of narratives that encourage ressentiment. For example, Salmela and Scheve (2018) argue that right-wing populism tends to involve the production of ressentiment: as they put it, right-wing populist narratives transform "fear and insecurity into anger, resentment, and hatred against perceived 'enemies' of the precarious self" (2018: 434). If my analysis is correct, and if we accept Salmela and Scheve's claims, this would imply that the relevant forms of right-wing populism are also productive of individual fanatics, and hence qualify as instances of group fanaticism.

How can a group promote individual fanaticism? There's a problem in the empirical literature on this topic: the mechanisms on which that literature focuses are too broadly applicable. They explain attraction to groups in general rather than extremist or fanatical groups in particular. However, I've suggested that there is a feature that seems present in many fanatical groups (and in many extremist groups, as well): the provision of narratives of ressentiment. Ressentiment encourages the emergence of individual fanaticism. By promoting ressentiment through promulgating certain kinds of narratives, groups can qualify as fanatical. Agents gripped by ressentiment define their identities in terms of a grievance against some out-group; the narrative encourages agents to see this grievance as encompassing most or all of the problems that the agent experiences; and the narrative presents reconciliation as impossible. It would be an exaggeration to claim that this is the only pathway to fanaticism, or that every fanatic exhibits ressentiment. Nonetheless, I have suggested that this is a common and underappreciated component of the fanatical mindset.

9
Irony, Affirmation, and the Appeal of Inarticulacy

I began this book by arguing that many people crave a particular form of devotion, which often comes at the expense of conventional goods such as pleasure and material comfort. In these cases, devotion isn't sought as a means to some further end; rather, devotion is valued for its own sake. Moreover, I suggested that the object of devotion is in some cases less important than the opportunity to manifest devotion. In a range of central cases, we do not first select ends and then decide that they merit devotion; rather, we (often inarticulately) seek to express devotion, and are attracted to ends that provide us with a way of doing so.

Devotion typically manifests itself as uncompromising commitment to ideals. These ideals have a distinctive structure, which distinguishes them from ordinary values. In particular, they are what empirical psychologists call "sacred values." Values count as sacred when they are seen as inviolable, incontestable, and dialectically invulnerable. The inviolable and incontestable nature of these ideals establishes a lexical ordering: because any perceived departure from the sacred value is seen as impermissible, strict compliance is mandated. Other values can be sacrificed or traded so as to secure greater goods; other values can be contested, problematized, and bracketed. But not sacred values. They enjoy a lexical priority over other values. (They can, of course, engender conflicts among themselves: if a person has two or more sacred values, she might face tragic dilemmas. See Chapter 2.)

A distinguishing feature of sacred values is that they are dialectically invulnerable. In other words, they are impervious to the usual effects of justificatory reflection; inquiry into the justificatory standing of the value has no effect on one's degree of commitment to it. Of course, as I pointed out in Chapter 5, we could avoid the need for dialectical invulnerability by uncompromisingly devoting ourselves only to those values that cannot be destabilized by critical reflection, values that are securely established by rational inquiry alone. But, I argued, any particular weighting of values can be problematized. So if weightings or prioritizations of values are to be utterly secure in the face of critical reflection, they need to be rendered dialectically invulnerable: our degree of commitment to them needs to be detached from questions about their justificatory standing. And if they are not—if we allow all values to be subject to the corrosive effects of critical reflection—then we risk Normative Dissipation, reducing what would otherwise be values with lexical priority into ordinary fungible values.

I then pointed out that this can be highly problematic: in detaching from the effects of critical reflection, in precluding tradeoffs and compromises, sacred values are likely to breed conflict. And not only that: under certain conditions they can produce a form of fanaticism, in which the agent gropes at some sacred value in an effort to preserve a fragile sense of individual or group identity. Moreover, this fragility is very easily provoked by a form of discourse that is depressingly widespread in our time: narratives of ressentiment. Chapters 6–8 addressed these points.

In short: I've argued that while sacred values play a key role in ethical life, enabling devotion and preventing normative dissipation, they also invite conflict and pathology.

We might simply leave it at that. There is no guarantee that our deepest needs are reconcilable; there is no guarantee that our story will have a happy ending. Perhaps we are riven by irreconcilable demands; perhaps this is our plight.

Or perhaps not. In this chapter, I want to ask whether there is a way of rendering commitments dialectically invulnerable, and thereby enabling devotion, without lapsing into the most problematic features of sacred values. I will suggest that there are non-fanatical ways of expressing devotion, ways that differ from fanaticism in that they enable the agent to recognize a form of contingency or optionality in her deepest commitments. I will investigate whether you can be devoted through irony; through affirmation; and through what I call the deepening move. Each of these stances preserves a degree of flexibility and openness in the objects of devotion; each one tries to preserve a wholehearted form of devotion despite this openness.

* * *

Recall that Normative Dissipation is a motivational problem that arises from a justificatory problem: because I see myself as lacking adequate justification for prioritizing my deepest commitments over alternative possible commitments, my commitments become etiolated. What was formerly treated as overriding, what formerly withstood comparisons and tradeoffs, what formerly seemed worthy of resolute commitment is gradually diminished, becoming on par with other, fungible commitments.

Because this motivational problem arises from a justificatory problem, the solution might seem obvious: address the justificatory problem. That is what I will examine below. The basic idea is this: we need to think more about what counts as *adequate* justification for a fundamental commitment. Perhaps it is only an inflated or misguided sense of what constitutes adequate justification that causes these problems to arise; or perhaps the way in which we are thinking about these justificatory issues needs reorientation. I will consider three strategies for developing this line of thought.

One strategy is *irony*. I understand irony as the stance in which a person is resolutely committed to some end, value, person, or activity, while simultaneously recognizing that this commitment is entirely contingent and optional, that nothing mandates continued adherence to it. There is a very long tradition of investigating this stance: versions of this position emerge in Schlegel, Kierkegaard, Sartre, Beauvoir, and, more recently, Richard Rorty, among many others. In Section 9.1, I analyze irony; investigate the way in which it can involve treating sacred values as internal to particular evaluative perspectives; and argue that an appeal to irony alone is unlikely to resolve the problem.

While irony alone doesn't seem likely to succeed, it does point us toward a potential solution. Perhaps we can look not for justification but for something else: a form of contentment with our commitments, which enables us to affirm them wholeheartedly. Section 9.2 investigates contentment, affirmation, and their connection to the preservation of commitments that are seen as contingent.

Another possibility is what I call *the deepening move*. Suppose you feel that you cannot justify your deepest commitments. There are ways of trying to escape that recognition. The most obvious way would be to distract yourself from appreciating that point, to engage in self-deception or willful ignorance. But there's another method: you convince yourself that although you presently don't have a full understanding of your commitment's objects, or presently don't have a way of justifying your commitment over possible alternatives, nonetheless some such explication or justification is available. The deepening move arises in unproblematic, everyday contexts; it is common in philosophy and in intellectual inquiry more generally. But when it is applied to fundamental commitments, the deepening move goes further: it involves a deliberate deployment of these dialectical or aspirational strategies in an effort to secure an otherwise problematized commitment. I investigate this strategy in Section 9.3.

To anticipate my conclusion: none of these strategies are entirely unproblematic. Irony is unlikely to succeed; the deepening move and the quest for contentment can work, but don't provide us with everything we might want.

9.1 Irony and Justification

Let's start with a specification of what we want and why we might not be able to have it. What we want is the ability to sustain confident, wholehearted commitment, without risk of this commitment being destabilized by critical reflection. What we worry about is the fact that all of our commitments can be destabilized by perceived lack of adequate justification for normative weightings. (Nietzsche: "the deeper one looks, the more our valuations disappear!" [Nietzsche 1977: Vol. 11, Section 25 [505]). If I am committed wholeheartedly to some end, but upon reflection am troubled by my perceived inability to find adequate justification either for maintaining that commitment or for prioritizing it over others, then my commitment may be destabilized. In particular, I may experience normative dissipation: while a vestigial form of commitment to the end may persist, the degree of commitment is likely to slacken (see Chapter 5). This is especially likely in cases where the person not only sees her justification for her current commitments as inadequate but also feels the attractions of competing commitments.

When this phenomenon is localized, it is manageable. A dissipation of one or two commitments needn't be worrisome; they can always be replaced by others. My commitment to running can be replaced by a commitment to yoga; my commitment to Christianity can be replaced by a commitment to philosophy. What's worrying is the global version of this phenomenon, in which facts about values (or normative entities) in general, rather than my particular values, generate the problem, so that the problem begins to affect one's deepest and most central evaluative commitments. As I pointed out in Chapter 5, the relative weightings of any particular value can be destabilized by critical reflection. For—I've been assuming—there are no successful non-circular, presuppositionless arguments for particular weightings of foundational values. Any argument for a foundational value will make certain assumptions, assumptions which can be questioned by a skeptic. Our justification for evaluative commitments is always defeasible.

One response to this is to alter our understanding of what counts as sufficient justification for maintaining an evaluative commitment. The higher one's standards for sufficient justification, the more likely it is that one's commitments will fail to meet those standards. If one insists that a commitment can enjoy sufficient justification only if one can answer all skeptical objections to it, then it will be easy to fall short. If, on the other hand, one lowers one's standards—allowing commitments to count as justifiable without insisting that they must be justified in a presuppositionless manner, that they be justified as preferable to any alternative commitments, that one needs to be able to convince a skeptic of their validity, and so on—then things will be easier. I raised a worry for this approach: the justificatory standards have to be made very low indeed in order for foundational normative commitments to be unaffected by normative weighting skepticism (the perceived inability to justify weightings or lexical orderings of competing normative claims).

Another approach to normative weighting skepticism is to disentangle perceived justification from degree of practical commitment. There are some commitments that we maintain despite seeing them as lacking adequate justification; in the most extreme cases, these commitments are dialectically invulnerable. No dialectical move will dislodge them. Rather than altering our epistemic standards, then, we divorce our deepest practical commitments from these standards.

How can we get to dialectical invulnerability? We might simply decline to reflect on the epistemic standing of certain commitments, thereby effectively rendering them impervious to critique. This is familiar in a number of settings: in political discussion, for example, attention can be deflected from contentious points to trivia or sloganeering. (No good arguments for tax cuts for millionaires? Focus on immigration instead!) In more complex cases, the dialectical invulnerability can arise because the relevant value is bound up with one's identity—distancing from it disrupts one's identity. So the invulnerability arises as a defensive mechanism against disruption of one's identity (either individual or group). And there are other strategies: willful ignorance, self-deception, distraction, and displacement are key mechanisms for maintaining potentially problematic commitments. If you don't look too closely at a commitment, or if your looking is skewed by these pathologies, it's going to be easier to maintain them.

But might it be possible to maintain dialectically invulnerable commitments without resorting to these strategies? Might we be able to admit in full consciousness that we lack adequate justification for some commitment and nonetheless sustain it without experiencing normative dissipation?

9.1.1 Irony

To do so would be to manifest Rortyian irony.[1] Rorty defines the *ironist* as the person who fulfills three conditions:

> (1) She has radical and continuing doubts about the final vocabulary she currently uses, because she has been impressed by other vocabularies, vocabularies taken as final by people or books she has encountered; (2) she realizes that argument phrased in her present vocabulary can neither underwrite nor dissolve these doubts; (3) insofar as she philosophizes about her situation, she does not think that her vocabulary is closer to reality than others...
>
> (Rorty 1989: 73)

---

[1] I focus on Rorty, but the view is older. Take Kierkegaard: "In irony, the subject is continually retreating, talking every phenomenon out of its reality in order to save itself—that is, in order to preserve itself in negative independence of everything...In irony...since everything is shown to be vanity, the subject becomes free. The more vain everything becomes, all the lighter, emptier, and volatilized the subject becomes" (1841/1989: 257–8). In Kierkegaard's lovely image, the ironical self risks becoming "volatized," in the sense that it may become ever more disengaged from its social roles, norms, and expectations, being emptied of content. In his later work, Kierkegaard lionizes Socrates for his ability to be both ironical and "earnest": while "his whole existence is and was irony," he does not become volatized (Kierkegaard 1970: 278). Jonathan Lear (2011) analyzes this Socratic form of irony as a detachment from local understandings of social practices, commitments, and so on, coupled with a deeper commitment to the ideal that seemingly underlies the local understanding. So, for example, I develop an ironical stance toward my commitment to being a philosopher, while groping for some deeper understanding of what that commitment is really meant to be. This is a version of what I will call the deepening move; I discuss it in Section 9.3.

By "vocabulary," Rorty simply means the words or concepts that we use to justify actions, beliefs, choices, and lives; these vocabularies count as final "in the sense that if doubt is cast on the worth of these words, their user has no noncircular argumentative recourse. Those words are as far as he can go with language; beyond them there is only helpless passivity or resort to force" (1989: 73). So, for example, if you are tempted by classical utilitarianism, Rorty would see "happiness" as part of your final vocabulary: there is no non-circular way of justifying the value that the utilitarian accords to this term. Or, if you're a Kantian, perhaps "freedom," "autonomy," and "dignity" will qualify as elements of your final vocabulary.

So, to meet condition (1), you'd have to employ a set of evaluative terms while having doubts about your ability to justify your commitment to these terms. To meet condition (2), you'd have to believe that you have no way of justifying your use of these terms in a non-circular fashion. To meet (3), you'd also have to believe that alternative sets of bedrock evaluative terms are equally appropriate. So, for example, you might be a committed Kantian, have doubts about the justifiability of the Kantian theory, and also think that incompatible theories such as classical utilitarianism are respectable alternatives. Or, for a political example, you might be a committed liberal but think that you have no non-circular way of establishing liberal societies as superior to illiberal religious regimes.

Rorty writes:

> I call people of this sort 'ironists' because their realization that anything can be made to look good or bad by being redescribed, and their renunciation of the attempt to formulate criteria of choice between final vocabularies, puts them in the position which Sartre called 'meta-stable': never quite able to take themselves seriously because always aware that the terms in which they describe themselves are subject to change, always aware of the contingency and fragility of their final vocabularies, and thus of their selves.   (Rorty 1989: 73–4)

This might seem like an odd stance. If you *really* think that your commitments are no better than alternative, incompatible commitments, why remain committed? Rorty's basic response is simple: thinking that a contingent commitment is problematized by its contingency depends on accepting the idea that there could be non-contingent commitments. But there can't. So there's no contrast between contingent and non-contingent commitments. As he puts it:

> Only the assumption that there is some such standpoint [such as using reason to discover which convictions are 'morally privileged'] to which we might rise gives sense to the question, 'If one's convictions are only relatively valid, why stand for them unflinchingly?'   (Rorty 1989: 50)

In other words, thinking that relatively valid commitments are tenuous depends on accepting an illegitimate distinction between relative and absolute perspectives. If all commitments are relatively valid, then the fact that your particular commitments are relatively valid can't be a good reason for abandoning them.

We can translate the relative/absolute terminology into more familiar language. Rorty's basic point is that there can be no such thing as presuppositionless justification for evaluative claims. Any purported justification for a claim will rest on certain presuppositions which can be questioned by a skeptic, and we won't find a non-circular way of answering the skeptical worries. Thus, Rorty writes that "there will be no such activity as scrutinizing competing values in order to see which are morally privileged. For there will be no way to rise above the language, culture, institutions, and practices one has adopted and view all these as on par with all the others" (1989: 50). And Rorty's point is simple: if *no* commitment can be justified in a presuppositionless manner, then the fact that *this particular* commitment lacks presuppositionless justification can't be an objection to it.

Now, I do think this is a good response in a certain context. Suppose I am committed to political equality, and then a skeptic comes along and convinces me that there's no presuppositionless standpoint which would show that I am rationally obligated to be committed to political equality. I start to worry. But then I read Rorty and see that what I was looking for, what the skeptic told me I couldn't have, was something that no commitment could ever have. This might render the skeptical arguments ineffective. For what seemed to be a problem with this particular commitment turns out to be a feature of commitments in general.

But this is not a satisfying response to another kind of predicament: if I am committed to some ideal, and see no way of privileging this ideal over some competitor, my commitment to the ideal can slacken. If I am a Baptist and come to believe that there is no reason for privileging the Baptist faith over Buddhism; if I am a liberal and see no reason for privileging liberal over illiberal values; then my commitments can be eroded (see Chapter 5). The Rortyan move won't help here, because my worry isn't based on the desire to find some presuppositionless ground for my commitment. The worry is instead based on the idea that there are too many possible competing commitments, that I can't sustain my attachment to any one of them. The problem, in short, is not foundational justification but *comparative assessment:* in light of my belief that there are many other justifiable commitments that conflict with or at least constitute alternatives to my own, I want a reason for maintaining my own commitments.

9.1.2 Irony vs. Sartrean Radical Choice

So I think Rorty mischaracterizes the real problem. Sure, if I am worried about the fact that my particular commitments can't be justified in a presuppositionless manner, showing me that *no* commitment could be justified in a presuppositionless manner might make me feel more secure. Or, more generally, if I have absurdly high standards for what counts as sufficient justification, you might point out that no commitment could ever meet those standards. But if I simply employ ordinary demands for justification and am primarily worried that my particular commitments can't be justified as preferable to available alternative commitments, then this response doesn't help. That worry, which I explored in Chapter 5, doesn't depend on overly demanding notions of sufficient justification.

We can use Sartre's reflections on radical choice to illustrate this point. Put simply, and abstracting from various complications, Sartre wants to say that we adopt our most basic evaluative commitments in acts of free, ungrounded choice. There are no antecedent reasons for these choices; reasons arise only within these basic evaluative stances, and hence cannot guide the adoption of them.

Notice that although Sartre would thus agree with Rorty that there's no possibility of presuppositionless justification for commitments, Sartre doesn't focus on Rorty's problem. We can see this by considering the characters who show up in Sartre's essays and novels. These characters do not insist on presuppositionless justification of their ends. Rather, they genuinely see the merits of two (or more) opposed evaluative perspectives and in light of this can't go on. Sartre's most famous example is given in "Existentialism is a Humanism." During World War II, a young student comes to Sartre and asks for advice. The student's brother had been killed by the Nazis, and in addition he viewed the Nazi regime as utterly evil. As a result, he wanted to join the French Resistance and do his part to fight the Nazis. However, his mother was severely ill and was completely dependent upon his care. So the student is faced with a choice: does he stay at home and care for his dying mother, or does he abandon her and join the French Resistance? And of course this choice is terribly difficult: if he stays with his mother, he will provide her with love and care in her final months; if he joins the Resistance, he might contribute to a great cause but also might achieve nothing at all, and his mother will be left to die alone. So he is faced with a choice: what is he to do?

Sartre runs through various options: the student can't appeal to religious commitments or to ethical theories, because these won't provide him with an algorithm for making his choice; he will still need to interpret the religious or ethical values, making a decision about how he sees these broader and more generalized values bearing on his particular case ("values are vague," they are "always too broad for the concrete and particular case we are considering" [Sartre 1948: 297]). The student can't appeal to his emotions or feelings or instincts or preferences, because these will be too vague to provide concrete guidance and will acquire determinacy only when he acts upon them ("the only way to determine the value of this affection is, precisely, to perform an act which confirms and defines it. But, since I require this affection to justify my action, I find myself caught in a vicious circle" [1948: 298]). The student can't go to others for advice, because he will need to decide both who to ask and what weight to accord to their advice ("if you seek advice from a priest, for example, you have chosen this priest; you already knew, more or less, just about what advice he was going to give you. In other words, choosing your advisor is involving yourself" [1948: 298]). So what's left? Here is Sartre's notorious answer:

> I had only one answer to give: 'You are free, choose, that is, invent.' No general ethics can show you what is to be done; there are no omens in the world.
> (Sartre 1948: 298)

There are no "omens" in the world. That is, there are no uninterpreted features of the world that will give us a determinate answer to questions about what to do. Our values, reasons, motives, preferences, the advice we seek, the theories we endorse—all of these rely on an act of interpretation. None of them can be taken as presuppositionless, uninterpreted data in terms of which choices can be made. So there is no *given* that would decide, for us, what we should do or what we should be. (The belief that there is—the belief that what you have in fact chosen is imposed on you independently of your choice—is what Sartre calls bad faith.)

Instead, Sartre tells us, we must choose ourselves. In his terminology, we must adopt some fundamental project that gives meaning and determinacy to these situational factors. Sartre's basic point, here, is that the world is imbued with normative significance only as a result of agents' desires, emotions, and goals. So, "the man who is angry sees on the face of his opponent the objective quality of asking for a punch on the nose" (Sartre 2003: 186); the world is perceived as normatively valenced in a particular way as a result of the agent's anger. This is a local and limited example, but Sartre wants to extend the point. He uses the term "fundamental project" to pick out the agent's adoption of basic ends that define his non-derivative values. Take the student: if he joins the Resistance, then ends such as fighting the Nazis, struggling for justice, and so on will be among his most basic commitments and will define his central values. Other things that he does—sabotaging a train, hiding ammunition, meeting secretly with certain people, avoiding the gaze of others, lurking in this alleyway, etc.—will be chosen because they are parts of or means to achieving these more basic ends. Sartre's idea is that these most fundamental ends will define the agent's derivative values, affects, motivations, and so on; they will imbue the world with normative and affective significance.[2]

Sartre claims that the adoption of fundamental projects cannot be understood as ordinary deliberation, because there are no reasons or motives on which the deliberation could be based: "We must insist on the fact that the question here is

---

[2] Webber 2006 offers a helpful introduction to Sartre's theory of action.

not of a deliberate choice. This is... because it is the foundation of all deliberation and because, as we have seen, a deliberation requires an interpretation in terms of an original choice" (Sartre 2003: 594). Instead, the free and unconstrained adoption of this fundamental project brings values and significances into the world:

> Our actual choice is such that it furnishes us with no *motive* for making it past by means of a further choice. In fact, it is this original choice which originally creates all causes and all motives which can guide us to partial actions; it is this which arranges the world with its meaning, its instrumental-complexes, and its coefficient of adversity. (Sartre 2003: 598–9)

So the student must constitute himself either as a caretaker or as a member of the Resistance. Nothing can tell him which choice is correct; nothing can absolve him of his responsibility for making this fundamental choice. Yet, once made, the choice will bring reasons into existence: if he chooses to be a caretaker, he will have reason to tend to his mother, to reject the temptations of fighting the Nazis, and so on.[3]

Just as nothing guides that original choice of fundamental project, so too nothing keeps the agent committed to the chosen project other than his own free continuous renewal of it. As Sartre likes to put it, "there is no inertia in consciousness" (Sartre 2003: 338). At any moment, the agent could reopen deliberation, deciding to alter his stance.

Recognition of this fact can give rise to *anguish*. Anguish occurs when we witness "this perpetual modifiability of our initial project. In anguish we do not simply apprehend the fact that the possibles which we project are perpetually eaten away by our freedom-to-come; in addition we apprehend our choice—i.e., ourselves—*as unjustifiable*" (Sartre 2003: 598).

In sum, then: the student's problem isn't resolved by pointing out that there are no ultimate justifications or presuppositionless starting points. True, the student would like there to be some "omen," some uninterpreted, presuppositionless feature that indicates one choice as superior to the other. But even when Sartre points out that there is no such thing, worries remain. For the student still needs to choose one over the other incompatible projects, where each excludes the other and each involves different evaluative perspectives. And, although Sartre poses this as a question that emerges at a moment of detached choice, he also emphasizes that it can arise at any moment after a commitment is made: the student

---

[3] When he's writing *Being and Nothingness,* Sartre seems to think this is true of *all* projects, but we don't have to follow him on this point. Suppose we think that in some cases, there's a decisive reason to choose project A over project B. Still, I think it's undeniable that there are *many* cases in which people choose between two or more incompatible projects, where each project is choiceworthy and neither is demonstrably superior.

might decide to fight the Nazis but be plagued, all along, with worries about whether he should have stayed home with his mother.

There are a number of questions that we could pose about the Sartrean account. But I want to focus simply on the core idea: our most basic evaluative commitments cannot be justified in a non-circular way as superior to their competitors. The student may commit to being a caretaker instead of joining the Resistance; but the other choice would have been equally rational. And notice that this point is perfectly general: it is supposed to apply to *all* choices of fundamental evaluative commitments.

While Sartre presents this recognition as profoundly disturbing, he also suggests that it is something that we can and must simply live with. We can persist in our commitments while viewing these commitments as ultimately unjustifiable over their competitors. And while his literary works do portray his characters as troubled by this kind of recognition—in *Nausea,* for example, Roquentin finds his projects serially collapsing in the face of this recognition—the characters ultimately find a way of going on with it, neither hiding the contingency from themselves nor letting it undermine their projects.

This is the very thing that I've suggested we cannot do without recourse to sacred values. I argued that recognition of this form of contingency tends to produce normative dissipation: the person might continue on with the same projects as always, but her commitment to these projects will be etiolated. The way to avoid this is to sacralize the commitments, to treat them as dialectically invulnerable. Let's reflect on these points.

9.1.3 The Entrenchment of Evaluative Perspectives

Sartre's phrasings suggest that the adoption of evaluative perspectives merely involves unconstrained choice: I back up and decide between fundamental projects just as I might select which shirt to wear. But when Sartre is being more careful—when he is less concerned with emphasizing the total freedom that we purportedly enjoy and is more concerned with analyzing lived experience—he focuses on the way that evaluative perspectives become entrenched in a person's way of experiencing the world. There is a feedback loop between the adoption of evaluative perspectives and one's experience of the world. Our basic evaluative commitments, including especially our sacred values, are bound up with affective orientations toward the world, habits, characteristic ways of thinking and acting. Because this is so, a genuine change in evaluative perspective involves not just an abstract dismissal of various values, but also a change—sometimes very dramatic—in one's affective orientation and one's patterns of activity. The person who adopts the project of joining the Resistance will acquire new habits (attentiveness, perhaps paranoia; secrecy; caution), will perform new kinds of actions, will live in different ways. The adoption of a new project is not just a moment of picking one option over another; it involves commitment to a particular form of life.

This comes across clearly in Sartre's discussion of the different ways of experiencing bodily sensations. His example: Sartre and several of his friends go on a mountain hike and all experience analogous amounts of fatigue; some view this fatigue as an inducement to continue climbing, others as a reason to give up and rest. Sartre himself has the latter reaction to fatigue, throwing himself down at the side of the trail and refusing to continue. His companion berates him for giving in to his fatigue, suggesting that he could see it instead as a way of being in touch with his body. The companion

> will explain to me that he is fatigued, of course, but that he *loves* his fatigue; he gives himself up to it as to a bath; it appears to him in some way as the privileged instrument for discovering the world which surrounds him, for adapting himself to the rocky roughness of the path, for discovering the 'mountainous' quality of the slopes... Finally the feeling of effort is for him that of fatigue overcome... Thus my companion's fatigue is lived in a vaster project of a trusting abandon to nature, of a passion consented to in order that it may exist at full strength, and at the same time as the project of sweet mastery and appropriation. It is only in and through this project that the fatigue will be able to be understood and that it will have meaning for him. (Sartre 2003: 586–7)

Sartre recognizes that he could modify his relation to the world and achieve this experience, but doing so would require "perceptibly modifying the organic totality of the projects which I am... it could be effected only by means of a radical transformation of my being-in-the-world." While he agrees that this transformation is possible, he asks: "*at what price?*" Sartre thinks the price would be high indeed: it would require a transformation of his most fundamental project. For "it is evident following our analysis that the way in which my companion suffers his fatigue necessarily demands—if we are to understand it—that we undertake a regressive analysis which will lead us back to an initial project" (2003: 588). And he continues: "Therefore if I apply this same method to interpret the way in which I suffer my fatigue, I shall first apprehend in myself a distrust of my body—for example, a way of wishing not 'to have anything to do with it', wanting not to take it into account... Hence my fatigue instead of being suffered 'flexibly' will be grasped 'sternly' as an importunate phenomenon which I want to get rid of" (2003: 589).

What's interesting about this discussion is that a seemingly localized, trivial episode—the way Sartre experiences fatigue while hiking—is linked to a deeper and more fundamental way of relating to his body and to the world, where these deeper features are explained by the fundamental project that he adopts. To put it a bit crudely: Sartre's fundamental project is or involves intellectual activity, and the body is seen in relation to this as a mere obstacle, as something that gets in the way. And, because the body is seen that way, the experiences of the body become troublesome, annoying, distracting. A feedback loop is generated: the fundamental project gives rise to certain kinds of experiences and then these experiences make the fundamental project seem justified.

For this reason, fundamental projects tend to become entrenched. Because fundamental projects and their associated values become entrenched, carrying with them ways of living and feeling, genuinely rendering the value vulnerable becomes increasingly difficult. The exit costs build up; over time it gets harder and harder to inhabit a moment of genuine fundamental choice. As Beauvoir puts it: "conversions [of fundamental projects] are difficult because the world reflects back upon us a choice which is confirmed through this world which it has fashioned" (1976: 40).[4]

9.1.4 Perspectival Sacred Values

I've been emphasizing the way in which Sartrean radical choice requires more than just choice: if it is to be genuine, it requires breaking out of entrenched ways of relating to the world. Suppose we treat the capacity for Sartrean choice as praiseworthy. No one would want to do this at each moment; no one would think that we should daily reevaluate our deepest commitments. But there is some pull to the idea that periodic assessments of our deepest commitments are praiseworthy. Rather than blithely carrying along in our commitments, we reassess them. This general stance has sometimes been associated with freedom, or autonomy, or open-mindedness.

We can understand this as a stance that oscillates between immersed engagement with and acceptance of sacred values, and a stance that involves trying genuinely to extract oneself from that immersed perspective, putting the values up for up grabs. In that moment of choice, if it is genuine, the value actually is rendered vulnerable: it can be abandoned or maintained, though only at the cost of abandoning or modifying one's perspective, in a way that would bring with it a new orientation toward the world.

---

[4] Merleau-Ponty objects to Sartre on precisely these grounds: "we must recognize a sort of sedimentation of our life: when an attitude toward the world has been confirmed often enough, it becomes privileged for us.... after having built my life upon an inferiority complex, continuously reinforced for twenty years, it is not *likely* that I would change.... This means that I am committed to inferiority, that I have decided to dwell within it, that this past, if not a destiny, has at least a specific weight, and that it is not a sum of events over there, far away from me, but rather the atmosphere of my present" (1945: 466–7). Prinz 2018 provides a helpful discussion. And of course Beauvoir, Fanon, and others analyze the way in which social structures and interpersonal relations reinforce this sedimentation, in some cases creating obstacles to fundamental choice.

Notably, there are cultural mechanisms that institutionalize this kind of alternation of perspectives. Consider the Amish *Rumspringa*: at a given age (which varies based on the community but is usually around 16), the Amish youth is no longer considered under the control of the parents and is not yet considered under the control of the church.[5] At this stage, some youths simply maintain their standard way of life; but others go out into the modern world, experimenting with it before deciding whether to commit to the Amish way of life. In a more diffuse way, teenage and college years in the US are analogous: one is encouraged, then, to put everything up for grabs, to reflect, to make these fundamental choices about what kind of life one will lead. And the midlife crisis is often portrayed as a moment at which people raise these questions about whether to go on with things as they are:

> At the age of forty the life you have lived so far, always *pro tem*, has for the first time become life itself, and this reappraisal swept away all dreams, destroyed all your notions that real life, the one that was meant to be, the great deeds you would perform, was somewhere else. When you were forty you realized it was all here, banal everyday life, fully formed, and it always would be unless you did something. Unless you took one last gamble. (Knausgaard 2013: 384)

Or Rilke, writing at the age of thirty-five: "I am sometimes astonished by how readily I have given up everything I expected, in exchange for what is real, even when that is awful" (Rilke 2009: 73).[6]

And of course there are other moments that encourage these reappraisals—self-help literature, new age movements, conversion/born again movements, personal trauma, illness, loss of loved ones, the recruitment to extremism, even comedy and certain forms of social disruption.[7] Some of these oscillations are shallow. But others are deep: others invite genuine assessment and potential abandonment of one's most basic commitments.

How should we understand this kind of oscillation, this movement between two perspectives with contrary demands? There are three possibilities: the oscillation could be inert, leaving everything as it is; it could result in a change in one's commitments; or it could result in a new manner of holding one's commitments.

---

[5] As an Anabaptist sect, the Amish believe that baptism is an unbreakable commitment to the church and must be entered into freely and knowledgeably; the Rumspringa is a prelude to this commitment. Schachtman 2007 provides an introduction to the topic.

[6] For philosophical discussions of the midlife crisis, see Hamilton 2009 and Setiya 2017.

[7] See Portilla's *Phenomenology of the Relajo* (commotion), translated in Sanchez 2012. Some have argued that features of modernity—its secularization, its pluralism, its multiculturalism, its emphasis on toleration as a central virtue—invite us to see even the deepest constituents of our identities as chosen rather than as imposed, and hence as variable. See especially Taylor 2007.

The first possibility is surely the most common. The Amish youth goes out in the world and then comes back.[8] The teenager revolts against his parents, full of grand plans for a more authentic life, and then returns to the same town and lives in the same way. The philosophy professor worries about his deepest commitments but nothing changes. We flip back and forth—either once or many times—between two incompatible perspectives, with neither impacting the other.

The second possibility is less common, but real. The person changes careers in midlife, or converts to a new religion, or gradually shifts toward extremism, or leaves the Amish community. The former project is abandoned and a new one arises to replace it.

The third possibility is the one that I want to examine. Rather than seeing the oscillation as inert (leaving everything as it was) or destructive (collapsing previous commitments and perhaps issuing new ones), we could see it as *transforming* one's immersed state. So, I back up and engage in Sartrean reflection on my fundamental commitments. I see them as optional: I could have chosen others, though doing so would have led to a different form of life. And something changes: my way of relating to those commitments is no longer the same. How might that be?

9.2 Contentment and Affirmation

Suppose I reflect on my commitments and the life they engender; and suppose I become dissatisfied with this life. I see it as cramped, or defective, or lacking opportunities for satisfaction. I don't want to consider a life where this is taken to an extreme. Certain lives are objectively problematic; certain lives look alienated, conflicted, full of despair and misfortune. It's easy to see why people might become disengaged from those lives. What I want to consider is a more run of the mill case: the life isn't obviously deficient in any respect; it involves no more than the ordinary share of disappointments and losses; it looks choiceworthy when considered in isolation. But, when compared to other possible lives, it breeds dissatisfaction.[9]

Let's consider an example, which I will borrow from Rahel Jaeggi. I will quote it at length:

> A young academic takes up his first position. At the same time he and his girlfriend decide to marry. That makes sense "because of the taxes." A short time later his wife becomes pregnant. Since large apartments in the city are expensive and hard to find, they decide to move to a suburb. After all, life outside

---

[8] About 80% of Amish youth return to the community following Rumspringa. See Schachtman 2007.
[9] See Miller 2020 for an interesting exploration of this phenomenon.

the city will be "better for the child." The man, a gifted mathematician, who until then has led a slightly chaotic life, oscillating between too much night life and an obsessive immersion in work, is now confronted with a completely new situation. All of a sudden, and without him having really noticed it, his life is now, as it were, "on track." One thing seems to follow ineluctably from another. And in a creeping, almost unnoticeable process his life acquires all the attributes of a completely normal suburban existence. Would he, who earlier ate fast food most of the time and relied on convenience stores for picking up milk and toilet paper as the need arose, ever have thought that he would one day drive every Saturday morning to the shopping mall to buy supplies for the week and fill the freezer? Could he ever have imagined that he would hurry home from work on Friday because the lawn needed to be mowed before the barbeque? At first he and his wife hardly notice that their conversations are increasingly limited to their child and the organization of household chores. Sometimes, however, he is overcome by a feeling of unreality. Something is wrong here... The life he leads... seems, in a strange way, not to be his own life. (Jaeggi 2014: 52).

Jaeggi treats the academic as alienated from his life, but that label won't be relevant for our purposes. What I want to point out is just that the academic is dissatisfied with a life that is not in any obvious way defective, a life that by conventional standards is choiceworthy; and he is dissatisfied with it in part because he feels entrenched in it, feels the exit costs building over time, and sees that other lives are possible. This, it seems to me, is one of the conditions that can sap motivation, leading to normative dissipation. Telling the academic that there's no ultimate justification for any set of commitments won't help; he's not worried about *that*. What he's worried about is the fact that his life seems deficient relative to some other perspective that he could, in principle, adopt, though the costs would be high. (Williams' Gauguin example, which I mentioned in Chapter 4, is analogous: there, a relatively conventional life is left behind, at high cost [a wife and children abandoned, etc.], in the effort to find something new.)

Entrenchment is part of the problem here: the academic makes little choices, wholly appropriate at the time, which set his life on a path that becomes increasingly difficult to modify. But entrenchment needn't be problematic. There are countless cases of people who are satisfied with entrenched lives. What generates the problem for the academic is the thought that some other life is available—some life that, at high cost, he could adopt—and he is unsure about how to relate to that thought.

What these examples drive home is just that life forces decisions upon us: there are multiple ways of living a good life, and we can't have them all. We have to pick and choose. Each choice has costs. Because each choice has costs, requiring us to forgo other valued options, we can be led to comparative assessment: is this life, the one I've led, really the one that I want to lead? Is it better than other possible lives?

Let's consider how these sorts of cases relate to normative dissipation. Although there is no necessity here, I don't think anyone would be surprised if the academic in Jaeggi's example experienced an attenuation of his commitments. A commitment that can be taken up only wearily and without interest is likely to lose some of its original motivational force, especially when the agent can see viable (though costly) alternatives to it.

But now let's consider something like the opposite case. Suppose we consider a person who is not suffering from dissatisfaction, alienation, or related maladies. She sees that her own evaluative perspective is at the deepest level arbitrary: she cannot justify her choice over certain available alternatives, as each would make possible a form of life that is internally consistent and that she would find acceptable. Nonetheless, she is fully satisfied with her own way of life, and thus fully satisfied with the values that make it possible. What does this involve?

One thing it involves is *contentment*. Cheshire Calhoun provides an illuminating account of contentment. Contentment is easy when you regard your situation as perfectly good: it's easy to be content with a lovely day at the beach. But Calhoun is interested in how we respond to imperfect situations. You reflect on your situation (which could be a particular moment of one's life, or one's life as a whole); you see that it could be, in various ways, better than it is. Some people will take the "it could be better" judgment to warrant discontentment; others, contentment. Those who are content might think that while their situation isn't perfect, it is good enough. Thus, Calhoun argues that contentment is a disposition to engage in counterfactual thinking about one's condition, which includes a "good enough" judgment; this good enough judgment will depend on the adoption of a particular "expectation frame," which specifies "the degree of goodness one is 'entitled' to expect and in relation to which one's present condition appears comparatively good, thus good enough" (2018: 149). She further treats contentment as involving not just judgments but also an affective dimension: "the contented affectively appreciate the goodness of their present situation" (2018: 157).

Let's apply this notion of contentment to our cases. Can I see two compelling yet incompatible evaluative perspectives—say, the ones involved in joining the Resistance or caring for my mother—and yet be content with whichever one I choose? To do so, I have to see that my perspective, though perhaps not best, is good enough. I might look with some measure of regret on my missed opportunities; I might bemoan the fact that I have to choose between incompatible values; but, insofar as I am content, I would not take this as a reason for dissatisfaction with my current perspective.

Would this prevent normative dissipation? Perhaps not. Contentment is a fairly low bar: I merely have to think that my perspective is good enough. But I can think something is good enough while being motivationally disengaged from it. Consider a dramatic example: suppose a committed, devout evangelical

Christian comes to think that his religion, while not manifestly superior to (say) Buddhism, is good enough. Will he still have the same fire, the same passion, when he comes into conflict with others or faces other costs? In Chapter 5, I suggested that the answer is no. It seems likely that his commitments will be attenuated.

Suppose, though, that we strive for something more than contentment: suppose we strive for *affirmation*. Affirmation is more demanding than contentment. To affirm something is not just to be content with it, but also to desire that it not be otherwise. Jay Wallace brings out this dimension. He argues that affirmation should be understood as follows: to affirm X is to judge that X is valuable (in some way) and to prefer on balance (taking everything into account) that it should not be otherwise (Wallace 2013: 65). For Wallace, this isn't an emotional state. For example, it doesn't require positive feelings. Rather, it's a matter of preferences and associated normative beliefs. It can be thought of as analogous to a conditional intention for the future: insofar as I am considering a choice, I would do just the same thing if I had it to do over again. Affirmation is an achievement: we can sometimes bring it about voluntarily.

Let's put the point this way:

(**Affirmation**) A value, activity, end, or relationship is *affirmable* by a person just in case the person making an informed fundamental choice would choose it again.

I say the person needs to be understood as making an "informed" fundamental choice in order to rule out cases of superficial confusion, errors, oversights, and so forth. Analyzing this notion would be a distraction, so I will simply rely on our intuitive understanding of it. The details won't matter for our purposes.

So affirmation and contentment can be understood as differing in the following way: whereas contentment involves the feeling that something is good enough, affirmation involves judging both that it's good enough and that one would not want it to be otherwise. These come apart: I could be content with my athletic abilities without affirming them, for I might wish that they were better than they are. I could be content with the Paris climate accord but not affirm it, for I might wish for a more demanding agreement. And so on.[10]

Let's apply this to perspectives and their associated forms of life. Affirmation seems to secure the perspective, together with its commitments, in a way that mere contentment does not. Contentment is a fairly low bar; it is compatible with disengagement. Even if Jaeggi's academic decides that he is content with his life,

---

[10] Wallace's notion of affirmation is based very loosely on Nietzsche's ideas about affirmation. But they differ. Nietzschean affirmation is more demanding than Wallace's affirmation, for Nietzsche includes a further feature: in addition to desiring that X not be otherwise, one must be delighted by the hypothetical thought of X recurring endlessly without variation. And Nietzsche associates this with the thought that X is perfect: if X is perfect, than not only does it make sense to want X, but it makes sense to want X endlessly. These subtleties won't be relevant for our purposes.

that it's good enough, he might become disengaged from it. But affirmation doesn't allow this. If I affirm my activity, I would choose it again. And if this is genuine—if one really would choose the activity again, in light of all its costs, in light of the abandonment of alternatives—then this seems to renew one's commitment to it.

Recall that Normative Dissipation was defined as follows:

(**Normative Dissipation**) Insofar as she is rational and lacks sacred values, an agent who formerly regarded normative commitment N_1 as outweighing normative commitment N_2, but who now believes that she lacks sufficient justification for assigning greater weight to N_1, will experience motivational and behavioral changes. In particular, there will be a reduction in the extent to which her motives, concerns, and behavior reflect the idea that N_1 is to be prioritized over N_2.

Suppose I seek affirmation. I come to believe that I lack sufficient justification for prioritizing N_1 over N_2. But I see that my life is built around my prioritization of N_1. And I affirm this life: I would choose it again. This might block normative dissipation. Insofar as the perspective demands a resolute commitment to some end, and insofar as one affirms the perspective, one has reason to affirm the commitment to that end. The motivational and behavioral changes might (I only say might) be blocked.

Of course, there are no guarantees. Human psychology is fickle and inconstant; I am not pretending to offer foolproof recipes for success. And we all know that even our deepest cares, concerns, and activities can be hostage to moods and unruly emotional states; even what is dearest to us can go dead for a time. But affirmation does generate some pressure toward the avoidance of normative dissipation. We oscillate out of an immersed perspective, seeing it and its constituent demands as up for grabs; and yet we affirm the life that the perspective makes possible, telling ourselves that we would choose it again; and, if all goes well, this carries some weight, recommitting us to the life.

So that is one potential solution: the quest for affirmation. You see that even if your values can't be comparatively justified as superior to others, they can be affirmed. You would choose them again.

Notice that affirming one's commitments is different than sacralizing them. Sacralized commitments exhibit three features: they are Inviolable, Incontestable, and Dialectically Invulnerable. The commitments that a person is capable of affirming needn't be Inviolable or Incontestable. They will, in a special sense, be Dialectically Invulnerable: *because* they are affirmed, the person's commitments will be impervious to the ordinary effects of justificatory reflection. To the extent that this form of affirmation is attainable, the person will have staved off normative dissipation without resorting to sacralization. So here we have a genuine alternative to sacralization, and it is the alternative outlined by Nietzsche: we preserve a form of devotion by affirming life.[11]

9.3 The Deepening Move and the Attractions of Inarticulacy

So far, I've been considering whether we can see our most basic evaluative commitments as not justifiable in preference to their competitors without this disrupting their force. I've raised some qualms about Rorty's approach, which emphasizes irony, and Sartre's approach, which emphasizes unconstrained fundamental choice. I've suggested that a quest for affirmation can stabilize evaluative perspectives even when the agent sees these perspectives as lacking adequate comparative justification. Indeed, we could even take this as a methodology: we allow critical reflection to proceed, to have effects, to erode certain commitments; but this typically leaves us with multiple possible evaluative perspectives that cannot be comparatively justified against one another; when we reach this point of comparative assessment, we switch to thoughts about affirmation rather than justification.

And yet this might seem unsatisfying: even if something is affirmable, some of us will still long for the comparative assessment of it and the justification of it as superior to other possible projects. We want something to anchor our choices. And I've suggested that at the deepest level, there is no way of meeting that need.

But if there's not a way of meeting it head-on, there might still be a way of preserving a substitute. Rather than confronting my inability to comparatively justify my normative commitments, I try to suppress recognition of the problem. I think this is by far the most common response to the problems I have canvassed.

This approach can take many forms. Some of them are obvious: we simply ignore contrary evidence, decline to reflect on certain arguments, and so on. We distract ourselves from these justificatory questions or simply never raise them in the first place. Or, going still further: we engage in self-deception and various forms of motivated reasoning. These are epistemically vicious ways of proceeding. But I want to look at something that hovers between epistemic virtue and epistemic vice. It combines the appearance of forceful, exemplary critical reflection on a commitment with the insulation of that commitment. This is what I will call *the deepening move*.

---

[11] Nietzsche's views are more complicated, however. He distinguishes affirming one's own life from affirming life as such; and his views on affirmation are entangled with his thoughts on will to power. For a discussion, see Katsafanas 2022.

9.3.1 The Deepening Move

Consider an entirely ordinary moment in a philosophical presentation. You've written a paper defending claim C. You think there are good arguments for C, but you also want to be open-minded and responsive to criticism. You want your degree of commitment to C to track C's justificatory standing, in the sense that you would abandon C if C were shown to be sufficiently problematic. So, you give the talk. Your audience offers various objections to C, criticisms of C, and so forth. Some of them are misguided or easily answered but others are not. Some of the objections are good. And I don't just mean that other people would consider them good: I mean that *you* recognize their force. You find yourself unable to answer these objections and criticisms in a convincing way. So, you are strongly committed to C, but you regard C as subject to a number of powerful objections that you see yourself as presently unable to answer. What happens next?

One option is to decrease your credence in C, perhaps to the extent that you abandon C entirely. Another option is to engage in what I call *the deepening move.* You convince yourself that although you presently don't have a full understanding of C, or presently don't have a way of justifying it, nonetheless some such explication or justification is available. You just haven't found it yet. So, you remain convinced that the claim is true, though you don't yet see how it can be shown to be true and perhaps don't even think that you've properly formulated or articulated the claim. You think you need to go deeper, developing a better understanding of the claim and its justification. Once you do, all will be well.

I take it that this is entirely familiar; this is how intellectual inquiry in general, and philosophy in particular, often works. Hegel says that what's distinctive of philosophy is that, in trying to understand some proposition, "we learn by experience that we meant something other than we meant to mean; and this correction of our meaning compels our knowing to go back to the proposition and understand it in some other way" (*Phenomenology of Spirit,* Section 63). He's right; this is a typical approach to philosophy. We think we understand something; we encounter an objection to the claim, a problem with it, a complication; and we go back, thinking that we actually must have meant something else. Reinterpretation or rearticulation begins.

Moreover, this approach seems epistemically praiseworthy. After all, we sometimes present some claim as true; we encounter an objection which we hadn't considered; we see that the criticism is a good one, potentially undermining our claim; we feel unable to answer the objection in the moment; but we feel that something is wrong with the objection, some response is available; and, later on, the response occurs to us. The objection fails and the claim is preserved. So it turns out that the claim was true; we just hadn't yet articulated its content, or its justification, or its connection to other claims to a sufficient degree. If we'd given up the claim, rather than pressing to understand it in a deeper way, we would have missed an opportunity for acquiring understanding.

So what I am calling the deepening move is this: when presented with good critiques of a claim, one takes these critiques as invitations to deepen one's understanding of the claim rather than as indications that one should decrease one's credence in the claim.

As I've indicated, this is sometimes a praiseworthy approach. The deepening move can involve engaging in exemplary, nuanced, flexible thinking about one's commitments; and it preserves a form of openness to revision of these commitments, so long as this revision can be understood as development or deepening rather than abandonment. Moreover, unlike some other forms of evasiveness, the deepening move is often epistemically virtuous in the sense that it involves engaging in patterns of thought that are conducive to acquiring a deeper understanding of one's commitments. But I want to draw attention to the way in which the deepening move can also be artifice; it can involve refusing genuinely to subject the commitment to critique. It can involve a form of dialectical invulnerability without the appearance of dialectical invulnerability.

Let me provide a philosophical example to illustrate these points.

Everyone will have their own favorite examples, but for me the deepening move comes up most clearly in discussions of Kantian ethics. The basic structure of Kant's moral theory is familiar: his Categorical Imperative, in its first formulation, is "act only on that maxim which you can at the same time will that it become a universal law" (*Groundwork* 421). In a recent review, Patricia Kitcher writes that despite the familiarity of this principle, "to this day, no one has a clear and plausible account of how Kant's argument for the formula of universal law...is supposed to go" (Kitcher 2004: 555). Many have offered theories.[12] There is some agreement on the most generalized version of the argument: in some way, Kant is moving from claims about rationality or freedom to claims about morality. But if you look at Kant's texts it is *very* hard to see what he takes himself to be doing; it's very hard to find a good argument at this point. There always seems to be some gap, some move that doesn't quite work.

Kant's central argument seems to me brilliant but unsuccessful: it's tantalizingly close to working but ultimately fails. I am just not confident that he has any real way of moving from claims about rationality or autonomy to substantive conclusions about what we should do. But, as anyone who discusses these matters with committed Kantians knows, Kantians have responses. Great philosophers can never be refuted: their proponents can always find traces of arguments in them, claims that seem to rebut whatever charge the critic wishes to levy against them. The Kantian might be unable clearly to articulate how rationality relates to the

---

[12] A few of the more influential readings: Allison 1990, Herman 1993, Korsgaard 1996, O'Neill 1975 and 1989, Wood 1999.

categorical imperative; but she sees this as a deficiency in her own presentation or her own understanding, rather than in Kant's argument. And of course this hagiographical approach has merits: it can deepen our approach to the texts, improve our arguments, and so on. So we have generations of commentators who have developed increasingly sophisticated readings of Kant's argument. These readings block the obvious objections, overcome certain difficulties, illuminate certain obscurities.

Many of the commentators on Kant are ingenious, displaying incredibly nuanced thinking and making deeply insightful points. Many depart from the letter of Kant's texts while purporting to remain committed to its spirit: they develop or make explicit points that remained inchoate or underdeveloped in the original. There can be no serious doubt that these commentaries are conducive to our acquiring a deeper understanding of the philosophical issues under discussion. All of this seems praiseworthy.

And yet when I study this literature, I am left with the thought: what has happened to the idea that there might be nothing here, that the argument might be hopeless? Kant is brilliant, but even the most brilliant people make mistakes or publish arguments that they are not absolutely confident about (Kant did, after all, write two different transcendental deductions!). But this possibility of error effectively disappears from much of the secondary literature; within this realm, this possibility is never seriously broached. In effect, the Kantian argument is taken as dialectically invulnerable: it can be critiqued, rephrased, developed, it can even be wrong on inessential points, but something of its core must be preserved.

Of course, I am just using Kant's ethics as an example; I might be wrong, and if you don't like that example you can use another. The point is simply that deploying the deepening move involves treating something—some claim, some presumed insight, some argument—as effectively insulated from critical reflection. And one way of insulating something from the effects of critical reflection is to treat your current grasp of it as inadequate, so that any flaws are attributed to your understanding rather than to the thing you aim to understand.

I don't think this is objectionable—if we want good defenses of positions, it helps to have people who are fully committed to them, people who doggedly persist in refining and developing these positions. (Individual vices are sometimes collective virtues.) But I think it does show something about philosophy and how it works. Central commitments in effect get treated as dialectically invulnerable. There are countless examples of this in subfields of philosophy, in which acceptance of some claim or principle is the price of admission to the debates (e.g., there's little reason to develop complex interpretations of Kant if you think he's just wrong). But there are also broader versions of the phenomenon: within different groups, we can see how dignity, equality, antiracism, gun rights, negative freedom, religious beliefs, and so forth get treated as foundational commitments, exempt from the typical effects of critical reflection. The crucial point is that there can be flourishing, lively debates, there can be a bustle of intellectual energy devoted to these topics, there can be good-faith skepticism and open-mindedness, and yet all of this reflection and intellectual energy can hold constant a deeper commitment, which is insulated from genuine critique.

Perhaps an example less close to home might illustrate the point: consider the debates between Christian theologians in—let's say—the first to the sixteenth centuries. Within this period there is probably no particular claim about God that is not critiqued, denied, or modified by some division or other. And yet in all of this something is held constant: a belief that the Christian God exists. The very idea that the whole system might be bankrupt, that the Christian God might be nothing more than fiction, that we might as well be debating the attributes of Zeus or Vishnu, is typically not entertained. To admit that thought into consideration—to take the possibility that all of these refinements, all of these discussions, all of these debates might be mere busyness—would be to step outside that system.

9.3.2 Is the Deepening Move a Form of Self-Deception?

I began Section 9.3 by distinguishing the deepening move from self-deception and motivated reasoning. Let me return to that point. There is a way of adopting an analogue of the deepening move explicitly and in full consciousness, so that you are perfectly aware that you are rendering certain commitments invulnerable. It's easiest to see this in the philosophy of science. As Imre Lakatos (1978), Helen Longino (1990), and others have long argued, normal scientific practice involves an intellectual division of labor, with scientists operating in different "research programs." Put simply, these research programs contain different and sometimes incompatible basic assumptions; when evidence seems to conflict with these basic assumptions, the assumptions are maintained, either by treating the evidence as anomalous, by developing ancillary hypotheses, or by other means. And we can extend the point beyond scientific inquiry to philosophy: it seems true that it's epistemically praiseworthy for there to be competing research programs, operating with different sets of fixed assumptions that are insulated from questioning. It's good, for example, that there are devoted Kantians and also devoted utilitarians; even if these devoted philosophers immunize certain core assumptions from questioning, their doing so enables the research programs to develop and increase in sophistication. This is conducive to acquiring understanding.

In light of this, we could imagine people explicitly deciding to treat certain beliefs or commitments as dialectically invulnerable. But notice that this will be *much* easier with respect to the investigation of descriptive claims than with respect to one's own normative commitments. For there are two crucial differences that arise when it comes to one's own fundamental normative commitments.

First and most obviously, the social costs tend to be higher in the domain of fundamental normative commitments. Suppose that we treat the political values of liberal democracy and authoritarian religious rule as constituting different research programs. This has grave consequences for the people affected by these "programs"; it would be absurd to tell the atheist who is being persecuted by an authoritarian religious regime that he should accept it as the cost of developing a research program. The fact that these social costs—these costs borne by other people—tend to be so high in the case of fundamental normative commitments can make it difficult for people to adopt them in the same way as they might adopt scientific research programs.

Second, even if we could find some benefit to a plurality of fundamental normative commitments, these could never be *my* reasons for taking up a commitment. I can't simply tell myself: "well, somebody has to be a Baptist, somebody has to be a Buddhist, somebody has to be an atheist, so I will just pick being a Baptist and go with that." In the scientific case, or even in the abstract philosophical case, you can tell yourself that even if the particular set of assumptions that you've chosen to operate with turns out to be a dead end, you will still be contributing to the acquisition of knowledge. (Even if Kant's argument fails, it's worthwhile to see that the *very best* version of that argument fails.) But in the case of one's own fundamental commitments, it is difficult to imagine an agent engaging in that kind of reasoning. In effect, I would have to tell myself: "My fundamental normative commitments might lead to my own life being a dead end (so to speak), but nonetheless I will insulate them from reflection." The recognition that these commitments might render one's life defective, problematic, or misguided will invite the problems of comparative assessment that the deepening move (as I presented it above) was designed to block.

So: whereas in the more straightforwardly epistemic cases you can explicitly tell yourself that you are rendering some set of beliefs dialectically invulnerable so as to pursue a research program, it will be difficult to do the same in the domain of fundamental normative commitments. There will be more pressures toward willful ignorance in the latter case: pressures to ignore the fact that some commitment has been rendered dialectically invulnerable, and to instead convince yourself that any justificatory problems with the commitment pertain only to your current understanding of it, and not to its deeper form.

9.3.3 The Attractions of Inarticulacy

I've been discussing the way in which the deepening move involves critical reflection while effectively insulating a core commitment from skeptical worries. I think this is a common move in philosophy, in religion, in politics, really in all areas of deep commitment. In this section, I want to consider how the deepening move fits with a characteristic feature of our central evaluative commitments: their inchoateness.

Every philosopher knows that the clearer and more precise a claim is, the easier it is to refute. Ambiguous, polyvalent claims are harder to refute than precise ones, for objections to them can more easily be seen as misrepresentations or misunderstandings.

Let me give an example. Back in Chapter 5, I illustrated Normative Dissipation with the example of Madeline. She was committed to a fundamentalist Christian outlook which she believed required her to reject premarital sex, homosexuality, and so on. But then she goes to college and encounters new points of view, makes new friends, experiences new pressures. I suggested that a common outcome in this sort of case is normative dissipation, in which the commitments to her prior values dissipate. She professes continued commitment to them, but they no longer play an important role in her life.

Yet there is another possibility: the deepening move. Suppose Madeline tries to rethink these commitments. Rather than seeing Christianity as focused on prohibitions against sexuality and the like, she sees it as expressing a deeper point, which she's tempted to articulate as follows: to love one's neighbor; to love people despite their foibles and frailties; to live in light of God's love. She sees Christianity as striving to comprehend the frailty of human nature; as giving us an image of what interpersonal love might look like; as holding up, against the bungled, defective stuff of actual life, an ideal toward which we might devote ourselves. And she sees the straightforward prohibitions as relatively unimportant: what matters, for her, is universal love.

So her ideal becomes at once more diffuse and more compatible with a variety of actions. She might genuinely remain devoted to it. Indeed, she might feel *more* devoted to it than she formerly did. And, because the ideal is amorphous and multivalent, she no longer experiences straightforward conflicts between action and ideal. She can remain devoted to the ideal, now in a rethought form. So the ideal, which seemed to be at risk of dissipation or even outright rejection, has been immunized from the effects of critical reflection by being rendered inchoate.

And it's easy to see how the same thing can happen at the collective level. It's no accident that political slogans, religious ideals, and self-help formulae often take inchoate forms.[13]

I've been belaboring a point that is perhaps obvious, though I think its importance for foundational normative questions is overlooked. The basic problem is this: when certain commitments are stated clearly, they're refutable. So there's a motivation to

---

[13] Consider Jonathan Lear on enigmatic signifiers: "We are by our natures susceptible to enigmatic signifiers—oracular utterances, if you will, which we can recognize as having a meaning—indeed, as having a special meaning *for us*—but whose content we do not understand" (Lear 2011: 223). "Precisely because these messages escape our understanding, they captivate us" (Lear 2011: 223). He is here drawing on work by Lacan, who introduces the notion of "master signifiers": the referent of the signifier will be understood as something enigmatic, something that no one individual can fully grasp. It's something that is initially taken as certain, as obvious, but which then turns out to be ineffable. Even if we can't precisely state the nature of the referent, we're sure that someone could.

keep them unstated, to treat them as ineffable. And this can always work, because it's difficult to be completely articulate about *any* of our commitments.

When we try to be articulate about our central commitments, we always feel that we are coming up short, that we are not really saying what we meant to say; and then we can always reinterpret and see ourselves as deepening our understanding of these commitments. So this approach tries to leave foundational claims fairly inchoate. This does preserve them from the corrosive effects of critical reflection. And it does pick up on something that's true: sometimes—indeed, very often—criticisms really do turn out to be based on superficial understandings, confusions, errors. Perhaps most people who object to Kant's ethics really do have superficial understandings of the terms, the arguments, the dialectical moves; indeed, perhaps nearly everyone does. It's a short step from there to concluding that there really must be something there, something that you perhaps cannot yet articulate but which you nonetheless sense. So the commitment—in this case, the Kantian argument—is rendered dialectically invulnerable, albeit in a way that gives it the aura of rationality.

So there's a way to avoid dissipation: preserve your commitments by treating the real form of those commitments as aspirational. You might not then describe yourself as having sacred values—you might not describe yourself as treating certain commitments as dialectical invulnerable. But, characterized from a more impartial point of view, that is in fact what you will be doing.

There's a risk that this approach will simply lead back to the earlier problems, to the possibility of fanaticism and dogmatism. But that risk needn't be actualized. The deepening move preserves commitment to a value with some degree of openness to its revision, and it does so by a kind of artifice: because there is no clear cut-off point in the continuum from articulating to deepening to revising to abandoning a value, it can present what's really abandonment of a value as its deepening. And, in so doing, it can oppose a kind of fixation or stasis. There is, after all, a crucial difference between the fanatic's pattern of reflection on his end and the Kantian's.

If this is right, then the deepening move can provide a form of insulation from the corrosive effects of critical reflection while simultaneously preserving some of the flexibility and openness that critical reflection promotes. In that latter respect, the deepening move differs from straightforwardly dogmatic or unreflective forms of dialectically invulnerable commitment.

9.3.4 The Dangers of Deepening

But this is not to say that the deepening move is always salutary. Just as we can deploy the deepening move to preserve widely accepted values, we can deploy it to preserve values that are widely regarded as misguided. To see this, let me mention two of the best explorations of what I'm calling the deepening move: Talbot Brewer on "dialectical activities" and Kyla Ebels-Duggan on inarticulate appreciation of values.

Brewer uses the term "dialectical activity" for activities that

> have a self-unveiling character, in the sense that each successive engagement yields a further stretch of understanding of the goods internal to the activity, hence of what would count as a proper engagement in it. If the activity's constitutive goods are complex and elusive enough, this dialectical process can be reiterated indefinitely, with each successive engagement yielding a clearer grasp of the activity's proper form and preparing the way for a still more adequate and hence more revealing engagement in it. (Brewer 2009: 37)

Brewer gives several examples: loving relationships, conversations, parenting, listening to music. In all of these activities, "we are initiating an activity whose value cannot be grasped with perfect lucidity from the outset, but must be progressively clarified via engagement in the activity itself" (Brewer 2009: 39). Although he doesn't defend the thesis, Brewer suggests that all activities that aim at intrinsic goods might have this structure (Brewer 2009: 39).

I do think there's something attractive about Brewer's picture, but again I want to emphasize that there's a difference between genuine deepening and misguided forms. One of Brewer's central examples is *love of the divine*. He notes that religious philosophers such as Gregory of Nyssa, Augustine, and Aquinas take love of the divine to be a dialectical activity capable of perhaps infinite deepening (Brewer 2009: 56–62). But suppose there's really no God; suppose the end to which these philosophers and theologians devote their lives is a fiction. Then what looks to Gregory or Augustine like deepening will amount to nothing more than spinning out an increasingly elaborate delusion.

Or, for a less controversial example, take a religious extremist like Abu Bakr al-Baghdadi (a former leader of ISIS), who maintained a lifelong devotion to the Islamic faith. From an early age, he recited scripture and studied the Quran; he earned graduate degrees in Quranic studies; during the US-led invasion of Iraq, he helped found an insurgency group; he was arrested by US forces in Falluja in 2004; after his release, he joined Al Qaeda in Iraq; in 2006, he participated in the formation of the Islamic State in Iraq; in 2010, he became the leader of the Islamic State in Iraq; in 2014, when ISIS declared the creation of the Caliphate, Baghdadi was proclaimed the Caliph and demanded allegiance from Muslims worldwide; he served as Caliph until his death in 2019. Reading biographical accounts of Baghdadi, it would be very difficult to resist the conclusion that he saw himself as progressively deepening his appreciation of the Islamic faith. And yet he was brutal: he supervised mass executions of prisoners, planned many successful mass terrorist attacks, championed the appalling tactics of ISIS, and kept many sex slaves. I assume most of us would say that what Baghdadi saw as the deepening of an evaluative commitment was in fact the increasing distortion or perversion of that commitment.

As these cases make clear, continued engagement with some intrinsic value needn't yield increased appreciation or understanding of that value; in fact, it can do the opposite. So we need to distinguish genuine deepening from the appearance of deepening. This is obvious even from the first person case: we sometimes realize, retrospectively, that what we took to be deepening was in fact a process of growing ever more misguided, being led further and further astray.

Let me put it this way: the deepening move is a *preservative*. It is indifferent to content: it can be deployed on any value of sufficient complexity. While I don't take Brewer to deny this, it does raise a problem: the opposite of deepening is stasis rather than error. Deepening opposes fixed, static thinking; but there is no guarantee that flexible thinking leads us to evaluative truth.

And that brings me to a second point. So far, my examples of deepening have involved people who accept an evaluative commitment, see themselves as unable to fully articulate either the commitment or its justification, and view this inability as a defect in their understanding rather than in the commitment itself. So I've been presenting the deepening move as motivated by failures of articulacy. But it can arise in other ways. As Kyla Ebels-Duggan points out, we can distinguish *being articulate* about a value from *appreciating* the value (2019). Ebels-Duggan claims that we can directly appreciate the value of certain things without being articulate about these values. For example, I might directly appreciate the value of my children, or the greatness of Shakespeare's works, without being able to articulate the content or nature of these values in a way that strikes me as adequate. Ebels-Duggan claims that direct appreciation of a value can count as an entirely adequate justification for holding it. If this is right, we can be adequately justified in holding certain values without being articulate about these values (or their justification). Moreover, Ebels-Duggan suggests, it's not always the case that pursuing greater articulacy will be desirable. Pursuing greater articulacy *might* lead to a deeper appreciation of the value, and then it is desirable; but there are other ways of deepening one's appreciation of values, which don't involve articulacy. For example, artistic engagement, literature, or direct experience can be paths to deeper appreciation of values even if they are dissociated from increased articulacy.

Consider how this bears on my points. On the one hand, Ebels-Duggan's position invites certain problems. Suppose al-Baghdadi claims to have direct appreciation of Islamic values; or suppose the fanatical neo-Nazi claims to have direct appreciation of the value of racial purity. What can we say? We might try to argue with him, to reason with him. We might press him to answer justificatory questions: why think you directly appreciate *that* value? Couldn't you be wrong? Couldn't you look at things differently? Insofar as we do this, we strive to make the agent articulate his justification for the putative value; and we present the lack of such justifications as a reason to modify or abandon the putative value. So here it seems that the quest to preserve one's commitments by citing direct appreciation can serve as an especially problematic form of insulation.

On the other hand, there are praiseworthy ways of pursuing direct, non-articulate appreciations of values. I can take myself to enjoy a direct appreciation of a value while being open to revisions in my understanding of what this direct appreciation involves. The key feature, here, is that I view my appreciation of the value as provisional and modifiable, rather than definitive and fixed. To the extent that this is so, I can preserve a form of flexible open-mindedness about the value while simultaneously remaining committed to it. So, even if we reject the idea that lack of articulacy about a value entails lack of justification for holding the value, we can deploy the deepening move by contrasting provisional forms of appreciation of a value with more complete forms of appreciation.

Regardless of whether we speak of dialectical activities, direct appreciation of value, or deepening, the key idea I have been exploring is that we sometimes preserve commitment to a value by treating our grasp of that value as inadequate. This has dangers: the deepening move preserves values, and it preserves them in a way that is indifferent to their contents. It can preserve problematic values as easily as admirable ones. But it does stave off fixity and leave us at least notionally open to revision even of our deepest commitments. It is not an antidote to error; but, when deployed in good faith, it can be an antidote to the fragile rigidity of fanaticism.

9.4 Conclusion

Let's review. To secure wholehearted commitment and avoid normative dissipation, there is a pressure to treat certain values as dialectically invulnerable. But dialectical invulnerability can breed problematic forms of rigidity, as in the case of the fanatic. It might seem that to avoid fanaticism and other forms of rigidity, you need to be capable of backing up to the Sartrean point, seeing that these commitments are freely adopted and freely sustained. But that Sartrean point, if taken seriously, risks collapsing the projects (and that's precisely Sartre's point in novels like *Nausea*). So we're riven by a dichotomy, an instability.

How can we respond to this instability? We might try to learn to live with the inability to justify our deepest commitments, striving for affirmation rather than comparative justification. Or we might go on with the quest for comparative justification, seeing our most important commitments as in need of deepening: one fine day, we tell ourselves, we will understand and justify them. Or, perhaps best of all, we might oscillate between the two, finding hope at times in affirmation, at times in deepening. As Freud says, "Every person must find out for himself in what particular fashion he can be saved" (Freud 1930/1961: 34).

10
Conclusion

I began this book by identifying two overlooked features of ethical life: our craving for devotion and the crucial role that sacred values play in sustaining commitment. If I am right, we long for things to which we can devote ourselves. But features of modern life—the plurality of values that seem genuinely available for choice, the perceived lack of any acceptable grounds for choosing between them, the idea that we should possess some justification for our commitments, the skepticism about values that were formerly taken for granted, the emphasis on tolerating normative commitments that differ from our own, the prioritization of autonomy and personal choice—make devotion problematic and uncertain. Nothing seems to offer adequate grounds for any particular case of devotion; and, when we take the absence of grounds seriously, our commitments risk becoming enervated. Reflecting on all of this, we can feel adrift, astray, lacking anything to which we might anchor our lives. We can be led to normative weighting skepticism, with our commitments gradually eroding, leaving us only with depleted attachments to trivial values.

But there are alternatives. One recourse—the traditional recourse—is maintaining sacred values. Sacred values entail devotion and hence answer our longing. In maintaining sacred values, we exempt certain evaluative commitments from the standard effects of justificatory reasoning. The person or culture that has a sacred value holds fast to that value, even when doing so is openly acknowledged as unjustifiable. These values provide fixed points, which structure and secure our evaluative perspectives. I have argued that despite their initially counterintuitive appearance, sacred values suffuse contemporary ethical life. They are everywhere, and we gain something by noticing this.

While sacred values forestall normative weighting skepticism and ground some of our deepest commitments, they are not innocuous. Under certain conditions, sacred values risk promoting fanaticism. The fanatic holds sacred values in a pathological manner: prompted by a sense of fragility both in her practical identity and in her value's status, the fanatic rigidly holds to a particular sacred value, seeing it as defining both herself and her group. Insofar as she is part of a fanatical group, she will tend to accept a ressentiment-fostering narrative, which promotes a sense of aggrievedness and portrays outgroups as threatening both her identity and her value. All of this fosters intolerance, hostility, and other forms of discord.

While fanaticism is a pathological form of devotion, it does get something right about sacred values. Having a sacred value involves treating it as Inviolable and

Incontestable, and there is a genuine tension between treating a value as sacred and tolerating the fact that others don't accept it. But in the last chapter, I suggested that we can avoid fanaticism in two ways: we can strive to affirm our commitments without treating them as Inviolable or Incontestable; or we can see ourselves as engaged in a quest to deepen our understanding of our own values, thereby preserving a form of flexibility even in the values that we treat as sacred. Insofar as we strive for affirmation, we manifest devotion without grounding it in sacred values; insofar as we strive for deepening, we preserve sacred values, but in a form that permits them to be indefinitely refined.

Here, then, is the ultimate recommendation: try to be devoted to something, for valuable facets of human life (including the avoidance of normative dissipation) require it. But don't be devoted through fanaticism—don't manifest a fragile attachment to your value's status or to your own identity. Instead, strive for a kind of existential flexibility: maintain devotion either by adopting sacred values that you see as open to deepening or by accepting values that enable affirmation.

This will always be precarious. What starts as deepening can drift into stultifying, dogmatic rigidity. What begins as a quest for affirmation can deform into a hostile rejection and resentment of alternative possible commitments. Nothing guarantees that either approach will succeed. But I hope to have provided some view of the costs of the alternative. The life sheared of devotion would be insipid; the life of fanaticism would be appalling. So we must try to navigate between the barrenness of normative dissipation and the horrors of fanaticism, turning at times to affirmation and at times to deepening, always aware of the dangers that lie to each side. To the extent that we can maintain this existential flexibility, we can answer our longing for invulnerable ideals.

References

Abramson, Kate, and Adam Leite (2011), "Love as a Reactive Emotion," *Philosophical Quarterly* 61(245): 673–99.
Abramson, Kate, and Adam Leite (2018), "Love, Value, and Reasons," in *The Oxford Handbook of Philosophy of Love*, ed. by Christopher Grau and Aaron Smuts. Oxford: Oxford University Press.
Adorno, T.W., Else Frenkel-Brunswik, Daniel J. Levinson, and R. Nevitt Sanford (1950), *The Authoritarian Personality*. New York: Harper and Row.
Alexander, L. (2000), "Deontology at the Threshold," *San Diego Law Review* 37(4): 893–912.
Allard, Ladonna Brave Bull (2016), "Why Do We Punish Dakota Pipeline Protestors But Exonerate the Bundys?," *The Guardian*, November 2. https://www.theguardian.com/commentisfree/2016/nov/02/dakota-pipeline-protest-bundy-militia.
Allison, Henry (1990), *Kant's Theory of Freedom*. New York: Cambridge University Press.
Al-Muhajirah, Umm Summayyah (2015), "Slave Girls or Prostitutes," *Dabiq* 9: 46.
Al Ushan, Isa Ibn Sa'd (2015), "Advice to the Mujahidin: Listen and Obey," *Dabiq* 12: 9–10.
Anderson, Elizabeth S. (1991), "John Stuart Mill and Experiments in Living," *Ethics* 102(1): 4–26.
Anderson, Elizabeth S. (1995), *Value in Ethics and Economics*. Cambridge: Harvard University Press.
Andreou, Chrisoula (2022), *Commitment and Resoluteness in Rational Choice*. Cambridge: Cambridge University Press.
Atran, Scott (2016), "The Devoted Actor: Unconditional Commitment and Intractable Conflict across Cultures," *Current Anthropology* 57(S13): 192–203.
Atran, Scott (2017), "The Role of the Devoted Actor in War, Revolution, and Terrorism," in James R. Lewis (ed.), *The Cambridge Companion to Religion and Terrorism*, New York: Cambridge University Press, 69–88.
Atran, Scott, and Robert Axelrod (2008), "Reframing Sacred Values," *Negotiation Journal* 24: 221–46.
Atran, Scott, and Jeremy Ginges (2015), "Devoted Actors and the Moral Foundations of Intractable Inter-group Conflict," in Jean Decety and Thalia Wheatley (eds.), *The Moral Brain*. Cambridge: MIT Press, 69–89.
Baron, Jonathan, and Mark Spranca (1997), "Protected Values," *Organizational Behavior and Human Decision Processes* 70(1): 1–16.
Baumeister, R.F. and K.D. Vohs (2007), "Self-Regulation, Ego Depletion, and Motivation," *Social and Personality Psychology Compass* 1(1): 115–28.
Beauvoir, Simone de (1976), *The Ethics of Ambiguity*, trans. B. Frechtman. New York: Kensington Press.
Beck, Jacob (2013), "The Only Good Reason to Ban Steroids in Baseball: To Prevent an Arms Race," *The Atlantic*, June 17.
Benatar, David (2017), *The Human Predicament*. Oxford: Oxford University Press.

Bennhold, Katrin (2015), "Jihad and Girl Power: How ISIS Lured 3 London Girls," *The New York Times,* August 17. https://www.nytimes.com/2015/08/18/world/europe/jihad-and-girl-power-how-isis-lured-3-london-teenagers.html.

Bentham, Jeremy (2007), *An Introduction to the Principles of Morals and Legislation.* New York: Dover.

Berger, J.M. (2018), *Extremism.* Cambridge: MIT Press.

Bergoglio, Jorge, and Abraham Skorka (2010), *On Heaven and Earth: Pope Francis on Faith, Family, and the Church in the 21st Century.* New York: Penguin.

Berlin, Isaiah (1990), *The Crooked Timber of Humanity.* Princeton: John Murray Publishing.

Bersani, Leo (2013), *Marcel Proust: The Fictions of Life and of Art.* Oxford: Oxford University Press.

Bhui, Kamaldeep, and Sokratis Dinos (2012), "Psychological Process and Pathways to Radicalization," *Journal of Bioterrorism & Biodefense* 5. doi: 10.4172/2157-2526.

Bloom, Mia (2009), "Chasing Butterflies and Rainbows: A Critique of Kruglanski et al.'s 'Fully Committed: Suicide Bombers' Motivation and the Quest for Personal Significance,'" *Political Psychology* 30(3): 387–95.

Branson-Potts, Hailey (2016), "In Diverse California, a Young White Supremacist Seeks to Convert Fellow College Students," *The Los Angeles Times,* December 7. https://www.latimes.com/local/lanow/la-me-ln-nathan-damigo-alt-right-20161115-story.html

Bratman, Michael (2012), "Time, Rationality, and Self-Governance," *Philosophical Issues* 22: 73–88.

Bratman, Michael (2018), *Planning, Time, and Self-Governance.* New York: Oxford University Press.

Brennan, Jason and Peter Jaworski (2015), *Markets Without Limits.* New York: Routledge.

Brewer, Talbot (2009), *The Retrieval of Ethics.* Oxford: Oxford University Press.

Brown, Wendy (1995), *States of Injury.* Princeton: Princeton University Press.

Busch, Patrick (2011), "Is Same-Sex Marriage a Threat to Traditional Marriages? How Courts Struggle with the Question," *Washington University Global Law Studies Review* 10(1): 143–65.

Bykvist, Krister (2017), "Moral Uncertainty," *Philosophy Compass* 12(3): 1–8.

Calhoun, Cheshire (2018), *Doing Valuable Time: The Present, the Future, and Meaningful Living.* Oxford: Oxford University Press.

Callimachi, Rukmini (2015), "ISIS and the Lonely Young American," *The New York Times,* June 27. https://www.nytimes.com/2015/06/28/world/americas/isis-online-recruiting-american.html

Camus, Albert (1955), *The Myth of Sisyphus and Other Essays.* New York: Random House.

Carlsson, Ulrika (2018), "Tragedy and Resentment," *Mind* 127(508): 1169–91.

Cassam, Quassim (2018), "The Epistemology of Terrorism and Radicalization," *Royal Institute of Philosophy Supplement* 84: 187–209.

Cassam, Quassim (2019), "The Epistemologies of Terrorism and Counterterrorism Research," *The Routledge International Handbook of Universities, Security and Intelligence Studies,* ed. Liam Gearon. New York: Routledge, 303–11.

Cassam, Quassim (2022), *Extremism: A Philosophical Analysis.* New York: Routledge.

Chang, Ruth (2014), "Value Pluralism," in James D. Wright (ed.), *International Encyclopedia of the Social and Behavioral Sciences, Second Edition,* Vol. 25. Oxford: Elsevier, 21–6.

Chang, Ruth (2015), "Value Incomparability and Value Incommensurability," in Iwao Hirose and Jonas Olson (eds.), *The Oxford Handbook of Value Theory*. Oxford: Oxford University Press, pp. 205–24.

Chappell, Sophie Grace (2017), *Knowing What to Do*. Oxford: Oxford University Press.

Chesterton, G.K. (1991), *The Collected Works of G.K. Chesterton, Volume XVII*. San Francisco: Ignatius Press.

Christensen, David (2010), "Higher-Order Evidence," *Philosophy and Phenomenological Research* 81(1): 185–215.

Colas, Dominique (1997), *Civil Society and Fanaticism: Conjoined Histories*, trans. Amy Jacobs. Stanford: Stanford University Press.

Crallé, Richard K. (1864), *Speeches of John C. Calhoun, Delivered in the House of Representatives and in the Senate of the United States, vol. II*. New York: Appleton and Co.

Crenshaw, Martha (1990), "The Logic of Terrorism: Terrorist Behavior as a Product of Strategic Choice," in Walter Reich (ed.), *Origins of Terrorism: Psychologies, Ideologies, Theologies, States of Mind*. Washington, D.C.: Woodrow Wilson Center Press, 7–24.

Crosson, Frederick J. (2003), "Fanaticism, Politics, and Religion," *Philosophy Today* 47(4): 441–7.

Cullity, Garrett (2018), "Weighing Reasons," in Daniel Star (ed.), *The Oxford Handbook of Reasons and Normativity*. Oxford: Oxford University Press, 423–42.

Deci, Edward L. and Richard M. Ryan (1985), *Intrinsic Motivation and Self-determination in Human Behavior*. New York: Plenum.

Dreier, James (2006), "Moral Relativism and Moral Nihilism," in David Copp (ed.), *The Oxford Handbook of Ethical Theory*. Oxford: Oxford University Press, pp. 240–64.

Dundon, Rian (2017), "Photos: It's Been 20 Years Since Julia Butterfly Fought Big Logging—by Living in a Tree," *Timeline*, December 8. https://timeline.com/photos-its-been-20-years-since-julia-butterfly-went-up-the-tree-748fe5f578f4

Durkheim, Emile (1915/1955), *The Elementary Forms of Religious Life*. New York: The Free Press.

Durkheim, Emile (1975), "Individualism and the Intellectuals," in W.S.F. Pickering (ed.), *Durkheim on Religion*. Cambridge: James Clark and Co. pp. 59–73.

Dworkin, Ronald (1995), *Life's Dominion: An Argument about Abortion and Euthanasia*. New York: Harper Collins.

Ebels-Duggan, Kyla (2011), Review of *All Things Shining*. *Notre Dame Philosophical Reviews* September 9 edition. https://ndpr.nd.edu/reviews/all-things-shining-reading-the-western-classics-to-find-meaning-in-a-secular-age/

Ebels-Duggan, Kyla (2019), "Beyond Words: Inarticulable Reasons and Reasonable Commitments," *Philosophy and Phenomenological Research* 98(3): 623–41.

Epictetus (2008), *Discourses and Selected Writings*, translated by R. Dobbin. New York: Penguin.

Folsom, Charles F. (1880), "Cases of Insanity and Fanaticism," *Boston Medical and Surgical Journal* 102(12): 265–71.

Forst, Rainer (2002), *Contexts of Justice*, J. Farrell (trans.), Berkeley and Los Angeles: University of California Press.

Foucault, Michel (1984), *The Foucault Reader*, ed. Paul Rabinow. New York: Pantheon Books.

Frankfurt, Harry (1988), *The Importance of What We Care About*. New York: Cambridge University Press.

Frankfurt, Harry (1998), "On Caring," in *Necessity, Volition, and Love*. New York: Cambridge University Press, pp. 155–80.
Frankfurt, Harry (2006), *Taking Ourselves Seriously and Getting It Right*. Stanford, CA: Stanford University Press.
Fraser, Nancy, and Axel Honneth (2003), *Redistribution or Recognition? A Philosophical Exchange*. London: Verso.
Freud, Sigmund (1961), *Civilization and its Discontents*, ed. James Strachey. New York: Norton.
Fried, Charles (1980), *An Anatomy of Values*. Cambridge: Harvard University Press.
Gaita, Raimond (1999), *A Common Humanity*. New York: Routledge.
Garfield, Jay (1995), *The Fundamental Wisdom of the Middle Way*. Oxford: Oxford University Press.
Gendler, Tamar (2008), "Alief and Belief," *Journal of Philosophy* 105(10): 634–63.
Ginges, Jeremy, and Scott Atran (2014), "Sacred Values and Cultural Conflict," in Michele J. Gelfand, Chi-Yue Chiu, and Ying-Yi Hong (eds.), *Advances in Culture and Psychology, Vol. 4*. Oxford: Oxford University Press, 273–301.
Goschke, T. (2014), "Dysfunctions of Decision-making and Cognitive Control as Transdiagnostic Mechanisms of Mental Disorders: Advances, Gaps, and Needs in Current Research," *International Journal of Methods in Psychiatric Research* 23: 41–57.
Graham, Jesse and Jonathan Haidt (2012), "Sacred Values and Evil Adversaries: A Moral Foundations Approach," in Mario Mikulincer and Philip R. Shaver (eds.), *The Social Psychology of Morality: Exploring the Causes of Good and Evil*. Washington DC: American Psychological Association.
Greenspan, Patricia S. (1983), "Moral Dilemmas and Guilt," *Philosophical Studies* 43: 117–25.
Haidt, Jonathan (2012), *The Righteous Mind: Why Good People are Divided by Politics and Religion*. New York: Random House.
Hamilton, Christopher (2009), *Middle Age*. Durham: Acumen Publishing.
Hampshire, Stuart (1983), *Morality and Conflict*. Cambridge: Harvard University Press.
Hanselmann, Martin and Carmen Tanner (2008), "Taboos and Conflicts in Decision Making: Sacred Values, Decision Difficulty, and Emotions," *Judgment and Decision Making* 3(1): 51–63.
Hare, R.M. (1972), "Nothing Matters," in R.M. Hare, *Applications of Moral Philosophy*. London: Macmillan.
Harman, Elizabeth (2015), "The Irrelevance of Moral Uncertainty," in R. Shafer-Landau (ed.), *Oxford Studies in Metaethics, Volume 10*, Oxford University Press.
Hassan, Ghayda, Sébastien Brouillette-Alarie, Séraphin Alava, Divina Frau-Meigs, Lysiane Lavoie, Arber Fetiu, Wynnpaul Varela, Evgueni Borokhovski, Vivek Venkatesh, Cécile Rousseau, and Stijn Sieckelinck (2018), "Exposure to Extremist Online Content Could Lead to Violent Radicalization: A Systematic Review of Empirical Evidence," *International Journal of Developmental Sciences* 12: 1–18. 10.3233/DEV-170233.
Healy, Jack (2016), "As North Dakota Pipeline is Blocked, Veterans at Standing Rock Cheer," *The New York Times*, December 5. https://www.nytimes.com/2016/12/05/us/veterans-north-dakota-standing-rock.html
Hegel, G.W.F. (1900), *The Philosophy of History*, trans. J. Sibree. New York: Wiley.
Heidegger, Martin (2002), *Off the Beaten Track*, ed. and trans. Julian Young and Kenneth Haynes. Cambridge: Cambridge University Press.
Henrich, Joseph, Steven J. Heine, and Ara Norenzayan (2010), "The Weirdest People in the World?," *Behavioral and Brain Sciences* 33(2): 1–75.

Herman, Barbara (1993), *The Practice of Moral Judgment*. Cambridge: Harvard University Press.
Hill, Thomas E., Jr. (1996), "Moral Dilemmas, Gaps, and Residues: A Kantian Perspective," in H.E. Mason (ed.), *Moral Dilemmas and Moral Theory*, New York: Oxford University Press, 167–98.
Hoffer, Eric (2010), *The True Believer: Thoughts on the Nature of Mass Movements*. New York: Harper.
Holton, Richard (2009), *Willing, Wanting, Waiting*. Oxford: Oxford University Press.
Honneth, Axel (1992), *The Struggle for Recognition: The Moral Grammar of Social Conflicts*, Cambridge, MA: MIT Press.
Honneth, Axel (2000), *Disrespect: The Normative Foundations of Critical Theory*, Cambridge: Polity Press.
Hopwood, Mark (2016), "Terrible Purity: Peter Singer, Harriet McByrde Johnson, and the Moral Significance of the Particular," *Journal of the American Philosophical Association* 2 (4): 637–55.
Huddleston, Andrew (2019), "Nietzsche on Nihilism: A Unifying Thread," *Philosophers' Imprint* 19(11): 1–19.
Hume, David (1739/2000), *A Treatise of Human Nature*, ed. David Fate Norton and Mary J. Norton. Oxford: Oxford University Press.
Hume, David (1985), *Essays Moral, Political, and Literary*. New York: Liberty Fund.
Jaeggi, Rahel (2014), *Alienation*. New York: Columbia University Press.
Jensen, Michael A., Anita Atwell Seate, and Patrick A. James (2018), "Radicalization to Violence: A Pathway Approach to Studying Extremism," *Terrorism and Political Violence* 32(5): 1067–90.
John Paul II (1995), *Encyclical Letter Evangelium Vitae*. Washington, D.C.: United States Catholic Conference.
Jollimore, Troy (2011), *Love's Vision*. Princeton: Princeton University Press.
Joyce, Richard (2001), *The Myth of Morality*. New York: Cambridge University Press.
Kahan, Dan M. (2013), "Ideology, Motivated Reasoning, and Cognitive Reflection," *Judgment and Decision Making* 8(4): 407–24.
Kant, Immanuel (1788/1996), *Critique of Practical Reason*, trans. Mary Gregor. Cambridge: Cambridge University Press
Kant, Immanuel (1797/2017), *The Metaphysics of Morals*, trans. Mary Gregor. Cambridge: Cambridge University Press.
Kant, Immanuel (1999), *Practical Philosophy*, ed. and trans. Mary Gregor. Cambridge: Cambridge University Press.
Kant, Immanuel (2001), *Religion and Rational Theology*, ed. and trans. Allen W. Wood and George di Giovanni. Cambridge: Cambridge University Press.
Kant, Immanuel (2007), *Anthropology, History, and Education*, ed. Paul Guyer and Allen Wood. Cambridge: Cambridge University Press.
Kashdan, T.B., and Rottenberg, J. (2010), "Psychological Flexibility as a Fundamental Aspect of Health," *Clinical Psychology Review* 30: 865–78.
Katsafanas, Paul (2015), "Fugitive Pleasure and the Meaningful Life: Nietzsche on Nihilism and Higher Values," *Journal of the American Philosophical Association* 1 (Fall 2015): 396–416.
Katsafanas, Paul (2019), "Fanaticism and Sacred Values," *Philosophers' Imprint* 19(17): 1–20.

Katsafanas, Paul (2022), "What Makes the Affirmation of Life Difficult?," in Keith Ansell-Pearson and Paul Loeb (eds.), *Nietzsche's "Thus Spoke Zarathustra": A Critical Guide*. Cambridge: Cambridge University Press.
Keller, Simon (2000), "How Do I Love Thee? Let Me Count the Properties," *American Philosophical Quarterly* 37(2): 163–73.
Kelly, Sean, and Hubert Dreyfus (2011), *All Things Shining*. New York: Simon and Schuster.
Kierkegaard, Søren (1841/1989), *The Concept of Irony with Continual Reference to Socrates, together with "Notes on Schelling's Berlin Lectures."* Ed. and trans. by Howard V. Hong and Edna H. Hong. Princeton: Princeton University Press.
Kierkegaard, Søren (1970), *Journals and Papers*, Vol. 2. Ed. and trans. by Howard V. Hong and Edna H. Hong. Princeton: Princeton University Press.
Kitcher, Patricia (2004), "Kant's Argument for the Categorical Imperative," *Noûs* 38(4): 555–84.
Klausen, Jytte (2015), "Tweeting the Jihad: Social Media Networks of Western Foreign Fighters in Syria and Iraq," *Studies in Conflict & Terrorism* 38: 1–22.
Klausen, Jytte (2016), *A Behavioral Study of the Radicalization Trajectories of American "Homegrown" Al-Qaeda-Inspired Terrorist Offenders*. US Department of Justice Grant Report, Document Number 250417. https://www.ncjrs.gov/pdffiles1/nij/grants/250417.pdf
Klein, Lawrence E. and Anthony J. La Vopa (1998), *Enthusiasm and Enlightenment in Europe 1650–1850*. San Marino, CA: Huntington Library.
Knausgaard, Karl Ove (2013), *My Struggle, Book 2: A Man in Love*. New York: Macmillan.
Koch, I., M. Gade, S. Schuch, and A.M. Philipp (2010), "The Role of Inhibition in Task Switching: A Review," *Psychonomic Bulletin and Review* 17: 1–14.
Kolodny, Niko (2003), "Love as Valuing a Relationship," *Philosophical Review* 112(2): 135–89.
Korsgaard, Christine (1996), *The Sources of Normativity*. Cambridge: Cambridge University Press.
Kruglanski, Arie, and Shira Fishman (2009), "The Need for Cognitive Closure," in M.R. Leary and R.H. Hoyle (eds.), *Handbook of Individual Differences in Social Behavior*. The Guilford Press, 343–53.
Kruglanski, Arie, D.M. Webster, and A. Klem (1993), "Motivated Resistance and Openness to Persuasion in the Presence or Absence of Prior Information," *Journal of Personality and Social Psychology* 65(5): 861–76.
Kruglanski, Arie, Xiaoyan Chen, March Dechesne, Shira Fishman, and Edward Orehek (2009), "Fully Committed: Suicide Bombers' Motivation and the Quest for Personal Significance," *Political Psychology* 30: 331–57.
Kruglanski, Arie, Michele J. Gelfand, Jocelyn J. Bélanger, Anna Sheveland, Malkanthi Hetiarachchi, and Rohan Gunaratna (2014), "The Psychology of Radicalization and Deradicalization: How Significance Quest Impacts Violent Extremism," *Political Psychology* 35: 69–93.
La Vopa, Anthony J. (1997), "The Philosopher and the *Schwärmer*: On the Career of a German Epithet from Luther to Kant," *Huntington Library Quarterly* 60: 85–115.
Lakatos, Imre (1978), *The Methodology of Scientific Research Programmes* (*Philosophical Papers*: Volume 1), ed. J. Worrall and G. Currie. Cambridge: Cambridge University Press.
Lear, Jonathan (2011), *A Case for Irony*. Cambridge: Harvard University Press.
Locke, John (1975), *An Essay Concerning Human Understanding*. Oxford: Oxford University Press.

Lockhart, Ted (2000), *Moral Uncertainty and Its Consequences*. Oxford: Oxford University Press.
Longino, Helen E. (1990), *Science as Social Knowledge: Values and Objectivity in Scientific Inquiry*. Princeton: Princeton University Press.
Lord, Errol and Barry Maguire (2016), "An Opinionated Guide to the Weight of Reasons," in Errol Lord and Barry Maguire (eds.), *Weighing Reasons*. Oxford: Oxford University Press, 3–24.
Loyd, Anthony (2019), "Shamima Begum: Bring Me Home, Says Bethnal Green Girl Who Left to Join Isis," *The Times of London*, February 13.
Lukes, Steven (2017), "Sacred Values in Secular Politics," *Analyze & Kritik* 39(1): 101–17.
Lynch, Kevin (2016), "Willful Ignorance and Self-Deception," *Philosophical Studies* 173(2): 505–23.
MacAskill, William (2014), *Normative Uncertainty*, Ph.D. thesis in Philosophy, Department of Philosophy, Oxford University.
MacIntyre, Alasdair (1984), *After Virtue*. Notre Dame, Indiana: University of Notre Dame Press.
Marcel, Gabriel (2008), *Man Against Mass Society*, trans. G.S. Fraser. South Bend, Indiana: St. Augustine Press.
Marcus, Ruth Barcan (1980), "Moral Dilemmas and Consistency," *The Journal of Philosophy*, 77: 121–36.
Martin, Glen (1998), "A Year in the Sky," *SF Gate*, December 6. https://www.sfgate.com/default/article/A-YEAR-IN-THE-SKY-Last-December-10-Julia-2974427.php
Martinich, A.P. (2000), "Religion, Fanaticism, and Liberalism," *Pacific Philosophical Quarterly* 81: 409–25.
Maslow, Abraham (1962), *Toward a Psychology of Being*. Princeton: Van Nostrand.
McBryde Johnson, Harriet (2003), "Unspeakable Conversations," February 16. *New York Times*. https://www.nytimes.com/2003/02/16/magazine/unspeakable-conversations.html
McCauley, Clark and Sophia Moskalnko (2017), "Understanding Political Radicalization: The Two-Pyramids Model," *American Psychologist* 72(3): 205–16.
McClelland, D.C., R. Koestner, and J. Weinberger (1989), "How Do Self-attributed and Implicit Motives Differ?" *Psychological Review* 96: 690–702.
Meiran, Nachshon (2010), "Task Switching: Mechanisms Underlying Rigid vs. Flexible Self control in Society, Mind, and Brain," in R.R. Hassin, K.N. Ochsner, and Y. Trope (eds), *Oxford Series in Social Cognition and Social Neuroscience. Self Control in Society, Mind, and Brain*. New York: Oxford University Press, 202–20.
Merleau-Ponty, Maurice (1945/2012), *Phenomenology of Perception*. New York: Routledge.
Mill, John Stuart (1861/1998), *Utilitarianism*, Roger Crisp (ed.), Oxford: Oxford University Press.
Miller, Andrew H. (2020), *On Not Being Someone Else: Tales of Our Unled Lives*. Cambridge: Harvard University Press.
Miyake, A., N.P. Friedman, M.J. Emerson, A.H. Witzki, A. Howerter, and T.D. Wager (2000), "The Unity and Diversity of Executive Functions and Their Contributions to Complex 'Frontal Lobe' Tasks: A Latent Variable Analysis," *Cognitive Psychology* 41: 49–100.
Molden, Daniel C. and E. Tory Higgins (2012), "Motivated Thinking," in *The Oxford Handbook of Thinking and Reasoning*, ed. Keith J. Holyoak and Robert G. Morrison. Oxford: Oxford University Press.

Moore, Michael S. (1997), *Placing Blame: A General Theory of the Criminal Law*. Oxford: Oxford University Press.
Moran, Richard (2017), "Frankfurt on Identification," in *The Philosophical Imagination*. Oxford: Oxford University Press, 136–57.
Morton, Jennifer M. and Sarah K. Paul (2019), "Grit," *Ethics* 129(2): 175–203.
Mueller, Benjamin (2019), "Shamima Begum, British Woman Who Joined ISIS in Syria, Wants to Come Home," *The New York Times*, February 14. https://www.nytimes.com/2019/02/14/world/europe/uk-isis-shamima-begum.html
Murdoch, Iris (1970), *The Sovereignty of Good*. New York: Routledge.
Nagel, Thomas (1979), *Mortal Questions*. Cambridge: Cambridge University Press.
Nietzsche, Friedrich (1974), *The Gay Science*, trans. Walter Kaufmann. New York: Vintage.
Nietzsche, Friedrich (1977), *Sämtliche Werke, Kritische Studienausgabe in 15 Bänden*, ed. G. Colli and M. Montinari. Berlin: Walter de Gruyter.
Nietzsche, Friedrich (1989), *Beyond Good and Evil*, trans. Walter Kaufmann. New York: Vintage.
Nietzsche, Friedrich (1997), *Daybreak*, trans. R.J. Hollingdale. New York: Cambridge University Press.
Nietzsche, Friedrich (2003), *Writings from the Late Notebooks*, ed. Rüdiger Bittner. Cambridge: Cambridge University Press.
Norman, Richard (2017), "Ethics and the Sacred: Can Secular Morality Dispense with Religious Values?," *Analyse & Kritik* 39(1): 5–24.
Olson, Jonas (2014), *Moral Error Theory: History, Critique, Defense*. Oxford: Oxford University Press.
O'Neill, Onora (1975), *Acting on Principle: An Essay on Kantian Ethics*. New York: Cambridge University Press.
O'Neill, Onora (1989), *Constructions of Reason: Explorations of Kant's Practical Philosophy*. New York: Cambridge University Press.
Ortega y Gassett, José (1927), "Le temps, la distance et la forme chez Marcel Proust," in *Hommage à Marcel Proust*. Paris: Gallimard.
Orwell, George (1968), "Review of *Mein Kampf* by Adolf Hitler," *The Collected Essays, Journalism and Letters of George Orwell*, ed. Sonia Orwell and Ian Angus, Vol. II. New York: Harcourt, Brace, and World, pp. 12–14.
Parfit, Derek (2011), *On What Matters*. Oxford: Oxford University Press.
Passmore, John Arthur (2003), "Fanaticism, Toleration, and Philosophy," *Journal of Political Philosophy* 11(2): 211–22.
Prinz, Jesse (2018), "Moral Sedimentation," in Gregg. Caruso and Owen Flanagan (eds.), *Neuroexistentialism: Meaning, Morals, and Purpose in the Age of Existentialism*. Oxford: Oxford University Press, 87–108.
Proust, Marcel (2003), *In Search of Lost Time,* trans. C.K. Scott Moncrieff. New York: Random House/Modern Library.
Railton, Peter (1997), "On the Hypothetical and Non-Hypothetical in Reasoning about Belief and Action," in G. Cullity and B.N. Gaut (eds.), *Ethics and Practical Reason*. Oxford: Oxford University Press, pp. 53–79.
Rawls, John (1971), *A Theory of Justice*. Cambridge: Harvard University Press.
Rawls, John (1993), *Political Liberalism*. New York: Columbia University Press.
Raz, Joseph (1986), *The Morality of Freedom*. Oxford: Clarendon Press
Raz, Joseph (1988), "Autonomy, Toleration, and the Harm Principle," in S. Mendus (ed.), *Justifying Toleration. Conceptual and Historical Perspectives*. Cambridge: Cambridge University Press, 155–75.

Reginster, Bernard (2003), "What is a Free Spirit? Nietzsche on Fanaticism," *Archiv für Geschichte der Philosophie* 85: 51–85.
Reginster, Bernard (2006), *The Affirmation of Life: Nietzsche on Overcoming Nihilism*. Cambridge: Harvard University Press.
Rilke, Rainer Marie (2009), *The Notebooks of Malte Laurids Brigge*. New York: Penguin.
Rorty, Richard (1989), *Contingency, Irony, and Solidarity*. Cambridge: Cambridge University Press.
Rosen, Michael (2018), *Dignity: Its History and Meaning*. Cambridge: Harvard University Press.
Roth, Kenneth (2015), "Slavery: The ISIS Rules," *The New York Review of Books*, September 24, 2015.
Sageman, Marc (2004), *Understanding Terror Networks*. Philadelphia: University of Pennsylvania Press.
Sageman, Marc (2008), *Leaderless Jihad: Terror Networks in the Twenty-First Century*. Philadelphia: University of Pennsylvania Press.
Salmela, Mikko, and Christian von Scheve (2018), "Emotional Dynamics of Right- and Left-wing Political Populism," *Humanity & Society* 42(4): 434–54.
Sanchez, Carlos (2012), *The Suspension of Seriousness: On the Phenomenology of Jorge Portilla*. Albany: SUNY Press.
Sartre, Jean-Paul (1948), *Existentialism is a Humanism*, trans. P. Mairet. London: Methuen & Co.
Sartre, Jean-Paul (2003), *Being and Nothingness*, trans. Hazel Barnes. London: Routledge.
Scanlon, Thomas (1996), "The Difficulty of Tolerance," in D. Heyd (ed.), *Toleration. An Elusive Virtue*, Princeton: Princeton University Press, 226–39.
Scanlon, Thomas (1998), *What We Owe to Each Other*. Cambridge: Harvard University Press.
Scanlon, Thomas (2007), "Structural Irrationality," in Geoffrey Brennan, Robert Goodin, Frank Jackson, and Michael Smith (eds.), *Common Minds: Themes from the Philosophy of Philip Pettit*. Oxford: Oxford University Press, 84–103.
Schachtman, Tom (2007), *Rumspringa: To Be or Not to Be Amish*. New York: North Point Press.
Schechtman, Marya (1996), *The Constitution of Selves*. Ithaca, New York: Cornell University Press.
Scheffler, Samuel (2013), *Death and the Afterlife*. Oxford: Oxford University Press.
Scheler, Max (1994), *Ressentiment*. Milwaukee: Marquette University Press.
Schopenhauer, Arthur (1844/1969), *The World as Will and Representation*, Vol. I, trans. E.F.J. Payne. New York: Dover Publications.
Schopenhauer, Arthur (1891), *Studies in Pessimism* [selections from *Parerga und Paralipomena*], ed. and trans. T. Bailey Saunders. London: Swan Sonnenschein and Co.
Sen, Amartya (1982), "Rights and Agency," *Philosophy and Public Affairs*, 11(1): 3–39.
Sepielli, Andrew (2009), "What to Do When You Don't Know What to Do," in R. Shafer-Landau (ed.), *Oxford Studies in Metaethics, Volume 4*. Oxford: Oxford University Press.
Sepielli, Andrew (2012), "Moral Uncertainty and the Principle of Equity among Moral Theories," *Philosophy and Phenomenological Research* 86(3): 580–9.
Sepielli, Andrew (2014), "What to Do When You Don't Know What to Do When You Don't Know What to Do..." *Noûs* 48(3): 521–44.
Setiya, Kieran (2014), "Love and the Value of a Life," *Philosophical Review* 123 (3): 251–80.
Setiya, Kieran (2017), *Midlife: A Philosophical Guide*. Princeton: Princeton University Press.

Shafer-Landau, Russ (2017), *The Fundamentals of Ethics*. Oxford: Oxford University Press.
Shaftesbury, Third Earl of (1999), *Characteristics of Men, Opinions, and Manners*, ed. Lawrence E. Klein. Cambridge: Cambridge University Press.
Sheikh, H., J. Ginges, A. Coman, and S. Atran (2012), "Religion, Group Threat and Sacred Values," *Judgment and Decision Making* 7(2): 110–18.
Sidgwick, Henry (1981), *The Methods of Ethics*. Indianapolis: Hackett Publishing.
Singer, Peter (1972), "Famine, Affluence, and Morality," *Philosophy and Public Affairs* 1(1): 229–43.
Singer, Peter (2009), "The Sanctity of Human Life," *Foreign Policy* (October 20, 2009).
Singer, Peter and Helga Kuhse (2002), *Unsanctifying Human Life: Essays on Ethics*. Oxford: Blackwell Publishers.
Sinnott-Armstrong, Walter (1988), *Moral Dilemmas*, Oxford: Basil Blackwell.
Skitkta, Linda J. (2010), "The Psychology of Moral Conviction," *Social and Personality Psychology Compass* 4(4): 267–81.
Smart, J.J.C., and Bernard Williams (1973), *Utilitarianism: For and Against*. Cambridge: Cambridge University Press.
Smith, Adam (1759/1976), *The Theory of Moral Sentiments*, D.D. Raphael and A.L. Macfie (eds.). Oxford: Oxford University Press.
Smith, Adam (1776/2000), *The Wealth of Nations*. New York: Modern Library.
Smith, Allison G. (2018), "How Radicalization to Terrorism Occurs in the United States: What Research Sponsored by the National Institute of Justice Tells Us," The U.S. Department of Justice, Office of Justice Programs, National Institute of Justice Reports. Washington DC: National Institute of Justice. https://www.ojp.gov/pdffiles1/nij/250171.pdf
Smith, Michael (1994), *The Moral Problem*. Oxford: Wiley-Blackwell.
Snyder, C.R. and Shane J. Lopez (2001), *Handbook of Positive Psychology*. Oxford: Oxford University Press.
Stack, Liam (2016), "How the 'War on Christmas' Controversy was Created," *New York Times* December 19, 2016.
Stern, Jessica (2003), *Terror in the Name of God: Why Religious Militants Kill*. New York: Harper.
Stern, Jessica (2016), "Radicalization to Extremism and Mobilization to Violence: What Have We Learned and What Can We Do about it?," *Annals of the American Academy of Political and Social Science* 668(1): 102–17.
Stern, Jessica, and John M. Berger (2015), *ISIS: The State of Terror*. New York: Harper Collins.
Stockdale, Katie (2013), "Collective Resentment," *Social Theory and Moral Practice* 39(3): 501–21.
Svavarsson, Svavar Hrafn (2014), "Sextus Empiricus on Persuasiveness and Equipollence," in Mi-Kyeung Lee (ed.), *Strategies in Argument: Essays in Ancient Ethics, Epistemology, and Logic*. Oxford: Oxford University Press, 356–73.
Swann, William, Jolanda Jetten, Ángel, Gómez, Harvey, Whitehouse, and Brock Bastian (2012), "When Group Membership Gets Personal: A Theory of Identity Fusion," *Psychological Review* 119: 441–56.
Taggart, Adam (2014), "Julia Butterfly Hill: Living With Meaning. How Our Actions Define Our Destiny," *Peak Prosperity*, April 26. https://www.peakprosperity.com/julia-butterfly-hill-living-with-meaning/
Taylor, Charles (1982), "The Diversity of Goods," in A. Sen and B. Williams (eds.), *Utilitarianism: For and Against*. Cambridge: Cambridge University Press.
Taylor, Charles (2007), *A Secular Age*. Cambridge, MA: Harvard University Press.

Tessman, Lisa (2014), *Moral Failure: On the Impossible Demands of Morality*. Oxford: Oxford University Press.
Tetlock, Philip E. (2003), "Thinking the Unthinkable: Sacred Values and Taboo Cognitions," *Trends in Cognitive Sciences* 7(7): 320–4.
Tetlock, Philip E., O.V. Kristel, S.B. Elson, M.C. Green, and J.S. Lerner (2000), "The Psychology of the Unthinkable: Taboo Tradeoffs, Forbidden Base Rates, and Heretical Counterfactuals," *Journal of Personality and Social Psychology* 78(5): 853–70.
Toscano, Alberto (2010), *Fanaticism: On the Uses of an Idea*. New York: Verso.
Uniacke, Suzanne (2004), "Is Life Sacred?," in Ben Rogers (ed.), *Is Nothing Sacred?* London: Routledge, 59–80.
Velleman, J. David (1999), "Love as a Moral Emotion," *Ethics* 109: 338–74.
Velleman, J. David (2000), "On the Aim of Belief," in *The Possibility of Practical Reasoning*. New York: Oxford University Press, 244–81.
Viedge, Nikolai (2018), "Defending Evidence-Resistant Beliefs," *Pacific Philosophical Quarterly* 99: 517–37.
Wallace, R. Jay (2013), *The View from Here*. Oxford: Oxford University Press.
Weatherson, Brian (2014), "Running Risks Morally," *Philosophical Studies* 167(1): 141–63.
Webber, Jonathan (2006), "Sartre's Theory of Character," *European Journal of Philosophy* 14(1): 94–116.
Webster, Donna M., and Arie W. Kruglanski (1994), "Individual Differences in Need for Cognitive Closure," *Journal of Personality and Social Psychology* 67(6): 1049–62.
Wedgwood, Ralph (2013), "The Weight of Moral Reasons," *Oxford Studies in Normative Ethics* 3: 35–58.
Wiggins, David (2006), *Ethics: Twelve Lectures on the Philosophy of Morality*. Cambridge: Harvard University Press.
Williams, Bernard (1965), "Ethical Consistency," *Proceedings of the Aristotelian Society* 39: 103–24.
Williams, Bernard (1981a), "Persons, Character, and Morality," in *Moral Luck*. Cambridge: Cambridge University Press, 1–19.
Williams, Bernard (1981b), "Moral Luck," in *Moral Luck*. Cambridge: Cambridge University Press, 20–39.
Wolf, Susan (2010), *Meaning in Life and Why It Matters*. Princeton: Princeton University Press.
Wolf, Susan (2012), "'One Thought Too Many': Love, Morality, and the Ordering of Commitment," in Ulrike Heuer and Gerald Lang (eds.), *Luck, Value, and Commitment: Themes from the Ethics of Bernard Williams*, Oxford: Oxford University Press, 71–92.
Wong, David (2006), *Natural Moralities: A Defense of Pluralistic Relativism*. Oxford: Oxford University Press.
Wood, Allen (1999), *Kant's Ethical Thought*. New York: Cambridge University Press.
Wood, Graeme (2015), "What ISIS Really Wants," *The Atlantic,* March 2015.
Zangwill, Nick (2013), "Love: Gloriously Amoral and Arational," *Philosophical Explorations* 16(3): 298–314.
Zimmerman, Michael (2014), *Ignorance and Moral Obligation*. Oxford: Oxford University Press.
Zmigrod, Leor (2020), "The Role of Cognitive Rigidity in Political Ideologies: Theory, Evidence, and Future Directions," *Current Opinion in Behavioral Sciences* 34: 34–9.
Zuckert, Rachel (2010), "Kant's Account of Practical Fanaticism," in Benjamin J. Bruxvoort Lipscomb and James Krueger (eds.), *Kant's Moral Metaphysics: God, Freedom, and Immortality*. Berlin: Walter de Gruyter, pp. 291–318.

Index

For the benefit of digital users, indexed terms that span two pages (e.g., 52–53) may, on occasion, appear on only one of those pages.

Abase, Amira 2–4, 53
Affirmation 204–9, 219–21
Al-Baghdadi, Abu Bakr 217–19
Al Qaeda 169, 174, 182–4
Alienation 87–93
American Identity Movement 184
Amish 152, 157, 187, 203–4
Arthurs, Devon 149–50
Articulacy 43–5, 210–16
Atomwaffen 164–7
Atran, Scott 11–12, 26–8, 154–5
Autonomy 147, 202

Beauvoir, Simone de 103–4, 192, 202
Begum, Shamima 2–4, 6–7, 53
Berger, J.M. 167
Breivik, Anders Behring 33, 133n.10
Brewer, Talbot 216–18

Calhoun, Cheshire 67–70, 206
Cassam, Quassim 158–60, 171
Close-mindedness 18, 145, 187
Cognitive closure 145
Commitment
    the nature of 67–9
    resolute commitments 96–8
Contagion model of fanaticism 170–1
Contentment 204–9
Cullity, Garret 52–3

Dabiq 3–4
Damigo, Nathan 184–5
Deepening move 209–21
Devaluation 56–63
Devoted Actor Hypothesis 155
Devotion
    connection to sacred values 7, 18, 85–7
    connection to dialectical
        invulnerability 78–81, 97–8
    connection to alienation and
        identification 87–93
    definition of 78
    distinguished from commitment 66–71

longing for 1–7, 190–1, 220–1
    reasons for 93–8
Dialectical activities 217–18
Dialectical Invulnerability 19–20, 32–9, 45, 47–8, 71–99
    clarifications concerning 82–5
    connection to devotion 64–6, 71–2, 78–81
    full definition of 77–8
Dogmatism 18, 20–1, 24–5, 32–9, 133–8, 216

Ebels-Duggan, Kyla 113–14, 218–19
Enlightenment account of fanaticism
    defined 133–8
    problems with 138–41
Environmental protection, as a sacred value 13
Epictetus 30
Extremism 33, 129–30, 141, 144–7, 152, 154–5, 158–60, 167–75, 187

Fanaticism
    connection to dogmatism 136–8
    paradigm cases of 129–33
    Enlightenment account of 127–41
    psychological account of 142–62
    see also: Group fanaticism; Intolerance
Fragility of the self 147–50, 159–62, 164, 186–7, 191, 220
Fragility of values 150–2, 159–62, 164, 187, 191, 220
Francis, Pope 139–41, 156–8
Frankfurt, Harry 88, 148
Freeman, Charles 130–3, 140–1

Gaita, Raimond 47–8
Ginges, Jeremy 11–12, 27, 155
Global Weighing Picture 52–3
Group fanaticism
    connection to ressentiment 177–88
    connection to individual fanaticism 175–6
    Generative View of 169, 175–6, 188–9
Gun rights, as a sacred value 13

Haidt, Jonathan 26–7, 40, 41n.18
Heidegger, Martin 23

INDEX

Heydrich, Reinhard 158–9
Hill, Julia "Butterfly" 4–7
Hoffer, Eric 140–1
Hume, David 25, 128, 134, 136–8

Identification 87–93
Identity
   and fragility 147–50, 186–7, 193–4, 220
   and fanatical groups 174–5
   and group orientation 133, 146, 152–6, 187–8
   and ressentiment 178–82, 186–7
Identity Evropa 184
Identity fusion 154–5
Importance, *see* Meaning
Inarticulacy 43–5, 210–16
Intolerance 132–3, 138–41, 144–5, 147, 155–8, 160–1, 164, 167–9, 173, 175, 220
Incontestability of sacred values 29–32
Inviolability of sacred values 25–9
Irony 192–7
ISIS (Islamic State of Iraq and Syria) 2–4, 129–32, 140–1, 143–4, 153, 167, 171–5, 182, 217–18

Judgment-sensitive attitudes 70–1, 88–94

Kaczynski, Ted 33, 133n.10
Kant, Immanuel 9–10, 25, 46–7, 128–9, 132–3, 135–40, 147–8, 150, 211–13

Life, as a sacred value 8–10, 23, 25, 41–2, 60, 125, 156–8, 176
Locke, John 128–30, 132–4, 136–8

Marriage, as a sacred value 150–2
McBryde Johnson, Harriet 58–61
Meaning 2–3, 5, 14–16, 42–3, 46, 103–5, 129–30, 174
Moral uncertainty 108–9
Moran, Richard 88–94

Narratives, fanatical 182–5
Nietzsche, Friedrich 18, 100–1, 104–6, 113, 119, 124–5, 132–3, 147–50, 177–81, 207n.10
Nihilism
   as the view that there are no moral facts 101–3
   as the view that life has no meaning 103–4
   as the loss of sacred values 104–6
   See also Normative Weighting Skepticism
Normative Dissipation 116–26, 190–4, 200, 205–9, 215, 221
Normative Weighting Skepticism 109–14, 193, 220
   effects of 116–24

Orwell, George 1

Proust, Marcel 65, 89–93

Radical choice 196–202
Radicalization 144–7, 170–5
Reflection, quantity of vs. effects of 75–7
Ressentiment
   the nature of 176–81
   and fanatical narratives 182–5
   and feedback loops 185–6
   and individual fanaticism 186–8
Rigid thinking 144–5
Rorty, Richard 194–7

Sacred values, full definition of 45–6
Sartre, Jean-Paul 103–4, 192, 196–202
Scanlon, T.M. 70
Scheler, Max 178–81
Self-deception 213–14
Shaftesbury, Third Earl of 128–30, 134–8, 170
Significance, *see* Meaning
Significance Quest Theory 146, 174
Singer, Peter 8–10, 58–61
Standing Rock 2, 6–7
Stormfront 154–5, 175, 182
Sultana, Kadiza 2–4, 53

Tessman, Lisa 33, 37n.14
Tetlock, Philip 11, 11n.12, 23, 27, 31–2
Tolerance 132–3, 138–41, 144–5, 147, 155–8, 160–1, 164, 167–9, 173, 175, 220
Tradeoffs, taboo 28–32
Tradeoffs, tragic 28–30, 32, 156–7, 190

Uncertainty, intolerance of 144–5
Uncertainty, moral 108–9

Voltaire 170

Wedgwood, Ralph 51–2
Weighting values 50–3
   As prohibited in certain cases 53–63
   See also: devaluation
Williams, Bernard 65–6, 72–6, 78, 78n.6, 99
Wolf, Susan 65–6, 69–78, 78n.6, 99

Zmigrod, Leor 144–5